PENGUIN BOOKS

POPE JOHN XXIII

Thomas Cahill, former director of religious publishing at Doubleday, is the bestselling author of the Hinges of History series, which includes *How the Irish Saved Civilization; The Gifts of the Jews; Desire of the Everlasting Hills: The World Before and After Jesus; Sailing the Wine-Dark Sea: Why the Greeks Matter;* and *Mysteries of the Middle Ages: The Rise of Feminism, Science, and Art from the Cults of Catholic Europe.* He and his wife, Susan Cahill, a novelist and anthologist, divide their time between New York and Rome. They have two children, a daughter who is a teacher in Oakland, California, and a son who is a filmmaker in Prague, and three grandchildren.

THOMAS CAHILL

POPE JOHN XXIII

A Penguin Life

A LIPPER™ / PENGUIN BOOK

PENGUIN BOOKS

Published by the Penguin Group

Penguin Group (USA) Inc., 375 Hudson Street, New York, New York 10014, U.S.A.
Penguin Group (Canada), 90 Eglinton Avenue East, Suite 700, Toronto,
Ontario, Canada M4P 2Y3 (a division of Pearson Penguin Canada Inc.)
Penguin Books Ltd, 80 Strand, London WC2R 0RL, England
Penguin Ireland, 25 St Stephen's Green, Dublin 2, Ireland (a division of Penguin Books Ltd)
Penguin Group (Australia), 250 Camberwell Road, Camberwell,
Victoria 3124, Australia (a division of Pearson Australia Group Pty Ltd)
Penguin Books India Pvt Ltd, 11 Community Centre, Panchsheel Park, New Delhi – 110 017, India
Penguin Group (NZ), 67 Apollo Drive, Rosedale, North Shore 0632,
New Zealand (a division of Pearson New Zealand Ltd)
Penguin Books (South Africa) (Pty) Ltd, 24 Sturdee Avenue,
Rosebank, Johannesburg 2196, South Africa

Penguin Books Ltd, Registered Offices:
80 Strand, London WC2R 0RL, England

First published in the United States of America by Viking Penguin,
a member of Penguin Putnam Inc. 2002
Published in Penguin Books 2008

1   3   5   7   9   10   8   6   4   2

Grateful acknowledgment is made for permission to reprint excerpts
from the following copyrighted works:
Journal of a Soul by Pope John XXIII, translated by Dorothy White.
Copyright © 1965, 1980 by Geoffrey Chapman, a division of Cassell Ltd.
Used by permission of Doubleday, a division of Random House, Inc., and Geoffrey Chapman.
Pope John XXIII by Peter Hebblethwaite. Reprinted by permission of Geoffrey Chapman.

THE LIBRARY OF CONGRESS HAS CATALOGED THE HARDCOVER EDITION AS FOLLOWS:
Cahill, Thomas.
Pope John XXIII / Thomas Cahill.
p. cm.—(A Penguin life)
Includes bibliographical references.
ISBN 0-670-03057-0 (hc.)
ISBN 978-0-14-311302-7 (pbk.)
1. John XXIII, Pope, 1881–1963.   I. Title.   II. Penguin lives series.
BX1378.2.C27   2002
282'.092—dc21   2001045435

Printed in the United States of America
Set in Cloister · Designed by Francesca Belanger

To Sister Helen Prejean

For the good are always the merry

The Three Secrets of John XXIII

The secret of everything is to let yourself be carried by the Lord and to carry the Lord.

—John XXIII at his coronation

The secret of my ministry is in [the] crucifix. . . . Those open arms have been the program of my pontificate: they mean that Christ died for all, for all. No one is excluded from his love, from his forgiveness.

—John XXIII on his deathbed

This was the secret of his personality: he loved people more than power.

—Yves Congar

CONTENTS

CONTENTS

INTRODUCTION

"Toward a New Order of Human Relationships"

"In the daily exercise of our pastoral ministry—and much to our sorrow—we must sometimes listen to those who, consumed with zeal, have scant judgment or balance," said John XXIII to the bishops of the world assembled in Saint Peter's Basilica as he opened the precedent-shattering Second Vatican Council (or Vatican II) in 1962. "To such ones the modern world is nothing but betrayal and ruin. They claim that this age is far worse than previous ages, and they rant on as if they had learned nothing at all from history—and yet, history is the great Teacher of Life. . . . We feel bound to disagree with these prophets of doom who are forever forecasting calamity—as though the world's end were imminent. Today, rather, Providence is guiding us toward a new order of human relationships, which, thanks to human effort and yet far surpassing human hopes, will bring us to the realization of still higher and undreamed of expectations."

This was uttered with his accustomed warmth and serene joy by a short man with sensuous lips and a hooked nose set in a flat Italian peasant's face framed by elephantine ears, a fat old man with twinkling eyes and a seductively resonant voice, robed with such extravagant dignity as to underscore the comedy of his figure. The glimpse he offered of the pope's daily trials of patience in the midst of an overheated clerical atmosphere proved too much for his handlers, the little, anonymous men of the Vatican. As John went on to ask his audience for "a leap forward" (*un balzo* in John's original Italian text) in insight (*penetrazione*) into the Church's teaching and a new coat of paint (*la formulazione del suo rivestimento*) in which to clothe the old doctrines, the little men made plans to censor the pope's text, to clip from the official transcript here and to add there, in order to prevent scandal to the faithful and to gratify their own outraged sensibilities. But the original text, before they could get their hands on it, was, like so many things John said, unlike anything any pope had said before or would say since; and this is because John was unlike any other pope.

We would not remember John at all were it not for the office he occupied in the last five years of his life: bishop of Rome, successor to Peter the Fisherman, the leading figure among Jesus's apostles. From this unique position John was able to cast a pebble into the pond of human experience that has continued to reverberate in ever wider rings. To understand his crucial importance to the world's one billion Catholics, his remarkable influence on Christians everywhere, and his effect on human hopes and happiness, we must spend some time retracing the long and labyrinthine history of the papacy, which gave him his platform.

PART I

BEFORE JOHN

✦ ✦ ✦

From Congregation to Church to Standard of Orthodoxy

VATICAN PROPAGANDA notwithstanding, Peter was never "bishop of Rome." In the five narrative books with which the New Testament begins—the four gospels and the Acts of the Apostles—Peter is given prominence, a prominence that would later be interpreted as his "primacy" over the other bishops of the primitive Church. But the early Church communities had a congregational structure, like the synagogues from which they sprang. The word *bishop* (*episkopos*, or superintendent, in Greek) was at first interchangeable with the word *elder* (*presbyteros*, from which we derive our word *priest*) and did not signify rule over others. After the death of the apostles, who had been the chief witnesses to Jesus's life and teaching, and under the pressure of bizarre heresies and the consequent need to establish a voice of orthodoxy within each community, the Churches of the late first century began to single out an *episkopos* to take doctrinal charge of each local Church. The Christian community at Rome, however, seems not to have adopted this strategy till toward the middle of the second century. The first man who can be designated "bishop of Rome" with historical certainty is Anicetus, who stands eleventh in the Vatican's somewhat fanciful list of early "popes" and who served from 155 to his death c. 166, weakening considerably the "claim" of Peter, who died a hundred years earlier.

But Peter did die at Rome, crucified during the first widespread persecution of Christians—under the emperor Nero—and his bones surely lie beneath the high altar of Saint Peter's Basilica, beside which John XXIII stood to deliver his address of welcome to the council fathers. Rome's possession of these bones, along with those of the other great martyr of the primitive Church, Paul—a rabbi converted to the new form of Judaism that would become Christianity and a missionary of such overreaching devotion that he was belatedly given the title "apostle"—would become in the generation after Anicetus the foundation of the Roman Church's universal prominence.

By the time of Ireneus of Lyons, who wrote in the last quarter of the second century, Rome had become the pilgrimage center of the Christian world on account of its shrines to the two martyred apostles, who were now imagined to have founded the Roman Church by shedding their blood (though there were Christian communities at Rome prior to their arrival there), and Rome's bishop was seen—at least by some—as final arbiter in disputes throughout the Christian world. For Ireneus, as no doubt for many others, the Church of Rome was already "the great and illustrious Church," and "every [other] Church—that is, the faithful everywhere—must resort to this Church on account of its pre-eminent authority, in which the apostolic tradition has been preserved without interruption."

Thus, within 150 years of Jesus's crucifixion, within 75 years of the last of the New Testament writings, there was a well-attested tradition that the Church of Rome in the person of its bishop was the most reliable bulwark against doctrinal error and the last court of appeal in any matter that could not be settled locally. If the "Petrine succession"—the monarchical succession of the long line of popes from the apostle Peter—is little more than wish fulfillment, it must be admitted that the roots of the Roman bishopric are ancient and most venerable, springing from the soil of the post-apostolic age, the age in which the Church as a whole took on a form of organization it would preserve to our day.

After Anicetus, a Syrian, there came to the bishop's chair one Soter (c. 166–c. 174), a Latin-speaking Christian and probably a Roman aristocrat, then Eleutherius (c. 174–c. 189), a Greek, then Victor (189–98), an African, all pointing up the cosmopolitan, multicultural quality of the Roman Church, which enabled it to express an earnest ecumenical concern for all Christians, wherever they were. "[We] greet you . . . with deepest concern, keep[ing] watch over all who call on the Name of the Lord," a letter to the North African Churches put it, a letter written by a committee of Roman Christians during a vacancy in the episcopacy caused by the brutal imprisonment and death of bishop Fabian (235–36) during the persecution of the emperor Decius.

Though in this early period the Roman Church was often seen as the common standard of orthodoxy, its orthodoxy was too flexible for many less elastic Christians. The bishop of Rome was often criticized for being too easygoing toward heretics and too forgiving toward sinners. Though Victor made a great fuss trying to get all the Churches to observe Easter on the same date, even briefly excommunicating the Asian Churches that kept their own separate tradition, bishop Callistus (c. 217–222), far more typical of the Roman bishopric in this period, sent his more rigid contemporaries into tizzies by ordaining men who had been married more than once, allowing marriages between partners of different social classes, and welcoming everyone to the Eucharist, even those who had lapsed during persecution. His critics favored purer priests, segregation by economic class, and lifelong penance for public sin. If it is easy for us to see that Callistus was closer in spirit to the views of Jesus, his critics saw no such thing, any more than the critics of John XXIII would acknowledge that he was simply following the Gospel and they were not.

For all the honor and status accorded Rome in the Church's early centuries, it was never imagined as unique among Churches, only *primus inter pares*, first in honor among equals. Other Churches, especially those with ancient bishoprics (like Antioch, Ephesus, Corinth, Alexandria, and Carthage), behaved more or less as Rome did, sending letters of encouragement and admonishment to younger, less distinguished Churches, offering monetary support, excommunicating when necessary. Bishops of the older metropolitan Churches tended to be addressed as *"papa"* (or pope), a title that in the Western Church was used as a form of address to all bishops—and in parts of the East to all priests—and would not be reserved to the bishop of Rome till well into the eleventh century. But all the bishops were seen as successors to Jesus's apostles, sharing apostolic responsibility for all the Churches and sharing also the apostolic power, which was unitary and indivisible, because it descended ultimately from Jesus, the Way.

Nor was criticism a one-way street that could be employed only by a greater Church against a lesser. In the midst of a raging controversy about whether it was necessary to rebaptize penitents who had lapsed during persecution, the African Churches, gathered under their unrelenting metropolitan bishop Cyprian, "the pope of Carthage," condemned the more flexible position of Stephen, bishop of Rome, in three overwrought synods, accusing Stephen of "set[ting] himself up as a bishop of bishops" and "exercis[ing] the powers of a tyrant to force his colleagues into obedience." Stephen replied serenely that he was Peter, the living representative of the first Peter, to whom Jesus had promised: "You are Peter [*Rock* in the Greek of the New Testament] and upon this Rock will I build my Church." Here we have, midway through the third century, the first instance in the historical record of a Roman bishop asserting an authority greater and different than that of other bishops.

Cyprian was unimpressed, though in fact his attitude toward the nature of Rome's authority waxed and waned over the course of his lifetime. The dispute was never settled because both the Roman bishop and his African opponent were about to enter the catalogue of saints, Stephen by natural causes in 257, Cyprian by his heroic martyrdom the following year. As will happen many times over in the life of the Church, death resolves the unresolvable.

The Imperial Church

THE HAND OF EMPIRE was shaping Churches not only by persecution, sometimes instigated by local imperial officials, sometimes by the emperor himself, but also by the occasional positive intervention of the emperor in ecclesiastical affairs. By the time Constantine wrested the imperial throne from his rival Maxentius at the battle of the Milvian Bridge in October 312, the Roman Church had nearly three centuries of history behind it, centuries of service to the poor and to peace certainly, but also centuries of lively, and sometimes deadly, controversy and contentiousness. It had had its share of episcopal martyrs, even of bishops who had abdicated or perished in times of persecution, leaving their see (or seat, the symbol of their authority) to be occupied by a committee. There had been bishops who in times of toleration had been able to build the wealth of the Church as well as its numbers. There had been many acts of courage, relatively few of cowardice. There had been two anti-bishops (known in later times as "anti-popes") and but one craven bishop, Marcellinus (296–304), who during the persecution of Diocletian had snapped, handing over his library of sacred books, thus becoming a *tra(d)itor* (one who "hands over"), and sacrificing to idols. There had been compromising bishops and uncompromising ones, peace-loving bishops and high-handed ones. There had even been the bishop of Alexandria's condemnation, solemnly confirmed by Rome's bishop Pontian (230–35), of the greatest theologian the Church had ever known, Origen, who was expelled from his teaching post, exiled from Egypt, and hounded out of the Christian priesthood.

The emperors were learning to live with the Church, sometimes persecuting it, but more often—as its growing numbers lent it undeniable social power—intervening for the sake of public order in violent disputes among clergy. On occasion, such intervention would even be invited by a regional conference of bishops. But collaboration between Church and emperor was about to take a new turn that would alter forever the Church's understanding of itself and its place in the world.

Prior to his victory at the Milvian Bridge on the outskirts of Rome, Constantine, commander of Rome's British garrison, had seen a sign in the heavens: a cross of light and the Greek words *en touto nika* (in this, conquer). This cross, formed by the so-called monogram of Christ—the Greek letters *XP* (chi rho), the first two letters of *Christ* in Greek—thereafter shone from his soldiers' shields and billowed on their banners. Constantine, a simple man, seems to have confused devotion to Christ with his own prior pagan practices, leaving us some evidence that he identified Christ with Sol Invictus, the Unconquered Sun of his father's paganism. But Constantine's mother, Helena, a barmaid whose husband on becoming emperor had divorced her for a more suitable consort, was an unswerving Christian convert; and by observing his mother's fervor Constantine may have picked up a notion of how this newfangled faith could be made to work on his behalf. No longer bemoaning, as his predecessors had done, the weakening of Rome's diffuse pantheism by this rude Asian upstart, Constantine viewed Christianity as a fresh form of energy that could be harnessed as a force to unify his empire, which was always threatening to break into fragments.

But as he looked closer at his chosen instrument of unity, the new emperor was disgusted to learn that Christianity was itself riven by deep theological divisions and the rigidity and mutual hatred that such divisions encourage. He must, at all costs, bring such nonsense to an end. A practical military man, he hit on an innovation that would probably never have occurred to churchmen: he would call a universal council of bishops and force them into agreement, of what sort he didn't much care. To accommodate the emperor, this council—the first ecumenical (or world) council—was convened in 325 at Nicea, Constantine's summer residence, not far from his glorious new capital of Constantinople—"New Rome," as it was called. Though the council appears to have been summoned without prior episcopal consultation and certainly without any by-your-leave to the bishop of "Old" Rome, the bishops came gladly from all parts of the empire, the Ecumene (or well-ordered world). Rome's bishop, Sylvester, did not come in person but sent two deputies to vote on his behalf. Constantine seems never to have noticed that bishops were not all of the same grade, and perhaps the bishops themselves never stressed to him the nuanced distinctions they treasured among themselves. Certainly, theological subtleties were beyond him. He just wanted to get the job done, and to this end he himself appeared at the council, the overbearing imperial presence no doubt stifling the partisan hysteria that would otherwise have erupted.

With Constantine's Edict of Toleration, issued in 313 and granting freedom of religion to all, theological controversy involving the *lapsi*—those who had betrayed the faith during previous persecutions—had quickly faded, giving way to a new dispute about the nature of Christ. Was Jesus of Nazareth just a man elevated by God, as the Arians claimed, or "one in being with the Father," as the Roman party insisted? In other words, was he truly God or not? Both sides of the argument built thickets of linguistic distinctions that must have caused the emperor to sneak a few naps. But in the end, the Arians were routed. Arius, an Alexandrian elder, and his fervent followers (many of them impassioned Egyptian nuns) were officially condemned by the council, which issued for the first time in the Church's history a "creed" or list of official beliefs (named from its first word in Latin, *Credo*, "I believe . . .") to which all Christians must subscribe. Unlike the usual, ambiguous, unending theological controversy, Nicea's result had all the elegant simplicity of a great general's successful strategy.

But Constantine was mistaken if he thought that churchmen could be deployed like soldiers. The defeated party slunk away, silenced but seething with resentment. The controversy would prove exceedingly durable, encouraging the Arian East to question whether the bishop of Rome, evermore the staunch upholder of Nicea, had any special authority over other Churches. Mutual retaliations followed, Eastern bishops excommunicating the bishop of Rome, he returning the favor, and the Western bishops declaring the bishop of Rome their "head." Constantine's son and successor Constantius would prove an Arian and would pressure the Western Church with gifts and threats to see things his way, even exiling the bishop of Rome to Thrace. Soon enough, in 366, an Arian anti-bishop, Ursinus, would be murdered in the streets of Rome by a rabble, urged on by the valid bishop, Damasus.

In 381, a new anti-Arian emperor, Theodosius, called a new ecumenical council at Constantinople, a council that no Western bishop attended but that confirmed Nicea and reformulated its creed with greater precision. This is the same creed still recited in Sunday liturgies. Though imperial interventions in the Church's affairs would hardly shut the door on theological controversy, the Church's new partnership with *imperium* would change the Church forever. Constantine had built splendid new churches around Rome, modeled on the basilicas, or public halls, long in use as law courts and places of assembly. He had made extravagant grants of rich farmland (as far away as Africa and Asia) and gifts of precious metals to the bishop of Rome. He had linked emperor and bishop in public display and private association.

Such association could only encourage the bishop to adopt a more regal, even an imperial style. The bishop took over the emperor's title of *Pontifex Maximus*, Supreme Pontiff or Bridge-builder (which the emperor had held as head of the city of Rome's college of pagan priests). Damasus began to call his fellow bishops "sons" rather than "brothers"; his immediate successor, Siricius (384–99), began to issue "decretals," normative rulings on ecclesiastical disputes throughout the empire, consciously modeled on the emperor's own decretals. In Rome, Damasus acted the part of the shady municipal politician, arranging the mob violence that cut down his Arian rival, Ursinus, following a little episcopal tête-à-tête with the city's chief of police. The bishop was now distinguished by the parallel purple stripes running down his shining senatorial robe. The wealthy matrons of the city vied for the prestige of his presence, a presence he was happy to lend their social gatherings in the hopes of cadging yet another benefice from their trembling hands. Damasus was known as *matronarum auriscalpius,* the matrons' ear-tickler; and the shenanigans of the episcopal party did not go unnoticed by more detached commentators, such as the pagan historian Ammianus Marcellinus, who describes the senior clergy of Rome as "forever secure, enriched with offerings from the matrons, riding out in their carriages splendidly bedecked, hosting banquets so lavish they surpass the tables of kings." Conveniently ignored was the example of the apostle Paul, who, despite his heroic missionary labors, had always worked at the humble trade of tentmaking, lest he "become a burden" to anyone or need to accept unseemly favors.

Here we have, already securely in place by the last quarter of the fourth century, the entitled, touchy, parasitical clerical culture that is with us still and to which John XXIII referred obliquely in his opening address at Vatican II. The bishop never allowed the matrons to get too close, of course. The sense of unspeakable distance was part and parcel of the "spiritual" aura that surrounded him. His intimate circle was exclusively male, composed of younger clergy whose only desire—to emulate their master—was announced by their own smartly striped dalmatics, the origin of distinctive clerical dress. Jesus's contemptuous description of "those who wear soft garments" was completely forgotten. God, it seemed, had created the Roman empire so that Christianity—this peculiar, hothouse Christianity—might triumph.

But there were storm clouds on the horizon. After Constantine, the empire was divided between East and West, an Eastern emperor residing at Constantinople, a Western one at Arles, Milan, or Ravenna—never again at Rome. If it was partly the emperor's absence that encouraged the bishop of Rome to assume the imperial style, this absence also left Rome more vulnerable. By the beginning of the fifth century, the barbarian hordes were already pouring into the empire from the north and east, and nothing attracted them more than the settled farmlands and sweet vineyards of the Italian peninsula. Leo the Great, a bishop of massive dignity, intelligence, and intentionality, the polar opposite of his trivial predecessor Damasus, had to travel north from Rome to Mantua in 452 to persuade the barbarian chieftain Attila the Hun not to march on the defenseless old capital. Leo employed every weapon in his considerable arsenal of words and panoply and so impressed the Hun that he agreed to desist. It was an encounter of mythological proportions that would bolster the bishop of Rome's reputation in the West for centuries to come. Peter could not be withstood; he was invincible.

There had now been four ecumenical councils, the third—in 431 at Ephesus, where Jesus's mother, Mary, was thought to have died—declaring that Mary could be addressed in prayer as *theotokos*, God-bearer, because Christ's divine and human natures were united in one person. The fourth council of the whole Church was held at Chalcedon a year before Leo's victorious encounter with Attila. Its principal achievement was a clear statement on the two natures of Christ, true God and true man. The statement was based on the precise formulations that Leo had used in his *Tome*, written to dispel confusion on the subject. For much of the West, Chalcedon's declaration was vindication of the claims of Rome's bishop to lead the universal Church. "Peter has spoken through Leo," said the council fathers after the *Tome* was read aloud to them. But for the "Eastern" bishops (from Antioch to Jerusalem, from Alexandria to Constantinople) this simply meant that this time out Peter had spoken through Leo. It was up to the bishops, gathered collegially, to decide when the bishop of Rome spoke true and when he did not. Thus was set for all time the two different ways of imagining how authority flowed through the Church. For Rome and its allies (especially the other Italian sees), Peter in the person of his successor was the last word. For the East and for not a few in the amorphous "West" that lay beyond the borders of Italy (whether in Gaul, Spain, or northwest Africa), the last word, the ultimate measure of doctrinal orthodoxy, could only be the bishops together, representing the whole Christian world as they deliberated in council.

The Romans and the Barbarians

IN 476, the last Western emperor is pulled from his throne. Thereafter, Western Europe is divided into an interlocking puzzle of barbarian chiefdoms, ruled by illiterates—sometimes animists, sometimes Arians, never (in Rome's discerning view) orthodox Christians. These petty kings can claim none of the legitimacy of the faraway emperor of the East; but the emperor is ever more distant from the political realities of the West, till he will eventually become in the minds of most of his putative Western "subjects" a figure as fabulous and remote as Kubla Khan. As the barbarians overwhelm the Roman civitates and the old, cultivated way of life, as the remaining Romans of the West dwindle in number before the barbarian population explosion, as violence, extortion, and abduction into slavery increase and education and even literacy decline precipitately, the bishops of Rome, like their brothers throughout the West, waste little time lamenting what is lost but take up the task of becoming not only standards of doctrinal orthodoxy but lonely beacons of culture, law, and literacy in this rough new world. As Lord Peter Wimsey, lost in a wild Fen snowstorm, remarks hopefully on hearing the peal of distant bells, "Where there is a church, there is civilization." Never in history was this so literally true as during Europe's Dark Ages between the fall of the Western emperor and the cultural flowering of the high Middle Ages. Any traveler making his way through the roiling barbarian sea knew that he had reached the cultivated security of a lost world when he came upon the little island of the bishop and his court.

The barbarian chieftains were generally open to such refined episcopal influence. After all, as Theodoric, the homely king of the Ostrogoths who now sat on the throne of the last Western emperor, put it: "Every able Goth wants to be a Roman; but no Roman wants to be a Goth." Though the unruly barbarians, in their ignorance and numbers, succeeded finally in destroying almost all vestiges of Roman civilization, this was not their intention. They just wanted in.

Meanwhile, the East, once the haven of the Arianism that had denied the divine nature of Christ, had become the protectorate of the monophysites, who denied Christ's human nature. Perhaps the Greek East, more diverse in its several ancient patriarchal sees, more intellectual, more "spiritual," more innovative, was also more naturally extremist. The Latin West, now solidly on the side of its single "patriarch of the West," the bishop of Rome, was more plodding and practical, more interested in questions of jurisdiction than rarefied theological speculation. It seems to have permanently absorbed something of Constantine's spirit: conserving of *Res Publica*, the Common Good, through adherence to law and tradition, open to innovation but unwilling to rewrite its history or its creed, striving to preserve unity through balanced common sense but without discarding anything essential. Jesus was God *and* man, not one or the other. If expressing this accurately created considerable verbal difficulties, this was no reason to manufacture a "purer" intellectual scheme by throwing out one pole or the other. In its obsession with abstractions, the Eastern Church sometimes seemed unable to hold more than one idea at a time. The Western Church, far less notional, was more comfortable living inside a theological universe that held opposites in tension.

This Roman balance, this sober assessment of the passing theological enthusiasms of the East, this unwillingness to go off half-cocked in one direction or another, would over the course of time only enhance Rome's reputation for dependable ortho-doxy—its "pre-eminent authority," in the words of Ireneus of Lyons. It is just this balanced maturity, this impermeability to the winds of fashion, whether of Arians to the left or monophysites to the right, that would one day encourage Victorian churchmen of the Oxford Movement to the unwelcome conclusion that the national Protestant Churches had got something seriously wrong, while Rome still stood where it had always stood—in the middle, at the center. "I saw my face in that mirror [of fifth-century theological controversy]," bemoaned the introspective Anglican curate John Henry Newman, the nineteenth century's greatest theologian, "and I was a Monophysite."

If the bishops of Rome felt no special love for the crude, dis-ruptive barbarian kings and secretly longed for the restoration of the Roman Ecumene, they were also forced—in their uncom-fortable political position between the ideal of the refined East and the reality of the harsh West—to notice a flaw in the politi-cal theory that had served the Church so well since the accession of Constantine. Whether or not the bishop of Rome was "head" of the college of bishops, there had never been any doubt that the emperor was head of the empire and that therefore every one of his subjects, including the bishop of Rome, was at his service and served at his pleasure. This is why Constantine could call a council of bishops without a peep of objection from them. But if

the emperor was now a heretic, a monophysite who, with an eye
to the eventual reunification of East and West, was attempting to
forge a compromise of words between Rome and his fellow
monophysites, was there not something misguided about the assumption that the emperor should control the Church?

Gelasius, upon his election to the Roman see in 492, did not
seek the emperor's confirmation (as had his predecessors) but
rather ventured to instruct the emperor in a novel political theory:

> There are, most august Emperor, two powers by which this
> world is chiefly ruled: the sacred authority of bishops and the
> royal power. Of these the priestly power is much more impor-
> tant, because it must render account for the kings of men
> themselves before the judgment seat of God. For you know,
> most gracious son[!], that although you hold the chief place of
> dignity over the human race, yet must you submit yourself in
> faith to those who have charge of divine things, and look to
> them for the means of your salvation. You know that it be-
> hoves you [in Church matters] to be obedient to ecclesiastical
> authority, instead of seeking to bend it to your will. . . . And if
> the hearts of the faithful ought to be submitted to priests in
> general . . . how much more ought assent be given to him who
> presides over that See which the most high God himself de-
> sired to be pre-eminent over all priests, and which the pious
> judgment of the whole Church has honored ever since.

So, the emperor should be subject to the bishop of Rome,
not the other way around. And though such language hardly
persuaded the emperor, it is the first salvo in a war that will see
skirmishes and pitched battles from Gelasius's day to the pontificate of John XXIII, when the Church will at last retire its antiquated weapons of words and embrace an alternative theory. But
Gelasius's theory is not so simple as may first appear: he sees two

realms, the temporal and the spiritual, the spiritual being the more exalted. Though it may be a short step from saying that the emperor should be subject to the bishop in spiritual matters to claiming that the bishop of bishops has universal jurisdiction over temporal rulers, Gelasius doesn't quite make such a claim. Many of his successors will; but it is just as possible to read Gelasius's instruction as the first attempt to articulate what will one day become the political doctrine of the separation of Church and state.

Despite Gelasius's august attempt to put some theoretical distance between his office and the emperor's, in the actual West of the late fifth century the Roman bishops and their supporters find themselves making whatever practical compromises are necessary for survival in the new barbarian world, even allowing the patently unorthodox king Theodoric, the Arian barbarian, to choose between two candidates for bishop, one presented by the Roman aristocrats who are hoping for the return of imperial rule even at the expense of doctrinal orthodoxy, the other favored by the rabble who are ardently orthodox and partisans of the jurisdictional claims of the Roman see. Theodoric goes with the people's choice (who is also, not incidentally, the anti-imperial candidate), Symmachus, who will occupy the bishop's chair from 498 to 514.

The political realities of this period become ever more complex for the bishops of Rome, who, though usually under the thumb of a powerful barbarian king, maintain some form of contact with the Byzantine court, always abuzz with subtle doctrinal intrigues. The emperor sometimes proves a piously orthodox believer, such as Justin, who forces the bishops of the East to accept the Formula of Hormisdas (514–23), Symmachus's successor. This doctrinal statement affirms the authority of Chalcedon as well as the primacy of Peter's "successors," all seen to be that same "Rock" on which Jesus meant to build his Church. At other times, the emperor turns out to be a monophysite sympathizer, such as Justinian, whose scheming and insatiable empress, Theodora, is determined to see a monophysite installed on the chair of Peter. What she gets for her machinations is Vigilius (537–55), not a true monophysite, just someone willing to appear in whatever guise is required to advance his ambitions—a thoroughgoing chameleon and the worst Roman bishop yet. Vigilius's attainment of his lofty episcopal goal does not improve his character: he flip-flops every which way over the subject of the two natures of Christ, pretending publicly to maintain some distance from the monophysite position but secretly caving in to pressure from the emperor, who finally turns over to the fifth ecumenical council, meeting at Constantinople, all of Vigilius's fulsome, duplicitous letters on the subject. The council, bowing to imperial pressure, condemns the writings of three deceased theologians who were among Chalcedon's most passionate defenders and condemns Vigilius himself, with whom the emperor breaks off communion. This excommunication is followed by similar action in the important Italian sees of Milan and Aquileia. The formerly warm relationship between Rome and Gaul enters a deep freeze. The bishops of Istria (northeastern Italy and Croatia) will remain alienated from Rome for the next century and a half. The prestige of the Roman see sinks to the lowest level since its establishment. Vigilius, under house arrest in Constantinople, is made to retract all his previous positions, after which the thoroughly disgraced bishop is allowed to return to Rome, where a murderous mob awaits him. Luckily for him, a vicious attack of gallstones does him in en route.

It will be thirty-five years before the Roman see can begin to recover some of the authority that Vigilius had frittered away. By the time of the accession of Gregory I (590–604), the power and panoply of Byzantium, as the Eastern empire was called, have become but a memory in much of the West, ever more deep in the camp of Germanic illiterates. Even if Rome remains officially imperial territory, a priest of Germanic stock has already sat on the throne of Peter, and many Germanic tribes, now settled on farms throughout the West and in the process of becoming Christian, look to papal Rome, not to Constantinople, for ultimate religious guidance.

Unlike Vigilius, the last thing Gregory wanted was to be bishop of Rome—a good beginning for greatness. He was the first monk to occupy the Roman see, a man known for his devotion to the poor and his personal care of the sick during one of Rome's many plagues (brought on by the brackish, undrained marshes that surrounded the city). He loved to pray and study and to care for those in need, and he much resented being forced to take on what seemed an impossible responsibility. It is amazing that the worldly Roman clergy would choose such a saint to lead them, but the choice was unanimous—which gives us a good idea of how desperate they had become for a sincere bishop who could raise them out of the noxious trough they found themselves in.

The Rome that Gregory inherited was no jewel. Though the city's position had made it a prize fought over by Byzantines and Goths, it was now, after so many battles, little more than a depressed and defeated backwater, its ancient Senate gone, its enormous population (which had once exceeded a million) reduced to a tenth of its former size, its marvelous water delivery system of ancient aqueducts in ruins over the hills from which water leaked into the plain, creating stagnant pools of disease. Communication with the outside world was blocked by the Lombard barbarians, who had come in droves to inhabit the northern half of the Italian peninsula.

But Gregory loved this city and its language and customs. Even when he had been the previous bishop's apocrisiary (or ambassador) to Constantinople for seven years, he had steadfastly refused to learn Greek. "How could anyone," he once asked, "be seduced by Constantinople, and how could anyone forget Rome?" Gregory was in many ways typical of the early Middle Ages, credulous of divine wonders, full of pious awe. But his many letters, still in the Vatican's possession, also show him to have been a *padrone* who combined medieval piety with the ancient Roman civic virtues of order, practicality, and hardheaded realism. He was required to engage in constant political haggles if only to save Rome from further depredations. He took his office as conserver of "Peter's Patrimony" most seriously, insisting that the farflung "Petrine" estates be administered justly and their bounty awarded to local people in need. "Promote not so much the worldly interests of the Church," he admonished the supervisors of these vast estates, "as the relief of the needy in their distress"—a sentiment one looks for in vain in subsequent papal pronouncements. He drew up an address list of every poor person in Rome, so that each could receive an adequate weekly food supply from the fruits of the episcopal farms. He saw to it that his own dinner table was populated by a dozen poor people each afternoon.

In regard to his office, he retained a wholly admirable humility, infrequent enough in his predecessors, hardly ever displayed by his successors. His favorite title was neither "pope" nor "patriarch of the West," but "servant of the servants of God." He admonished the patriarch of Constantinople for styling himself "the Ecumenical Patriarch" and objected strenuously when the patriarch of Alexandria addressed Gregory as "Universal Papa" (that is, Pope or Father). "Away with these words," exclaimed the bishop of Rome, "that increase vanity and weaken love!" A bishop should be ever "a minister, not a master," one who attempts "to subdue himself, not his brethren."

Gregory lived to see orthodox Christianity make fresh inroads among the Lombards, among the Visigoths of Spain, and—with Gregory's careful intervention—among the pagan Angles and Saxons, who had recently wrested southern Britain from its Celtic Christian population. Having spied some young Angles on sale in the Roman slave market and thinking their blond beauty made them "not Angles but angels," Gregory sent his librarian, Augustine, off to evangelize Angland (or England). The nearsighted, sedentary scholar was hardly the ideal apostle, and the wretched man tried to wriggle out of his assignment more than once. But Gregory was used to making do with whatever was available. Augustine, who arrived in England quaking with fear and expecting to be eaten, ended up doing a creditable job and rewarding Gregory's faith in him.

As Christianity took root in these barbaric realms, Gregory the lover of Rome sent forth a steady stream of letters offering advice, telling his friends and representatives in various places not to be too fussy about keeping to Roman custom, even daring them to be creative in altering the customs of the Roman Church to fit local sensibilities. "My brother," he urged the cautious Augustine, now ensconced at Canterbury as primatial bishop of the English nation, "customs are not to be cherished for the sake of a place, but places are to be cherished for the sake of what is good about them." In other words, adapt—and love your neighbor as he is, even if he is an Anglo-Saxon.

Gregory's care for all the Churches, expressed in his constant outpouring of thoughtful letters to every part of the known world, undoubtedly shortened his life, for he died in his early sixties, an exhausted man happy in the knowledge that he had done his best in an impossible job. His nimble mind was bent on solving problems wherever he met them. But his love of prayer and contemplation impelled him, even in this time of upheaval, to collect and document the Roman Church's musical traditions, leaving his name in permanent association with the ethereal beauty of "Gregorian" chant. He lived in a time of political and cultural change so rapid that many, including Gregory himself, believed the world was approaching its end. But even had he lived in a more settled age, his understanding of his role as one of universal concern would probably have shortened his life. Though he rejected the title of "universal father," he came closer to fulfilling it than any of his predecessors. Nor would any of his successors come near to realizing such a description till the advent of John XXIII.

The death of Gregory the Great brings us to the opening decade of the seventh century—about a third of the way through Christian history. Gregory is a kind of hinge, for with his "reign" the Western Church definitively turns its back on the postclassical Greco-Roman world, turning its face toward the barbarian nations—the Celts, Germans, Vikings, and western Slavs who will come to represent its future. The once-unified empire had always had a cultural fissure running through it, dividing those who spoke Greek from those who spoke Latin. This fissure was made only more emphatic when the emperor abandoned Rome for the oriental lavishness of New Rome, empowering a new patriarch at Constantinople, who could often rival the bishop of Old Rome—who had previously been held in evident honor above the bishops of the other ancient patriarchates of Jerusalem, Antioch, and Alexandria, all thought to be of apostolic origin.

Greek cultural superiority was a given of the ancient world: Greeks knew they had no intellectual rivals, and even Romans tended to accept their superiority, if more than a little grudgingly. This cultural hegemony made it difficult for even the bishop of

Rome, speaking, as it were, on the bones of Peter and Paul, to assert clear leadership over the Greek East, especially in intellectual—that is, theological—matters. Given Byzantium's growing isolation and cultural stasis, its increasing political irrelevance to the West, and the infusion into the Western Church of the rude but vigorous barbarians, the stage was set for a complete break. It would be four and a half centuries more in coming, but from the time of Gregory little more than lip service would ever again be paid to the Eastern empire, and an invisible but permanent wall of estrangement was building between the Churches of the Greek East and the Church of the Latin West.

In the East, where the emperor held all political power, a synodal or conciliar form of Church government had become the norm: decisions of importance could be made only by the bishops gathered in council, who were bound to be guided by their own most revered traditions. In the West, the bishop of Rome, the West's sole patriarch, will increasingly be elevated as *il papa*, *the* pope, despite great Gregory's rejection of the title; and the other Western bishops will correspondingly shrink in stature. It is in some ways an inevitable, even a natural, development. In the land of the blind, the one-eyed man is king. In a rough, illiterate society, full of talismans and superstitions, the civilized island of Roman culture, redolent of holiness and continuity with the ancients, could only increase in importance. In a world of warriors and petty strongmen, devoid of intellectual traditions or any notion of conciliar-parliamentary polity, kingship will take on ever more hallowed associations. And who can be more kingly than Peter's successor, the only man on earth who can be said to speak on behalf of the King of Kings?

To Peter, Jesus had given—in the metaphorical language of ancient Palestine—"the keys to the Kingdom of Heaven" and the power to "bind" and "loose" in heaven and on earth. These last were translated by Jerome (whose fourth-century translation of the Bible would be used in the West for more than a thousand years) as *ligare* and *solvere*—technical legal Latin suggesting that Peter's successors had authentic juridical claims over the Kingdom of Heaven itself and certainly over the kingdoms of Earth.

The Two Swords

WHEREAS IN THE EAST the relative power of the episcopate was always exercised in the shadow of an all-powerful emperor (who customarily thought of himself in the spirit of Constantine as the "Thirteenth Apostle"), in the West there was a political vacuum left by the gradual receding of empire, a vacuum that would be filled uncomfortably by a chessboard of jostling medieval figures: barbarian kings of growing territorial power, bishops who continued to embody what remained of the old traditions of Roman law and literacy, and the bishop of bishops. It is not so hard to see how in this new Western political environment the office of Roman bishop would loom ever larger till, to the estranged East, it would come to seem an overbearing monstrosity, an unhealthy and damnable weed that for lack of proper cultivation had grown to endanger the garden of Christendom.

Byzantium, however, which continued to shrink in size, could not fix its attention on the upstart West. To the east of Constantinople, matters were even more unsettled: Slavic barbarians were invading the Balkans and driving the Greek-speaking inhabitants into the sea; Persia was once again on the rise, its Zoroastrian troops capturing (at least for a time) the Byzantine cities of Antioch, Damascus, and Jerusalem; most frightening of all, the whole Arab world was being transformed into a great army of conquest, propelled by the visionary revelations of a camel driver named Mohammed. This new force would in time conquer and convert to Islam nearly all of the Eastern empire (what we call today the Middle East), turning the Mediterranean into a Muslim sea and seriously threatening the cultural survival of Christian Europe.

Despite these looming woes, the Byzantine emperors continued to act as though they were superior to the bishops of Rome, issuing religious decrees supposedly binding on all Christendom and even (in one instance) arresting a Roman bishop, Martin I (649–53), at his own altar in the Lateran Basilica and forcing him to Constantinople, where he was publicly humiliated, physically abused, and then deported to the Crimea to die. A new Eastern theological movement—Iconoclasm (or Image-Breaking)—drove another wedge between East and West. Despite the fact that virtually every formerly revered icon—every representational Christian image—throughout the East was destroyed by the iconoclasts (usually with the emperor's encouragement) on the theory that God had in the Book of Exodus forbidden the making of "graven images," the illiterate West was by this point too much in love with religious images—their vivid colors, their emotional power—ever to give them up. To Westerners, especially those concerned with religious matters, it was simply that the East was at it again, agitated by another exaggerated enthusiasm, advancing another cockamamie theory. "You have no business issuing dogmatic constitutions [in favor of Iconoclasm]," Gregory II (715–31), bishop of Rome, wrote to the emperor Leo, as if to an outrageously naughty boy. "When it comes to dogmas, you haven't the brains; yours are too crude and militaristic."

Islam's advance into Europe, after overrunning Visigothic Spain, was brought to a decisive halt in 732 at Poitiers in southern Gaul by the forces of Charles Martel. The patriarch of the West could only be grateful and sent a delegation to Charles asking protection for Peter's Patrimony—the territories of central Italy clustered around Rome and Ravenna, territories threatened by Lombard incursions. Though Charles made no reply, this was the first uncertain step in a collaboration that would refashion the power structure of Europe and influence its politics ever after.

Charles was not yet king of the Franks but Mayor of the Palace to the Merovingian kings, who were kings in name only. What did the bishop of Rome think? asked Charles. Shouldn't he who wields the power hold the title? By all means, Rome replied and supplied its loyal missionary Boniface to anoint and crown the upstart king. Then, on January 6, 754, the old feast of Christmas, Stephen II, two years after his election as bishop of Rome, arrived at Ponthion for a meeting with Pepin, Charles's son and successor and now (with Rome's help) undisputed king of the Franks. They got on famously, Pepin willingly leading the mounted bishop's horse as if he were a stable boy. The bishop anointed Pepin, bestowed on him and his male heirs the newly minted title "patrician of the Romans," and swore the Franks to eternal allegiance to this family. Pepin then vowed to restore Peter's Patrimony to its rightful owner.

And Pepin was as good as his word. The next two years saw the creation of a new kingdom, carved out by Pepin's sword, encompassing as much of the west coast of Italy as modern Lazio, running through the heart of the Italian peninsula, and spreading north along the Adriatic from Ancona almost to Venice. Here we have the origin of *lo Stato della Chiesa*, the Papal States. Of course, the Byzantine emperor objected, crying feebly that this territory was rightly his, now wickedly alienated from the Roman empire by barbarian upstarts. And, indeed, there is mystery here. The bishop of Rome had long held extensive properties, farms that fed the poor and supported the far-flung activities of the see of Peter. But the bishop had never before claimed to be anything more than a landowner, certainly not a monarch. Yet here was Stephen accepting the absolute rule of considerable territories at the hands of a self-styled king.

About this time, there came to light a document known as the Donation of Constantine, which presented the first Christian emperor as setting the bishop of Rome once and for all time above all other bishops and bestowing on him "all the privileges of our supreme station as emperor and all the glory of our authority." Constantine's donation included all of Italy, as well as "the Western regions"—that is, the whole of Europe west of Italy. The document was completely bogus, but to eighth-century eyes it looked reassuringly authentic. It became the theological and political basis for the papal role in subsequent Western history: the pope (and we should probably begin calling him this now even if "pope" as his exclusive title still lies three centuries in the future) was, in effect, not only patriarch but emperor of the West, ceded this role by Constantine himself. The pope was—to say the least!—entitled to the territories of central Italy; moreover, imperial rule lay in his gift. Who devised the forgery no one can say for sure.

Before the modern period and the selling of "shares," all wealth lay in land ownership. The saying of Jesus that "you cannot serve both God and money" was relegated to the outer darkness; and the wealth of the Papal States brought into being fresh horrors not known before, as the principal Roman families set in motion an unending mafia war over whose candidate would sit on the throne of Peter—whose stock had spiked with the Donation of Pepin—and which family would get its hands most deeply into the papal pork barrel. From this time on, the halls and dungeons of Old Rome would echo with never-ending cries of torture, betrayal, poisoning, murder, and maiming, all in hopes of making a pope or thwarting a candidacy. The goal of the pope in acquiring a kingdom was security for the papacy, but this earthly kingdom would make the papacy more insecure than ever. The ghoulish intrigues that we associate with the Renaissance Borgias begin right here in the middle of the eighth century.

Collaboration between the pope and the Frankish king grew even closer when on Christmas Day 800 Pope Leo III solemnly crowned Pepin's son Charlemagne as Holy Roman Emperor of the West—a title that would serve its bearers for more than a thousand years—in a singular ceremony in Old Saint Peter's. The less-than-reliable Frankish account of this scene includes the detail that the pope then prostrated himself on the floor before Charlemagne, as protocol required before the Byzantine emperor. Whether or not this act of humility occurred, Charlemagne, the greatest of his line, had no doubt that his authority came directly from God, not the pope, and felt himself free within his own demesnes to make significant religious decisions, such as adding a key word to the consecrated age-old text of the Creed. (The word, *filioque,* expressed the belief of the West that the Holy Spirit "proceeded" from the other two Persons of the Trinity. But since in the original conciliar formulation the Spirit had proceeded only from God the Father, this addition was seen by the East as further proof of the West's heretical tendencies.) The pope's objections to this innovation carried no weight with the Emperor of the West. All the same, the pope had succeeded in establishing papal anointing (and therefore papal approval) as a prerequisite for imperial rule in the West.

In the centuries after the crowning of Charlemagne, the question of who was on top, pope or emperor, would remain unsettled. This question of sovereignty, of which sword was absolute—the spiritual or the temporal—was to be threaded through all the European political tensions of succeeding centuries until the clear emergence of powerful nation-states in the sixteenth century would render the Sword Spiritual an anachronism.

But the pope, considering not only the proper arrangement of the temporal powers of this world but the inner workings of his Church, had other fish to fry. Another forgery—this time an elaborate collection of letters of earlier "popes" and canons (or decrees) of ancient councils, some authentic, others spurious, many nonsensical—emerged around 850 under Frankish auspices. The purpose was to undermine the traditional power of metropolitan archbishops over smaller dioceses by asserting that all power in the Church had always derived from the pope and that the bishops were only vicars—his representative spokesmen—in regions where he could not personally reside. A pope could appoint or remove anyone and had the right to hear any appeal, the judgment of competent local authority, whether spiritual or temporal, notwithstanding. These false "Decretals of Isidore of Seville," which departed so strikingly from the customs of the ancient Church (in which all bishops were seen as sharing in the unitary power of the apostles) were taken for the real thing. From them—and not from the New Testament or from the life of the ancient Church—issue the extraordinary theological claims, still made in canon law, that the pope's jurisdiction over the Church—and, therefore, in the last analysis over all Christians—is "full" (that is, total), "supreme," "ordinary" (that is, constant), and "immediate." In the course of the two and a half centuries since the death of Gregory the Great, the Church had gone from viewing the pope as the servant of all and an exemplar to others ("a minister," as Gregory had said, "and not a master") to setting him up, in theory at least, as absolute monarch of the whole world.

The first pope to act as if the False Decretals were true was Nicholas I (858–67), the third and last bishop of Rome to be given the title "the Great." Nicholas cut a great swath through his time, demanding—and getting—obedience from powerful archbishops, who had formerly thought themselves autonomous, even extracting obedience from the emperor Lothair himself, forcing the emperor to abandon a fertile concubine he was planning to raise as empress and return to Theutberga, his barren wife. He instructed the Eastern emperor in his duty of obedience to Rome and excommunicated the embarrassingly young patriarch of Constantinople, who had been illegitimately appointed by the emperor because he needed a yes man. The patriarch, Photius, retaliated by excommunicating Nicholas, but the pope never heard of the excommunication. He died before the news reached Rome.

The mutual excommunications of pope and patriarch, which severed the Eastern from the Western Church, did not become final and unalterable till 1054, two centuries after the age of Nicholas. But by his time, communication between the two branches of Christianity had all but stopped completely. In language, culture, and obedience, the two Churches had grown so separate that they felt they no longer had anything to say to each other. And the see of Rome, after the brief respite of Nicholas's reign, descended once more to the cesspool of intrigue to which it had grown accustomed.

Inconvenient popes were dispatched mafia-style or left to live on as terrifying examples, minus eyes, lips, tongue, hands—or, in one case, all the above. As such occurrences became almost commonplace, the ne plus ultra scene was no doubt the trial, ordered by Stephen VI (896–97), of the corpse of his predecessor, Formosus. For the occasion of this "Cadaver Synod," the putrid mummy of the dead pope, whose name means "One Beautifully Formed," was arrayed in full pontificals and deposited on a throne. In due course it was found guilty of many crimes, had the blessing fingers of its right hand chopped off, and was thrown into the River Tiber, whose green sludge serves as the unhallowed final resting place of not a few popes. Stephen would come to his own grisly end after two years in office, deposed, imprisoned, and choked to death.

But the theory of papal supremacy, as well as its practice during the pontificate of Nicholas the Great, had become an established feature of the medieval landscape. Because there now was in place, nearly a full millennium after the time of Jesus, most of the privileges claimed by the historic papacy, we may say that the construction of the platform from which John XXIII would speak to the world was well on its way to completion. It needed only to be reinforced and more splendidly decorated. It also, however, had to undergo a long history of abuse and neglect.

The Need for Reform

THE PAPACY had become a corrupt political institution and with only a few bright moments would remain so from the middle of the eighth century till Paul III would convene the Council of Trent in 1545. This means that for eight centuries—more than a third of its history—the Roman bishopric or "Holy See" was to be fatally tainted by the power politics of Europe and by the grasping atmosphere of papal Rome, as well as by the venal motivations of the men who sat on its throne, a spiritual seat in name only. "Kings who incarnate an idea," muses the Prince in *The Leopard*, Giuseppe di Lampedusa's great novel of the Italian Revolution, "should not, cannot, fall below a certain level for generations; if they do the idea itself suffers." So, too, with the papacy, so much so that the historian is hard put to make his selection among the abundant riches of outrageous incidents: which scandal to include, which abomination to forgo. It is diffi-

cult indeed, even for the doggedly professional researcher, working systematically through this increasingly dreary eight-century
saga, to keep straight the difference between one conniving papal
mistress and another, one set of highly beneficed papal nephews
and another, one family fortune and another, which boy cardinals were placed on the papal throne to satisfy which families,
which pope built which splendid palace, who thought up each
new method of increasing papal revenues, which popes died in
their beds at an early age from an excess of early morning sex.

There were, even during this long period, reforming popes,
though their reforms tended to stop well short of the sort of
remedies that were actually called for. Leo IX (1049–54), for instance, who walked to Rome for his papal coronation all the way
from his episcopal see of Toul in Alsace, was resolved to make
the papacy more than a familial Roman institution. He traveled
to northern Italy, Germany, and France, holding reforming synods to deal with the evils of simony, lay investiture, and clerical
marriage (or, where marriage was not a viable possibility, concu-
binage). Though of these, only simony (the selling of Church offices to the highest bidder) is likely on the face of it to strike the
modern reader as a genuine evil, "lay investiture" had come to
mean not the democratic election of a priest or bishop (the common practice of the primitive Church) but appointment by the
prevailing strongman, whether duke, king, or emperor.

Leo's innovative view of his office—"proactive," we might be
tempted to call it in contemporary terms—also left room for the
pope as commander in chief of papal armies, a role that popes
would resort to with catastrophic results in coming centuries. In
Leo's case, the catastrophe was the defeat of his inexperienced
forces in 1053 and his arrest by the Normans, who had expelled
the Muslims from southern Italy and were threatening the freedom of the Papal States. The Byzantine empire (or what was left

of it) greatly resented this papal intervention into what it still thought of as imperial territory, and Leo's disastrous military campaign supplied the occasion for the final break between Rome, henceforth center of "Catholicism," and Constantinople, henceforth center of "Orthodoxy."

Not many years later, a successor of Leo's, Nicholas II (1058–61), set out a new mode for electing popes. Up to now, they had been selected in all sorts of ways—originally elected by the priests and people of Rome, later appointed by emperors, kings, or Rome's most distinguished mafia families. Now, a new pope was to be chosen by seven electors, the cardinal (or "hinge") bishops of the principal Roman churches, his election confirmed by the cardinal priests and deacons of Rome, with final confirmation to be obtained by the acclamation of the Roman people. Though "cardinal" was already a term in transition, an honorific whose precise meaning would continue to evolve, this mode of election represented a break with lay investiture and the corruptions of power politics; and it forms the basic procedure for papal election to this day (though the laity are now completely excluded).

The greatest of the medieval popes was Hildebrand, a monk who had been deeply influenced by a monastic reform movement generated by the Abbey of Cluny in Aquitaine and who took the name Gregory VII (1073–85). Cluny's reforms would hardly strike us as radical. The charter it was awarded by its founder, the generous and thoughtful William, Duke of Aquitaine, enabled it to remain free of local political control and to answer only to the pope. Thus liberated from the need to spend their energies in endless political machinations, the monks of Cluny had time to devote to spiritual and aesthetic considerations, such as art, architecture, and liturgy capable of inspiring devotion. Cluny's achievement was to embody faith in ritual and stone. It was unique in its day because it took religion seriously.

Monkish Hildebrand was the pope who, after more than a thousand years of Christian tradition, made lifelong celibacy mandatory for clergy throughout the West, upsetting the families of priests everywhere, as wives were declared whores and children bastards with no claim on inheritance. Indeed, the incremental loss incurred by Churches as ecclesiastical property fell more and more into the hands of priests' heirs played no little part in Hildebrand's insistence on celibacy. But it was not his whole reason.

Heretofore, the obligation had risen and sunk fitfully. Peter, as is clear from the New Testament, had a wife who shared his ministry; and this was true of other apostles as well. The New Testament's Epistle to Titus even advises local congregations that whoever they elect as their priest should be the "husband of *one* wife," rather than of several. But early in Christian history—as early certainly as the apostolate of Paul—the idea that celibacy is superior to marriage began to gain adherents. Paul's exaltation of the single life may have been practical (how could he have covered so much missionary territory with a wife and children?) and feminist (women, especially, were freer to live a life of the spirit if they were not limited by the enslaving demands imposed on a wife in a male-dominated society). But Paul was exceptional in many ways, and there is evidence that even bishops of Rome continued to have wives at least into the early fifth century (and afterward, as the idea of married bishops became unthinkable, mistresses). The shift in direction to an all-celibate clergy was gradual, modeled initially by monk-bishops, who were much influenced by the atmosphere of Eastern monasticism, which was in its turn much influenced by Platonism—and particularly by the dualist strain in Platonism that saw the material world (and therefore the human body) as inimical to immortal spirit, something to be dominated and, insofar as possible, ignored. For all that, even Hildebrand's reform was unable to eliminate clerical marriage altogether, as lonely priests simply invented new terms. Their wives became "housekeepers," their children a gaggle of "nephews" and "nieces"—and their sympathetic parishioners conspired in this innocent ruse.

Thinking the elimination of lay investiture the heart of reform, Hildebrand wasted little time in setting forth a bold assertion of papal prerogatives in the teeth of the claims of emperors, kings, and lesser princes. In 1075 he published the *Dictatus Papae*, a set of twenty-seven propositions that included such old standbys as: the pope is Christendom's final court to whom anyone may make appeal over the heads of local bishops or monarchs and, concomitantly, the pope may be judged by no one but God. But there was much in these dictates that was novel: only the pope is to be called "by right, universal" (thus forgetting Gregory the Great's vigorous rejection of such a title) and may, therefore, depose even an emperor and absolve his subjects from their obedience; only the pope can depose or transfer a bishop, add to or alter the canons of Church law, or call an ecumenical council (thus dismissing the precedents of the ancient Church); the pope is supreme over all bishops and councils; even his legates take precedence over any bishop. Most startling of all are the assertions that "the Roman Church has never erred" (conveniently ignoring Vigilius and a couple of others), it "will never err to all eternity," and the pope is by virtue of his office a living saint. Though the pope hasn't tried to depose an emperor recently, just about all the other claims are still in force, however innovative most of them were in the eleventh century. The Vatican is too politically astute to claim publicly nowadays that the pope is a living saint, but the etiquette of addressing the pope as "Your Holiness" or "Holy Father," a vocative locution expected of everyone who meets the pope (regardless of personal belief), goes a long way toward suggesting that even this dictate remains in effect. In fact, the only planks yet to be added to the papal platform after the *Dictatus* were the pope's incontestable right to appoint all bishops (which Hildebrand could never have gotten away with because so many cities, cathedral chapters, and princes were well aware of their time-hallowed rights in this respect) and the doctrinal infallibility not just of the Roman Church but of the pope alone.

Hildebrand's greatest success was the sight of Henry IV, the German king (who styled himself Holy Roman Emperor), standing barefoot in the snow for three days in the courtyard of Countess Matilda of Tuscany at Canossa in the Apennine mountains, while the pope, Matilda's guest, decided whether or not he would forgive him. Henry's sins were egregious: he had attempted to make his own candidate bishop of Milan without consulting the pope and, after the pope had castigated him, had forced the German and Lombardian bishops, over whom he held control, to "depose" the pope. Unexpected political consequences, especially the subsidence of support for his throne by independent-minded bishops and princes, drove Henry to his knees. The image of the king, the most powerful man in Christendom, as a painfully humiliated beggar would live on in medieval imagination with the same force that the image of Leo the Great confronting Attila once had for the people of late antiquity.

Hildebrand forgave Henry—reluctantly. But the pope's remarkable luck did not hold. He was to die at Salerno, a fugitive from Rome, cursed by the Romans who had once loved his steely courage, now blamed for his unbending obstinacy in provoking against them not only the emperor's forces but the cutthroat Normans, who nearly leveled the city. Hildebrand never doubted the course he had taken. "I have 'loved righteousness and hated iniquity,'" he maintained, quoting Psalm 45. "For this, I die an exile."

Though the Vatican reveres his memory, the contemporary reader is likely to find Hildebrand insufficiently "spiritual." It is instructive, however, to ask ourselves what else the man might have done in the circumstances. The great fight of the Middle Ages was over real estate; and the Latin tag *Cujus regio, ejus religio* (The ruler decides the religion of his realm) had overwhelming force long before the Reformation. If the pope wanted to avoid being reduced to court chaplain, either to the emperor or to some magnate closer at hand, he had to assert—vigorously and often—that he possessed unique prerogatives not conferred by any man. Since no one had yet conceived of "rights," civil or otherwise, that could be written into law to protect the individual against the whims of the monarch, it is hard to imagine how Hildebrand could have insisted on the special privileges of the spiritual realm except as he did. Had he given in to Henry and admitted that the Cross was simply the creature of the Crown, would the Church have anything left today?

It is in this context that we should consider the last important title that the pope would claim for himself. For ages, he had been acknowledged as Peter's "vicar" or stand-in. But Peter was thought to have been bishop of Antioch, perhaps of other ancient Churches as well, before coming to Rome. As the life of the Eastern Churches (such as Antioch and Alexandria) faded from Western memory and as the cold necessities of European *Realpolitik* closed their iron lock on the Roman Church, the pope—in the person of Innocent III (1198–1216)—was moved to proclaim: "We are the successor of the prince of the apostles but we are not his vicar, nor the vicar of any man or apostle, but the vicar of Jesus Christ himself." If such a grand pronouncement can only make Christians uneasy today—what, in this theory, could be said to have happened to Christ, who had promised to remain always present among his disciples, what had happened to the Holy Spirit?—the pronouncement makes splendid sense as an affirmation of the primacy of the spiritual realm over the mundane exigencies of the temporal order. That the spiritual realm should be localized in one man was probably also inevitable, given the limits of medieval imagination, in which a consecrated individual (whether king or bishop) stood for a whole mass of men. The English king was addressed, at least by other kings, as "England," the French king as "France," and so it went throughout Europe. That the pope should be imagined to be Christ's visible stand-in is logical. As England needed the visible figure "England," the Church required a visible figure of its own—and who but the pope could fill such a role?

Of course, the new concentration of power that resulted from Hildebrand's exaltation of the pope's role within the Church quickly lent itself to new forms of corruption: if Rome was the court of last resort in cases that had once been dealt with locally, if more and more postings within the Church had to be approved by the pope, more and more palms had to be greased, and more and more ducats found their way to the papal purse. To understand these currents of power in their medieval context, it is useful to compare this age with that of modern Africa, its nearest contemporary equivalent, where the leaders tend to be village chieftains raised to national status and the led are often illiterate and unable to discern subtle shifts in power or to exercise much in the way of political effect. As a discouraged Kofi Annan, the recently retired UN Secretary General, remarked of his home continent: "For everything you want, you need a permit. The person who gives you a permit wants a bribe. The person who's going to make an appointment for you wants a bribe. And so on." Though the Holy See did make most of its money through fees for permits and similar services (as well as through taxes leveled on beneficed bishops and priests), these were not bribes precisely, since they were generally known from officially published price lists. But the prices were steep. Until the reforms of Vatican II, for instance, only wealthy Catholics could expect to obtain marriage annulments, because only they could afford the endless list of "fees" required.

The crusades, convoked by powerful popes (in their newly fashioned role as executive spokesmen for Christendom) to win back the Holy Land from Muslim control, also created fresh opportunities for money to change hands and, as war inevitably does, opened the way for cruel men to practice barbaric atrocities on vast populations of the innocent and helpless. Not only could you massacre to your heart's content, you were, while in arms, a sort of temporary cleric under the pope's protection (and therefore technically exempt from prosecution in a secular court); and when you died you went straight to heaven, all your sins having been forgiven you by the pope's plenary indulgence.

Innocent III, who straddled the twelfth and thirteenth centuries, was the most powerful pope of the Middle Ages, a man who knew how to extract large concessions (especially on the issue of ecclesiastical appointments) from kings in return for throwing his weight to them as the occasion demanded. It was Innocent, therefore, who roundly condemned Magna Carta— the fragile beginning of the world's first parliamentary system— nullifying it as an illegal encroachment on the privileges of God's anointed monarch.

But it was also Innocent, "adorned in jewels and silk, crowned with gold, mounted on a white horse," as Bernard of Clairvaux reprovingly described the pope, who gave his blessing to Francis of Assisi's peculiar experiment in absolute poverty. Indeed, it was saints such as Bernard and Francis, Peter Damien and Hugh of Cluny, living far from the centers of power, who were the real strength behind the medieval reform movement. Pope Innocent, worldly, sharp, and ironic (never more so than in his choice of name), knew in his heart that what integrity the Church possessed rested on such people. In a dream he could never forget, Innocent saw the Lateran Basilica—the pope's own cathedral church and symbolic seat of all his power—about to fall to the ground, held up only by the strong arm of *il Poverello*, the little poor man from Assisi. It was this dream that induced the effulgently adorned Innocent to give his seal of approval to a company of gray-clad wretches, who would become known as "Franciscans" and who were usually preceded by their own body odor and a host of circling fleas—and who believed their way of life an imitation of the earthly Jesus. In a world of illiterates who lived by images rather than words, such commitment served as a living witness, condemning the "way" of the popes more eloquently than words could ever do. A scant two years after Francis died, Innocent's nephew, reigning as Gregory IX (1227–41), would "canonize" *il Poverello* as a saint.

The authority to make a saint, traditionally in the power of the local community—the people who had known the man or woman—was now, like so many other things, reserved exclusively to the papacy. One of Innocent's lasting effects was the enormous expansion of the Code of Canon Law, an expansion completed under his immediate successor that reserved one right after another to the pope alone, excluding not only kings and princes but bishops, priests, and ordinary people from a participation that had been considered normal in the ancient Church.

Innocent's lasting shame, however, lies in his crusades, one against the Albigensians of Spain and southern France, during which he offered an indulgence from sin to all who took part. They took part with abandon, slaughtering men, women, and children. The Albigensians held austere beliefs not unlike those of the Franciscans, but they made the fatal mistake of denying the efficacy of the Catholic system of sacraments—which was intolerable to Innocent. Heretics, he reasoned, those denying an essential doctrine of the Church, had to be exterminated before they infected others, as if they were rats carrying plague. Under his immediate successor, Honorius III (1216–27), this idea would blossom into the evil flower of the Papal Inquisition, which, like so many papal initiatives, took precedence over local authority and came to interrogate, torture, and execute with impunity. Innocent also preached the Fourth Crusade to Jerusalem. In the event, the attention of this savage army was diverted to Constantinople, and the population of Greek Christians was attacked with the same fervor that one might have expected to be reserved for French and Spanish heretics.

If Innocent III may be taken as an example of a strong pope who did at least some good and had some sense of his own limitations, the thirteenth century closes with Boniface VIII (1293–1303), a papal megalomaniac who understood only his own importance. Like Caesar Augustus, he erected statues of himself everywhere and was fond of dressing up as a Roman emperor. He remodeled the papal crown, which had been an elongated cone with a single diadem, symbolizing priestly power, into the triple tiara, symbolizing the powers of priest, king, and emperor. The triple tiara has been worn by popes ever since, till Paul VI sold his and gave the money to the poor. Before his pontificate, Boniface had been highly regarded as a canon lawyer (could there be a worse training ground for a pope than a lifetime of narrow legalisms?); and he was smart about money, initiating the first Jubilee Year, which brought countless thousands of pilgrims to Rome, so many that, according to an eyewitness account, the sacristans in the major basilicas had to spend *"notte e giorno . . . con in mano rastrelli e raccoglievano . . . senza fine"* (night and day . . . with rakes in hand as they harvested . . . without end) the monetary offerings left by the faithful. He brought the papal indulgence machine to its basest level yet, bestowing plenary indulgences on anyone willing to join his vendetta against the powerful Colonna family. Rumored to be an atheist and an insatiable pederast, he secured the undying hatred of many, including Dante, the greatest poet of the Middle Ages, who in the *Inferno* gives us Boniface hanging upside down in the perpetual fire of the devil's oven. In the papal bull (from the Latin *bulla,* for lead seal) *Unam sanctam* (One, Holy), he formally taught that subjection to the pope is "utterly necessary for the salvation of every human creature." Thus did this horrifying creature think to grab hold of not only the purse but even the soul of each human being. And he knew perfectly well from which direction he could expect obstruction. In another bull, *Clericis laicos,* he started off with this earth-shattering insight: "All history shows clearly the hostility of the laity toward the clergy." Can't imagine why.

A close successor to Boniface was John XXII (1316–34), who so identified himself with both Christ *and* his own immense riches that he was moved to teach that the earthly Jesus and his apostles had not been so poor as to own nothing at all. Since this was completely at variance with the well-known Franciscan interpretation of the gospels, John found he had to suppress the most severe branch of the Franciscans, known as the "Spirituals." The Inquisition went to work, and in due course four innocuous Franciscans were burned at the stake. John succeeded, in fact, in making enemies of the entire Franciscan movement, including the philosopher William of Occam, the most discerning writer of the day.

It's seldom wise to make an enemy of a writer. William got busy at his trade, refuting John's theology point by point; and by the time of the pope's death, John was held throughout Europe to be that rare bird, a pope who had actually fallen into heresy. Despite his literary success, I would not wish to inflate Occam's importance in this controversy. Rather, it would seem that, even in a time of few books and sparse literacy, even so august a personage as a pope could not win the great mass of people over to a view of Jesus that contradicted the plain sense of Scripture. "Foxes have their holes and the birds of the air their nests, but the Son of Man has nowhere to lay his head," said Jesus of himself. He had nothing. People high and low might have had trouble defining the proper role of a pope, but this pope went too far when he tried to foist on them a portrait of Jesus contrary to the gospels.

John XXII did not rule from Rome. He was second in a line of popes who took up residence in the French town of Avignon. Boniface's fulminations had in the end proven impotent to protect the papacy from the growing power of nationalism, and Boniface himself was hounded to an early grave by the forces of France's Philip the Fair, who had no patience for anyone asserting power over *him*. (The humiliated Boniface found himself toward the end surrounded in his hometown of Anagni, south of Rome, where he became the only pope in history to be slapped publicly—the famous *schiaffo d'Anagni*, the slap of Anagni.)

It was the powerful magnet of the French monarchy that first brought the popes to Avignon, where they were to remain for seventy years—most of the fourteenth century—captives of the king surely, but living better than popes had ever lived, erecting dazzling villas and concerning themselves with their admirably efficient estates. "My predecessors," exclaimed the cheerful Clement VI (1342–52) on his way to another *fête*, "just didn't know *how* to be pope!"

The one lasting, if dubious, achievement of the Avignon popes—needless to say they were all Frenchmen—was to give the Curia (or papal court) a more rational structure, creating the basic dicasteries (or departments) of the papal bureaucracy, as well as the Sacred Rota (or marriage tribunal), all of which remain in existence to this day. One great saint crosses the story of the Avignon papacy (or "Babylonian Captivity of the Church," as it was known to those who disapproved): Catherine of Siena, a mystic and charmer of the first rank, who in her letters addressed the pope as *"dulcissimo babbo mio"* ("my sweetest da-da") but was not afraid to sail into Avignon and wag her finger under the pope's nose, while instructing him in his solemn duty to return to Rome.

Unfortunately, the return to Rome encouraged only further disintegration, in the form of the Great Western Schism, with a pope at Rome, a "pope" at Avignon, and at length a third "pope" striding about. The schism was able to get off the ground because the valid pope, Urban VI (1378–89), the first to be elected by the Roman cardinals since the supposed end of the Avignon papacy, turned out to be a screaming madman once installed. By the time a solution was reached, the schism had lasted nearly forty years. In the end, no one could keep straight who the real pope was. The century and a decade that stretched from the beginning of the Avignon papacy to the end of the schism had brought the papacy to the lowest esteem in which it had ever been held. There must, everyone thought, be a better way of organizing Christianity than this.

The seemingly obvious solution was Conciliarism, the old belief of the Eastern Church that the bishops in plenary council, not the pope, were the whole Church's final arbiter. It was indeed a council—the Council of Constance in the Swiss Alps—that at last put an end to the schism, managing to retire three extant popes and electing a single new pope, Martin V (1417–31). Theorists like Occam went even further, speculating that, in the final analysis, authority issued not from the pope nor even from the bishops gathered in council but simply from the Church as a whole because the power to "bind" and "loose" was given not to Peter alone but to the whole Church. Thus the Church—that is to say, all Christians together—could structure the Church in any number of ways and could delegate authority as it wished. Such a theory grew out of late-medieval experiments in republican government but also provided a far more faithful description of the actual functioning of the Church of the apostolic and postapostolic ages right through the time of Gregory the Great than did the medieval theory of papal supremacy.

The Council of Constance, however, which was a council of bishops, did not mean to go so far in disestablishing episcopal prerogatives. Rather, like the English barons who wanted to limit their king by the rules of Magna Carta, the council fathers intended only to rein in papal power so as to increase their own. They decreed that ecumenical councils had to be held regularly, every five to ten years. But once the fathers of the council had returned to their far-flung sees, who would call such councils? The popes, reduced in both prestige and income, bided their time and quietly saw to it that this question would never be answered.

The Council of Constance, in what it thought of as its reforming zeal, also condemned the saintly Czech reformer Jan Hus. This was a terrible mistake, and the Catholic Church is still paying the consequences in the tepid regard of the Czech people. The things that Hus fought for—allowing the laity to drink from the chalice, the Bible accessible to all, participation by all the laity in the affairs of the Church, reform of the openly scandalous lives of the clergy, informed preaching and teaching— seem unremarkable today, certainly not sufficient reason for the flames that lit the walls of Constance on the night they burned Hus alive, despite a specious promise of safe conduct, which had brought the Czech to Constance and had been guaranteed by the emperor himself.

These flames were portents, for we have now reached the Renaissance and its necessary concomitant, the Reformation.

The broken and bankrupt city that Martin V took possession of was about to get a face-lift. As the conciliar movement lost adherents through the sheer impossibility of making it work, humanism—the rediscovery of the art and literature of the pagan past and the inspiration these lent to a fashionable new intellectual force—began to drive all before it. Nicholas V (1447–55), the first humanist pope, was a master at consolidating political ties, which gave him not only breathing room but new income. This he used to begin the transformation of the old city. He abandoned the decaying Lateran, made the Vatican his official residence, and began to redecorate. He restored Castel Sant'Angelo and the ancient buildings of the Capitol; he brought in Fra Angelico to do up the new Vatican palace. Inspired by a confidence that was sweeping over Italy as it began to recover the magnificence of its own past, Nicholas had no doubt what he was about: "to create solid and stable convictions in the minds of the uncouth masses." If his authority were to be "visibly displayed in majestic buildings, lasting monuments, and testimonies that seem to have been planted by God's own hand, faith will grow." In the end, "the whole world will accept and revere [the pope]." His successors can only thank him for giving them such a stage set.

His immediate successors waded into the fashions of humanism like hippos to mud holes, and the religious sensibility of the papacy became so beclouded with the enthusiasms of the day that at times it was impossible to tell a pope from a pagan. Alexander VI (1492–1503), the second Borgia pope, had his Vatican apartments decorated with pictures of the mysteries of Osiris to please his current mistress and fathered nine acknowledged bastards, marrying off the females to princes and installing the males as dukes on papal lands. One of these, Cesare Borgia, served as Machiavelli's model of the ideal Renaissance prince.

Curial documents began to refer to God as "Jupiter," to Mary as "Diana," and to the pope as "God's Consul." The Latin of these documents, imitative of the worst rhetorical excesses of late antiquity and so pretentious as to be indecipherable, was largely given over to an elaborate obsequiousness toward the "Supreme Pontiff" that must have appeared as distasteful then as it does now. Had Peter risen from his grave beneath the basilica and appeared among the living once more, he would never have recognized this court of oriental sycophants as the inheritors of his Church. Papal ceremonial and literary style underwent a similar metamorphosis. Thus was initiated the allusive, refined pompousness that was to mark papal discourse right through the mid-twentieth-century reign of Pius XII, John XXIII's immediate predecessor: never a short sentence, seldom an active verb, impenetrable paragraphs clotted with ornamentation and indirection, a language of effete churchiness, parading itself as imperial, far removed from biblical sounds and themes, and requiring a specialized education if one were to unlock its meanings and intentions.

The most amazing Renaissance pope was Julius II (1503–13), known as *il Terribile*, a commanding, athletic figure who led his troops into battle while clothed in silver armor. He was not the first warrior pope; and, it must be confessed, he was more selfless than his predecessor, Alexander VI, since some of his battles were for the sake of winning back territory that Alexander had alienated from Peter's Patrimony by awarding large parcels to Borgias. By the end of Julius's reign, the French had been driven from the Italian peninsula, and the northern border of the Papal States was approaching the Alps.

An overbearing man of overreaching appetites, he was an enthusiastic patron of the arts and of Michelangelo in particular, who celebrated his patron's fierceness in the great statue of Moses that was intended for Julius's funerary memorial (and was banished by jealous successors to a side aisle of San Pietro in Vincoli). It was Julius who commissioned a new Saint Peter's to replace the Constantinian basilica that was falling down. This Saint Peter's is the one that still stands today, a building that would take nearly half a century to complete. An acute businessman who replenished the papal treasury that had been plundered by Alexander, Julius knew that financing the new Saint Peter's would require funds from an extraordinary source. A sale of indulgences seemed to him the very thing—and in this way the building of the basilica, the quintessential monument to papal power, became the direct cause of the Reformation, the ultimate challenge to this power.

Martin Luther, a sensitive young German friar, had come to Rome on pilgrimage and been scandalized by what he saw of the uncaring, materialistic lives of high-ranking clergy who were supposedly the heart of the Church. But Luther was more than a scrupulous monk; in a time of cold theological aridity, he was much admired as a dynamic theologian of uncommon warmth and creativity. And he was nothing if not earnest. He came to believe that what passed for religion was a jerry-built system of automatic salvation. Though Luther lived long before vending machines, they give us his essential metaphor: the Church preached that its system enabled the devotee to put money (or ritual or some rigmarole or other) into the machine at one end and out would pop personal salvation at the other end. You could even work the machine on behalf of others, especially your dead friends and relations now suffering the fiery tortures of purgatory. If only you were to buy them an indulgence they could pass from the flames to the bliss of heaven. How could you refuse to save your own loved ones from pain (and at the same time help the Supreme Pontiff to build his beautiful new church)? Heaven, insisted Luther, was not a purchasable commodity.

Looking back to this moment of intellectual and moral crisis that would forever split Western Christendom, it is easy to see that Luther was right and the pope (Julius's successor, Leo X, who understood nothing of theology and was interested only in political and financial consequences) wrong. However one refines one's interpretation of these events—claiming, say, that Luther was too sensitive, too unworldly, too confrontational, even too parricidal, and that the reigning pontiff was an unusual blockhead even for a pope—one comes out the same door in the end: somebody had to blow the whistle on these impostors and point the way back to the spirit of Jesus—and whoever did the whistle-blowing had better have all his ducks in a row and all his defenses secure if he did not mean to end like Hus. Luther's ducks were his own bracing ideas, flung like gauntlets before a flabby papal establishment shockingly unprepared for such a challenge. His defenses were German nobles, who offered him their protection either because they were convinced by his theological positions or because they saw in them the more mundane possibility of increasing their own power at the expense of the Church. Luther, who proved to be quite worldly as time went on, was especially good at playing the nobles to his permanent advantage.

What had begun as a series of academic theses by an obscure theologian turned quickly into a movement for radical reform. At each step, as positions hardened on both sides, the rhetoric of the controversy became more and more extreme till, in a short time, there could be no turning back, no compromise. Luther was, in papal rhetoric, "a leper . . . and the son of a bitch, born to bite and snap at the sky with his doggish mouth," all his writings "heretical, scandalous, or offensive to pious ears." To Luther, the papacy was seen more and more as so corrupt as to be irreformable, and the pope was "the whore of Babylon" and the Antichrist prophesied in the Book of Revelation. It was not long before Luther began to claim that the official, visible Church—and therefore the papacy itself—was not founded by Jesus but was the result of historical accidents. Because the Christian clergy had for so long shown themselves to be unreliable guides to spiritual health, *sola scriptura*, Scripture alone, was the single incorrupt authority. He set himself the task of translating the Bible into German, a spectacular achievement given currency by a new invention, the printing press, which enabled the humblest reader to examine the Bible in his own language for the first time, as well as Luther's zesty manifestos. The new invention did what the Internet is now doing to dictatorships throughout the world. It broke the tyrant's monopoly on the truth.

But Luther, none of whose main theological assertions would be rejected by the majority of Catholic theologians and biblical scholars today, was only the beginning. Beyond the Lutheran territories of Germany and Scandinavia (and, from the beginning of the seventeenth century, England, whose Elizabethan Anglicanism retained much of Catholic form and substance), far less Catholic forms of Christian faith were aborning, especially the Calvinism that was to become the dominant species of Protestantism. John Calvin, a much more severe figure than the earthy Luther, managed—almost entirely by sheer willpower—to remake the Swiss city of Geneva into his vision of a model Christian community, where public vice was not tolerated and even private sin was extirpated. Dancing, singing (especially if the lyrics suggested less than total respect for Calvin), and fortunetelling could all bring severe fines or imprisonment on the malefactor; adultery, if discovered, led to execution; laughing during a sermon could get you into major trouble. Geneva became the only city in Christendom without a working theater; and prostitution, formerly a principal Genevan industry, was eliminated. Calvin, the "pope of Geneva," taught that God was so Other that his purposes were unfathomable to mere human beings. The Catholic "domestication" of God—in ritual, art, sacrament, and extravagant devotion to the saints—was an abomination. The terrifying Calvinist God permitted no such mediations (not even the celebration of Christmas) and in fact had predestined every human being from all eternity either to salvation or damnation—and there was nothing you could do about it. Needless to say, Geneva wasn't much fun.

Calvin's spiritual children would fan out in many directions, forming the Dutch Reformed and Scottish Presbyterian Churches, becoming the Huguenots in France and the Puritans in England, who, distressed at the lingering Catholicism of the Anglican Church, finally crossed the Atlantic to establish new Genevas in New England. The division of Western Christianity into warring camps created whole new industries of propaganda, fed by printing presses and reaching ever lower depths of invective. Catholics were seen in Protestant lands as pagans and agents of Satan and their religious practices as forms of black magic. To Catholic eyes, Protestants were rebels who, like Adam, had refused to obey and thus brought on a formerly happy Christendom all the anguish of disunity. Neither side would willingly accord the other the appellation "Christian." It was in this context that the reformers who remained within the Catholic fold set out to do their work.

Though the urge to reform had hardly been confined to those who turned Protestant, the rise of Protestantism and the permanent alienation of whole provinces and countries from the Roman obedience lent undeniable urgency to the need for Catholics to clean up their own house. Not surprisingly, this Catholic Reformation (or Counter-Reformation, as it was more commonly called till recently) was initiated not by the pope but by a series of extraordinary individuals who brought new life to medieval orthodoxy, carefully pruning its evident excesses and giving it bold new directions. Of these the most important was Ignatius Loyola, the Basque soldier who became general of the Jesuits, a new military-style religious order that put itself completely at the service of the Holy See. These men were filled with a new kind of missionary zeal, ready (like Francis Xavier, who blazed a trail of baptisms through India, Malaysia, and Japan and died at the gates of China) to set off for the ends of the non-Christian earth. Within Europe, the Jesuits engineered themselves into smart bombs, focused, flexible, and adept at hitting heretical targets. But many new (and renewed) orders and movements began to give Catholicism a new look, among them the cheerful Italian Oratorians of Philip Neri and the mystical Spanish Carmelites of Teresa of Ávila and John of the Cross. French-speaking Europe had its own Catholic innovators, among them the witty Francis de Sales, who as bishop of Geneva won back many Calvinists to Catholicism. His protégée Jane de Chantal founded the Visitation Sisters; and the compassionate Vincent de Paul founded both the Congregation of the Mission and (with Louise de Marillac) the Sisters of Charity, the first vowed religious women not confined to cloister. These figures (all of whom would become the leading patron saints of a revitalized Catholicism) and their movements created a new ambience for Catholicism that would endure into our own time, an ambience of serious, activist clergy and religious, chaste and often forbidding, allowing themselves few pleasures beyond the overgorgeous Baroque sanctuaries they built and populated, covered in New World gold.

The New World was, indeed, part of their plan. Though they managed to recover some of Europe for the papacy—the Poles, the unwilling Czechs, most of France, and large parts of Germany and the Low Countries—the percipient head-counters saw that the future lay beyond Europe. For the whole of the seventeenth century, Catholic missionaries were the only missionaries; and it is especially the adherence of Latin America and large parts of Africa to the Catholic Church that today gives Catholicism its numerical edge over other forms of Christianity—Orthodox worldwide: 250 million; Protestants: 400 million; Catholics: 1.1 billion (as well as 350 million or so Christians who don't fit easily into one of the three major categories).

It took the papacy a while to get with the new program. Still bedazzled by the glories of their surroundings, the popes continued to live as entitled Renaissance princes. Paul III (1534–49), who saw himself as a patron of the arts and of his several illegitimate children, thought the way forward lay in reestablishing the hated Inquisition. This gruesome papal instrument, eventually supplemented by the Congregation of the Index, which listed all the books one could not read without being brought before the Inquisition, did indeed suppress almost all suspected deviancy in Spain and Italy, though it was hardly a positive step. But the same pope was also responsible for calling a council. He did so reluctantly, ever fearful that the old papal bugbear of Conciliarism would once more raise its head. The council convened at

Trent in the Italian Alps, and it was by conciliar standards a modest affair, only thirty-odd bishops participating at the outset. It took Trent, seldom in session, eighteen years (1545–63) to complete its work, and when it had done so the Counter-Reformation was complete, for the Council of Trent gave to Catholicism the exact shape it would maintain till the calling of Vatican II, a shape which would in time be mistakenly received by conservative Catholics as eternal and unalterable.

Trent did indeed reform Catholicism in that henceforth the lives of the clergy, especially the higher clergy, and of the members of religious orders would never again be the source of open and unchecked scandal they had so often been before. Strict, even punitive standards were set in place for the formation of clergy and vowed religious, and these were gradually implemented to the letter, rooting out the more public forms of sexual laxity and worldliness that had afflicted the Church for so long. By the close of the council, it was inconceivable that a sitting pope would ever again create his bastards cardinals (though popes would, for several decades to come, continue to sire bastards). Beyond this, all of Trent's reforms were reactionary, designed to be specifically anti-Protestant. Against Luther, Tradition, in addition to Scripture, was held to be determinative of faith. A human being's justification was not by faith alone; good works were also necessary. The constitution of the Church was monarchical and God-given (the laity were there only to obey), its sacraments were seven (no more, no less), instituted by Christ. Only its duly ordained priests could turn bread and wine into Christ's body and blood in the Sacrifice of the Mass (no talk of the "Lord's Supper," please), and this central act of the Roman Church would continue to be carried out in the now-hallowed (and unintelligible) language of Latin, as would the other major rituals. On all these matters, compromise might once have been forged, especially since (as theologians on both sides have discovered since Vatican II) the issues were virtually all a matter of terminology rather than of substantial disagreement. But forty-seven years had passed since Luther had first spoken out, and Europe (apart from the Orthodox East) was permanently divided into two armed camps. What Trent had to do was prove that the Catholic Church—saving the expectable moral flaws of some of its members—had been right all along. No quarter could be given, and none was.

The Pope Alone

IF THE PERMANENT EXISTENCE of Protestant kingdoms within Europe meant that the pope could no longer claim to be master of the world (Europe being the only world that had ever really mattered), the post-Reformation popes were determined to be masters of the house that was left to them. Under the exceedingly antipathetic Paul IV (1555–59), a man obsessed with heresy (and who had earlier in his career denounced as a heretic even so blindly loyal a son of the Roman communion as Ignatius Loyola), cardinals were imprisoned on suspicion of heresy, and the Jews of Rome, who had long counted on the popes as protectors, found themselves confined to a ghetto and compelled to sell their property and offer up their sacred books to the bonfires. Pius V (1566–72), a Dominican who introduced the papal fashion of wearing white, solemnly excommunicated Elizabeth, Queen of England, absolved her subjects from their allegiance, and forbade them from recognizing her as their sovereign, all of which only heightened English prejudice against Catholics and made their lives more precarious. Sixtus V (1585–90) helped finance the Spanish Armada against England and generally encouraged the Catholic crowns to war against the Protestant powers and to persecute their Protestant subjects, as would several of his successors. From Sixtus's day forward, all bishops were to come to Rome and kiss the feet of the pope before taking up the duties of their diocese and were to return periodically to report to the pope on their management of their charge. Thus was power to be seen as flowing from the pope, not from the Church, the Assembly of the People, as the ancient theology had held.

Within the Holy City, Sixtus demanded the execution of any religious who broke the vow of chastity (in comic ignorance of the lives of his predecessors) and even tried to execute any layperson discovered in adultery (in direct contravention of the example of Jesus). It was said of Sixtus's Rome that there were more heads on display along the Sant'Angelo Bridge than there were melons for sale in the markets. If such a grisly show seems more characteristically Genevan than Roman, it must be said that Europe had become a continent full of change and full of fear, which now spread to the Americas. Burnings, hangings, and decapitations served absolute monarchs everywhere as their chief tools for enforcing social compliance.

Despite the illusion of absolute control, however, the pope was one absolute monarch who was in the course of being relativized. As Cardinal Richelieu, the French king's *éminence rouge* in the first half of the seventeenth century and the Henry Kissinger of his day, put it: "We must kiss [the pope's] feet and bind his hands." More and more, the Catholic powers paid the pope elaborate homage, kept their own counsel, and went their own way—often at variance, even at war, with one another. In the same period, the bellicose Urban VIII (1623–44) made what is probably the most famous papal error when he placed Galileo, one of the greatest scientists of all time, under lifelong house arrest for "dar[ing] to meddle in matters beyond his competence" by teaching that the earth revolved around the sun—rather than the other way around, as had been thought. It was, in fact, the pope, not the astronomer, who was "beyond his competence."

Urban emptied the papal treasury with gifts to his relatives and an ill-considered war, waged on the advice of his nephews, against an enemy family. And the monarchies of Europe, in the face of toothless papal condemnations, continued to exercise ever greater control over Church appointments, Church property, and religious practices within their realms. Nowhere was this truer than in the kingdom of France, whose "Gallican" Church, though professedly Catholic, was every bit as nationalist as England's Anglican Church.

One pope knew how to live within these new constraints, the amused, ironic Benedict XIV (1740–58), who enjoyed his leisurely strolls around Rome during which he would chat with whoever crossed his path. He took a realistic view of European power politics, securing the liberties of the Church wherever he could, surrendering gracefully and making the best deal when someone else held the upper hand. He was the first pope to employ the encyclical letter as his standard literary form. An insightful theologian, he protected not a few theological innovators, truthful historians, and spiritual guides from their more vindictive critics and modernized both the agricultural methods of the Papal States (substantially increasing revenues) and the machinery of papal governance (markedly improving efficiency). Everyone loved him. Even Protestants found themselves admiring him, and Voltaire, of all people, dedicated a play to him. He belongs as much to the eighteenth century as Dr. Johnson and Ben Franklin. Approached one day during his *passeggiata* by a wild-eyed friar, who told him that the Antichrist had been born, Benedict inquired with apparent interest as to the age of the Antichrist. "Three," came the assured reply. "Ah," smiled the pope benignly, "in that case I shall leave the problem to my successor."

But Europe's century and a half of sectarian wars had taken their toll. Men high and low were fed up with the claims and counterclaims of Churches. More and more, the idea that religion should be a private affair, not interwoven with matters of state, was gaining ascendancy. Voltaire, the most prominent exponent of the new secularism that came to be called the Enlightenment, had concluded that the pope should not be permitted to interfere in other countries or be a temporal ruler of any kind. By 1773, papal power was at an ebb. The cowardly Clement XIV (1767–74) felt forced by the combined pressure of the principal Catholic monarchies to suppress the Jesuit order, which had served the popes so well but was seen, in one royal court after another, as interfering with the rights of the crown. Jesuit "interference" had especially rankled over the issue of the human rights of the native peoples of Latin America and the Caribbean, which the Jesuits championed and which the crowns of Spain, Portugal, and France found it economically expedient not to consider. But we have now reached the age in which the Divine Right of Kings runs into mortal conflict with an appealing new slogan, "the Rights of Man"—appealing to the put-upon many, horrifying to the privileged few.

Voltaire, despite the demonizing he has suffered at the hands of Catholic apologists, was a moderate thinker, a penetrating and entertaining controversialist, and a religious, if idiosyncratic, soul, who made a deathbed confession to a priest and allowed himself to receive Final Anointing. But he saw with piercing clarity that the functions of the state had to be disentangled from those of religion. He rightly loathed the fanaticism and obscurantism of the clergy, whether Catholic, Lutheran, Reformed, or Anglican, and found repellent the common "Christian" practices of torture, hanging, decapitation, and incineration of those accused of impiety. Most radically, he and the fellow *philosophes* of his circle believed that all men were equal before God and should be equal under the law. For Voltaire, this was not in itself an anti-monarchist proposition; he had no quarrel with kingship as such. But he was soon followed by less moderate men (and women) who pushed his lively—and bestselling—speculations to more revolutionary conclusions.

It is not as if only Voltaire and his friends marched under the banners of intelligence and justice, while the entire political-religious establishment of Europe was ranged against them. The ideas of the *philosophes* soon affected the air that everyone breathed. And just as the Roman political-religious establishment had once adopted the fashions of humanism, many crowned heads and Church leaders throughout Europe found themselves drawn to the new ideas. As anticlericalism becomes for the first time an *articulated* factor in European politics, we witness the paradoxical emergence of anticlerical clergy and even, as the Enlightenment grows more fierce in its assertions, atheist clergy. When King Louis XVI declined to transfer the archbishop of Toulouse to the see of Paris, he defended himself by saying that, even if it were unremarkable to appoint atheists to lesser sees, surely the arch-bishop of *Paris* "must at least believe in God."

The Enlightenment was about to hatch the messy egg of rev-olution and its even messier siblings, regicide and class warfare. The first time revolution struck—in the British colonies of North America—it hardly raised a blip on continental Europe's radar. It was all to do, Europeans thought, with matters Anglo-Saxon, Anglican, Atlantic, and faraway. No one in a position of power foresaw what was coming next. For Louis XVI, even July 14, 1789, the very day the Bastille was stormed, was a day with-out incident. In his normally abundant diary he could find but one word to write, *"Rien"* (the same single word the poor blunderer had posted years earlier to describe the night of his wedding to Marie Antoinette).

The mounting chaos in France—the eventual execution of the foolish king, the hated queen, and the haughty nobles, the hunting down of clergy high and low and good and bad, the blithe confiscation by local and national assemblies of virtually all monastic and ecclesiastical property, the retributive purges (afterward known as "the Terror") against anyone deemed insufficiently "revolutionary" (not unlike the Stalinist, Maoist, and Pol Pottist purges of our own time), the forced paganization of public life—gave nightmares to the crowned heads and to anybody who had the least stake in the status quo. In the imagination of Europe—of have-nots as well as haves—all of France was steeped in blood. Whether this vision elated or repelled you depended on where you stood in society. Needless to say, it had little appeal for the papacy.

Revolution rumbled fitfully across Europe. The Italian peninsula, for so long divided and redivided into various kingdoms and continually beset by shifting alliances with the larger Catholic powers of Austria, Spain, and France, would not be remolded by the full force of France's new ideas till the middle of the nineteenth century. In the meanwhile there was General Napoleon Bonaparte to contend with. This Corsican upstart, who fancied himself the new Alexander (or, at the least, the new Charlemagne) intervened decisively in the political chaos and gave the French Revolution a new twist, allowing the "Republic" to keep its democratic, secular, anticlerical posture, while insisting that he, Napoleon, was its natural leader. Since he meant to conquer the world, the popes could hardly avoid dealing with him.

Occupying much of northern Italy, especially the cities of Ravenna and Bologna, so essential to papal solvency, Napoleon established the Republic of Milan and boasted that he would at last "free the Roman people from their long slavery." This was saber-rattling. Instead, he made terms with the humiliated pope—Pius VI (1775–99), as close to being a nonentity as popes ever get—alienating from Peter's Patrimony the fat cities of the north and the papal reservation of Avignon, levying an exorbitant ransom of some 45 million scudi, and carrying off many of Italy's most precious manuscripts and works of art from places as diverse as the Vatican museums and the early medieval Irish scriptorium of Bobbio in the Apennines. Pius VI, who had been born Giovanni Braschi, ended his days as "Citizen Braschi" (one is almost tempted to say "Comrade Braschi") in the French city of Valence, where he, though terminally ill, had been forced by his French guard. There, in the closing months of the eighteenth century, the local clergy, now called "constitutional" and in the pay of the French state (all their benefices having been confiscated), refused the pope's body burial in consecrated ground.

The Revolution had overstepped and inadvertently created a martyr, giving the papacy a new mystique that would become its salvation for the next two hundred years. For the pope, deprived of his pomp and even his property, was on his way to becoming the purely spiritual figure, suffering on behalf of goodness and truth, that fourteen centuries of imperial pretensions had been unable to make of him.

The deadlocked conclave of cardinals that after three months of meetings in Venice, under the watchful patronage of the Austrian emperor, elected Pius VI's successor saw that the times required a flexible pontiff. Their choice, which horrified imperial Austria, was the bishop of Frenchified Imola, dubbed "the Citizen Cardinal" because of the lengths to which he had gone to accommodate himself to the Revolution, teaching that God did not favor a particular form of government and that the ideals of democracy—liberty, equality, fraternity—were ideals first enunciated in the Christian Gospel. But the new pope took the name Pius VII (1800–23), giving a clue that he was committed to continuity rather than revolutionary departure. Refusing the emperor's invitation to Vienna, the pope set out for Rome. While Pius made his journey south on an antiquated barge, not being permitted to travel overland lest he generate a popular uprising, Napoleon succeeded in defeating the Austrians at the Battle of Marengo and expelling them from all of northern Italy, where he now reigned supreme.

Pius went as far as he could to accommodate Napoleon, even traveling to France, where his predecessor had been abused and defeated, to preside at Napoleon's coronation as Emperor of the French, an event that outraged Austria's Holy Roman Emperor. Napoleon, needing the pope's presence to confirm his legitimacy but, unwilling to concede that the pope had any power to confirm him emperor, placed the crown of empire on his own head and another on the head of Josephine, his wife, as depicted in the famous David painting in which a youthful Pius is shown seated behind Napoleon, a little dazed, two fingers raised in languid blessing. He may have been dazed not just to find himself in such circumstances but by the triumphal progress he had made by carriage from Rome to Notre Dame de Paris. All along the way, the roads had been lined with kneeling men and women, begging the papal blessing. The same would be so on the way back. Europe had never seen such devotion. The pope was indeed becoming a sacred figure, somehow above the petty politics of kings and nations.

The coronation was to prove the high point of papal-Napoleonic cooperation. Not long after the scene in the cathedral of Notre Dame, Napoleon began declaring himself "King of All Italy," made moves against the remaining Papal States, and ordered the pope to block his ports against "the Church's heretical enemies"—England and Russia, coincidentally Napoleon's enemies as well. Pius VII replied that "We are the Vicar of a God of peace, which means peace toward all without distinction." From this point on, the relationship between the two deteriorates till the Citizen Pope is made to undergo a replay of his predecessor's sufferings.

Pius is first barricaded in his palace on the Quirinal, then forced to languish in isolation at Savona on the Gulf of Genoa not far from the French border, then bundled into a coach and dragged over the Alps to Fontainebleau, dressed in the black soutane of a simple priest so there could be no recurrence of his earlier triumph—despite the fact that a chronic papal urinary infection requires the party to stop every ten minutes. What Napoleon wanted was that the pope relinquish all his temporal power, that the papacy be moved to France, and that the pope put the ultimate power of episcopal appointment throughout French territories in the hands of the emperor. Pius, alone, exhausted, and bullied beyond his power to resist, gives in to much of this, then recants. But by early 1814 Napoleon's run is nearly over, his army lost in a Russian blizzard, the Austrians closing in on the "French" republics of northern Italy. The pope is able to return to Rome. Soon after, rather less charitably disposed than he had been toward Republicanism, which had destroyed the Church's economic foundation as well as its leadership, he restores the Jesuits, the trusty defenders of papal rights. In the following year, the Congress of Vienna restores to the pope most of the territory he had lost, Avignon excepted.

Europe, swept by Republicanism, is now swept by a reaction against it. This reaction will often take the form of extreme devotion to the pope as the living foundation stone of European society. As Joseph de Maistre, a Corsican count, puts it in his popular book *Du Pape:* "There can be no public morality and no national character without religion; there can be no Christianity without Catholicism; there can be no Catholicism without the pope; there can be no pope without the sovereignty that is properly his." Thoughts like this fill the minds of many and come to be called Ultramontanism, or South-of-the-Alps-ism, which sees the Papal States as the seedbed of Europe's blessedness, the unalterable land that is the absolute guarantor of all monarchical stability. The Revolution, which destroyed the previously unassailable power of metropolitan bishops throughout Europe, has left one still standing.

The next pope, Leo XII (1823–29), is a stranger to his predecessor's moderation and reasonableness, and Rome soon takes on the fearful darkness of the most repressive Puritan settlement. Games, drinking, suggestive apparel, even public spontaneity can bring one a prison sentence. Religious indifferentism, toleration, and Freemasonry are condemned. The Jews, whose civil disabilities had been largely lifted, are clamped down on once more. Throughout papal Italy, due process is suspended, anonymous denunciation to authorities encouraged, and even summary execution initiated for a time. *Lo Stato della Chiesa* has become a police state.

Gregory XVI (1831–46) is even worse. In his infamous encyclical *Mirari vos arbitramur* (We Perceive You Are Astonished), he denounces freedom of conscience, freedom of the press, and the separation of Church and state. He argues that his sovereignty over the Papal States is divinely mandated. He condemns Félicité de Lamennais, a forward-looking French priest and the founder of liberal Catholicism, who is engaged in trying to reconcile religious liberty, universal suffrage, and other positive Enlightenment developments with traditional Catholic theology. Lamennais, like

THOMAS CAHILL

many before and since, tries at first to bend his mind to the reproving papal teaching. But when he hears that the pope has condemned the Polish uprising against the czar, which conforms to all of Lamennais's political principles, he leaves the priesthood and the Church, remarking that the Catholic hierarchy has "divorced [itself] from Christ, the Savior of the human race, in order to fornicate with all his torturers." His departure is an unnecessary tragedy, for virtually all of Lamennais's thought will find expression in the decrees of Vatican II.

In June 1846, following Gregory's death, the cardinals meet once more in conclave, the *intransigenti* in support of a reactionary candidate, the more numerous *liberali* resolved to find among their number a man capable of meeting with an open mind the challenges of the new age. Thanks partly to repressive papal regimes and partly to the fermentation of Enlightenment principles, Italy is in the process of a great transformation: more and more men are in favor of ending the peninsula's fragmentation into small kingdoms and duchies and of allowing it to coalesce into a united country with an Enlightenment constitution. The cardinals choose Giovanni Maria Mastai-Ferretti, a genial nobleman of fifty-four whose presumed liberalism had raised the previous pope's suspicions. "Even his cats are liberals," sneered Gregory.

As it turns out, not even his cats are liberals. The new pope takes the name Pius IX, in Italian Pio Nono—and "no, no" will prove to be his favorite response to practically everything. His papacy will endure for close to thirty-two years (1846–78); and when he finally dies at the age of eighty-six, he will have had the longest run in all of papal history. He begins well enough, allowing an elected municipal government for Rome and a constitution for the Papal States that calls for an elected assembly with lay representatives, lifting some of the Jewish disabilities, modernizing methods of farming, introducing gas lighting to the

64

streets of Rome, and even permitting the construction of rail-ways—which Gregory XVI had forbidden, calling them *chemins d'enfer* (roads of hell), punning on the French *chemins de fer* (roads of iron), because he feared people would gather under their trestles to plot sedition. For his first two years the new pope is wildly popular throughout Italy, and cheap cartoons begin to appear everywhere showing Pio Nono, flanked by Victor Emmanuel II (the constitutional monarch of Piedmont) and the red-shirted revolutionary Giuseppe Garibaldi, arms linked, suggesting the desirability of a united Italy brought about by the magnanimous cooperation of these three.

In 1848, as all Europe seems to rise in revolution, the pope is pressed to lead an army to expel the Austrians from northern Italy. "No," says Pio Nono—not against a Catholic power. He condemns the aspiration to a federated Italy and tells the Italians to obey their God-given monarchs, no matter who they are. It now appears that all the pope's reforms had been strategic—to allay unnecessary opposition—and did not spring from Enlightenment conviction or a sense of patriotism desirous of a united Italy. The tide of popular opinion turns against him, for he is not the man people had thought him to be. Rome itself is now on the brink of revolution, and in November Count Rossi, the pope's prime minister, is assassinated on the steps of his chancery, as revolutionary nationalists surround the papal palace on the Quirinal. Pio Nono barely escapes, disguised in black soutane and shovel hat. Garibaldi (who now calls his horse "Mastai," the pope's surname) and his compatriots proclaim a republic that lasts but half a year, when French troops overcome the forces of revolution (that take France as their model!) and restore Rome to the pope.

Pio Nono would continue to rule the recalcitrant Romans for twenty years, propped up only by French and Austrian firepower. He now saw clearly that any concession to democracy was misguided and could only result in further concessions and final defeat. The forces of the *Risorgimento* (Resurgence) that were amassing to deliver a united Italy were in the service of Satan. The pope, ruling the middle of the peninsula, would never give in. Though liberal Catholics from Europe to the Americas found the pope's stance a painful embarrassment, simple folk throughout the world saw in his courtly defiance the courage of true holiness. As his political power shrank ever smaller, his spiritual stature continued to wax.

In 1864, Pio Nono solemnly issued his "Syllabus of Errors," condemning Freemasonry, Socialism, and all forms of rationalism. Indeed, eighty separate "errors" were condemned, including this one: "That in the present day, it is no longer necessary that the Catholic Church be held as the only religion of the State, to the exclusion of all other modes of worship: whence it has been wisely provided by the law, in some countries nominally Catholic [read especially "France"], that persons coming to reside therein shall enjoy the free exercise of their own worship." The most memorable "error" reads: "That the Roman Pontiff can, and ought to, reconcile himself to, and agree with, progress, liberalism, and modern civilization." Here was a badly frightened old man who existed in a sealed environment, utterly out of touch with the age in which he lived.

Nothing condemns Pio Nono more than his kidnapping of a six-year-old Jewish boy and refusal to return him to his parents. This hideous intervention occurred in 1858, ten years after the abortive Roman Republic and six before the "Syllabus." The child, Edgardo Mortara, had been secretly baptized by a Catholic serving girl who worked in the Mortaras' house in Bologna. The occasion for the rite was Edgardo's illness, which the servant feared might prove fatal—which to the servant (and, unfortunately, to most Christian theologians of the day, whether Catholic or Protestant) would mean that little Edgardo would be condemned eternally to hell, final home of the unbaptized. So the pope had no choice but to seize the now-saved child and raise him as a Christian, so that he could not be lost again.

The horrors of the story are manifold. The servant was addled and unreliable, so her story of the secret baptism may have been fanciful. In any case, she told it in secret to the Inquisition—which always operated in secret, so that, when the child was seized, the Mortaras were given no reason for this destruction of their lives. They were never allowed to recover their son. He was raised in the papal household as Pio's darling and became a priest.

It has been objected recently by defenders of this pope that he must be understood "in the context of his time"—which would mean absolving him on account of his good intentions in Edgardo's regard. He only meant, after all, to save the boy from eternal damnation. But "the context" of our time offers a strikingly similar drama. The Edgardo Affair had for 1858 all the tension, posturing, and self-justifying fanaticism of the recent Elián Affair, in which American relatives of a Cuban boy attempted to prevent his permanent return to his father on sheerly ideological grounds. Like Elián, Edgardo was entranced by the wealth and panoply of his new surroundings. Like Elián's Miami relatives, the pope complained bitterly that he was the victim of vicious propaganda—in his case, from Freemasons, revolutionaries, Jews, and, as Pio put it, a conspiracy of "freethinkers, the disciples of Rousseau and Malthus."

To a delegation of Jews who had come to plead with him for the return of the child, Pio threatened to "make you go back into your hole"—that is, reimpose the full range of Jewish disabilities, such as compelled attendance at Christian sermons, confinement to the ghetto, and disbarment from the professions. But no, his wondrous image of himself would prevent such harshness. "Don't worry," he reassured them. "My goodness is so great, and so strong is the pity I have for you, that I pardon you." A difficult character to pardon, whatever the historical context. But what finally gives the lie to such a defense is that, knee-jerk papalists aside, the whole world—that is, the context of his time— turned against Pio Nono over this outrage. The American president, James Buchanan, was kept from public condemnation of the pope only by his realization that in the slave states of his country black children were regularly separated from their parents for motives far less supernal than Pio could offer.

In order to put an even more authoritative stamp on his retrograde opinions, Pio Nono now called a general council—the First Vatican Council (or Vatican I)—which was expected to anathematize the modern world. While Ultramontanists were overjoyed, liberal Catholics prepared for the worst. As the time for the council's opening drew near—on December 8, 1869, the feast of the Immaculate Conception, a celebration of the doctrine that the Virgin Mary had been born without the human stain of original sin, a dogma Pio Nono had proclaimed on his own—it looked more and more as if a ringing affirmation of papal infallibility would prove to be Pio Nono's hidden purpose in calling the council. After all, if the council fathers would assent to such a doctrine, the impervious cloak of infallibility could be placed retroactively over the dogma of the Immaculate Conception and the "Syllabus of Errors," as well as over anything the pope might do or say. Once this maneuver was accomplished, there would be no further theological need for bishops, except as implementers of papal decrees.

The *idea* of infallibility had been around a long time. Because Jesus had promised to be with his Church "to the end of the world," it was assumed—by almost all Christians through most of Christian history—that the Church as a whole could not fall into permanent theological error. The question remaining was: In what or whom did this so-called infallibility reside? In the apostolic and post-apostolic Church, the answer was obvious. The Church was the Church, that is, the Assembly of God's People; and so, the Church's "infallibility" (though the authors of the New Testament would have shunned such a term as inflated, exclusivist, inflammatory, and bizarre) lay in the consensus of the Assembly. In the imperial period of the great ecumenical councils, such "infallibility" (though, again, the term was never used) would have been presumed to lie with the assembled bishops, elected by the people of each locale as their representatives. It was only with the rise of the pope in the guise of a divinely anointed medieval monarch—as the personal embodiment of Christendom—that anyone could have imagined that "infallibility" accrued to him in some exclusive sense. But, in truth, no one in the early Middle Ages ever uttered the word. In the thirteenth century, some dissident Franciscans invented the term in the hopes of getting a papal decree on their preferred form of poverty declared "infallible." In the fourteenth century, the "infallible truth of the teaching of the Roman pontiff in matters of faith" was proposed by a single theologian, Guido Terreni, but the idea remained a novelty without much currency. It was only the vibrant growth of competing ideologies—Protestantism, rationalism, revolution, democracy, Socialism, atheism—in the pope's backyard that triggered the widespread adoption of this defensive theological tool.

The pope intervened in the council at every turn, scheming with his advisors and twisting episcopal arms. Though Pio Nono, now approaching his twenty-fifth year on the papal throne, had appointed a majority of the bishops in attendance, he was leaving nothing to chance. Contrary to the tradition of general councils, the topics to be discussed and the ground rules for discussion were drawn up before the bishops arrived and were presented to them as *faits accomplis*. Only the pope would be permitted to propose new topics. Pio Nono then set about to influence bishops one by one. He threatened poor bishops with the withdrawal of financial support, pressured others by placing items in the Vatican newspaper, intimidated others with nocturnal visits from the papal police. With still others, he gave himself over to hysterical fits. In Saint Peter's Basilica, where the council was being held, Cardinal Guidi, the best theologian on the pope's side, made the mistake of offering concessions to the opposition by proposing that the dogmatic formula speak of the infallibility of the pope's doctrinal definitions rather than of his personal infallibility and that a clause be inserted obliging the pope to examine the existing doctrinal tradition (which would imply the necessity to consult his brother bishops) before proclaiming a dogma. When Pio Nono got poor Guidi alone, he asked him stridently what on earth he could be thinking of. *"Tradizione?"* screamed the pope. *"La tradizione son' io! La chiesa son' io!"* (*"I* am the Tradition! *I* am the Church!"*)—not far from Louis XIV's *"L'état, c'est moi,"* and pointing to the receding tradition of monarchical absolutism that provides the underlying historical context for this corrosive theological development.

The dying Count Montalembert, a distinguished liberal spokesman who had remained faithful to Rome after Lamennais's departure, published a letter in which he characterized the council as an attempt to "sacrifice justice, truth, reason, and history as a holocaust to the idol they have set up in the Vatican." John Henry Newman, a convert from Anglicanism and the greatest Christian theologian of the century, called the council majority an "insolent and aggressive faction." In the end, this council of rubber stamps still possessed enough free men for 60 bishops—Germans, Austrians, Frenchmen, and Americans—to refuse to vote with the majority. They were pressed to return to their dioceses before the final vote, so that the 535 bishops remaining would constitute the necessary "consensus" that had been the constant tradition at ecumenical councils.

With all this, the pope did not get everything he wanted. His newfound infallibility was severely hedged about: he had become infallible only when speaking *ex cathedra* (that is, officially) on a doctrine of faith or morals; and his "gift" of infallibility was not exclusive but a participation in the infallibility thought to have been implied by Christ in his promise to remain with his Church. Pio Nono's precious "Syllabus of Errors" did not meet the test, even if the dogma of the Immaculate Conception seemed to. (Only one more papal definition has since been deemed infallible: Pius XII's oddball definition of the dogma of Mary's bodily "assumption" into heaven.)

On July 18, 1870, as the voting concluded and Pio Nono read out the new dogma, a violent storm broke overhead, sending rain thundering down on the great basilica and filling the shadowed aula with garish bursts of lightning. The next day, the Franco-Prussian War erupted. As bishops hied themselves quickly back to their dioceses, France, in need of all its troops, withdrew its garrison from Rome, leaving the pope to fend for himself. On September 20, the Rome of the popes fell to the revolutionaries, soon to be declared the capital of a united Italy. The pope withdrew into the Vatican, refusing to recognize the new state or to have any dealings with it. Likewise, he forbade Italian Catholics from any participation in their state—even by voting—under pain of excommunication. In Pio Nono's absolutist stance some may discern, as the Ultramontane cardinal Manning put it, "the beauty of inflexibility."

Henceforth, the pope would be the self-styled "prisoner of the Vatican," a mysterious figure in white, whose isolation, sufferings, and inflexibility made him beloved of unschooled Catholics everywhere. The modern world, which Pio Nono so despised, gave the pope by its inventions the means of coming in contact with his millions of admirers. They flocked to him as pilgrims by steamship and rail, kneeling at his feet (as only their bishops and princes had once done), and he came to them by printed pictures, newspapers, and telegraph and would soon arrive by telephone, film, and radio. By the time Pio Nono died, in February of 1878, the world was on the threshold of a revolution that would reconfigure modern reality beyond the wildest dreams of the *philosophes*, a communications revolution that would for the first time in history enable the enshrining of individual human beings as international icons. Already, many Catholic homes and businesses throughout the world gave pride of place to a printed portrait of the old pope (often sentimentally situated between pictures of Jesus's Sacred Heart and Mary's Immaculate Heart). The Papal States had made the pope a temporal ruler, seldom enough a good one, and encouraged him to imperialist fantasies. Their final loss began to remake him into an exalted global figure, powerless in political and economic terms but capable of moving mountains.

PART II

ANGELO THE MAN

✠ ✠ ✠

From Peasant to Priest

IF ONE WERE to travel by time machine to Pio Nono's last days—to the crash of lightning around Saint Peter's and the bitter withdrawal of the old man into his Vatican enclave, as far away as possible from the tempests of the world—it would seem impossible to imagine that any subsequent pope could teach his Church to love this world and embrace modern insights as John XXIII would do. Even a revolutionary pope needs a precursor, someone to whom he may point as having thought his thoughts before him, someone with whom he may establish continuity, someone to give him the "cover" of previous tradition. For John XXIII, that pivotal predecessor was Leo XIII, the pope who would follow Pio Nono and the pope of John's first years of life.

John XXIII was born Angelo Giuseppe Roncalli in the Lombardy village of Sotto il Monte on November 25, 1881, nearly four years into the papacy of Leo XIII. Since popes, however august, have no influence on newborns, it is more important to consider the circumstances of Angelo's birth before examining the post-Pio atmosphere of the united Italy in which he was raised.

The Roncallis were farmers, industrious in their habits and pious in their religious practices. Though their family had lived for centuries in the hills around Sotto il Monte (literally "beneath the mountain"), Angelo's parents, Giovanni Battista and Marianna (née Mazzola), were still tenant farmers, dependent on the counts Morlani of Bergamo, the small city that was the market hub around which hamlets like Sotto il Monte were clustered. As had been the case for the sharecroppers of Italy from the time of Charlemagne, from the time of the Caesars, and even before, half the Roncalli output—in milk, veal, and the product of their silkworms—went as rent to their landlords. Only in their later years—and largely as a result of legislation flowing from the republican social reformation—would the Roncalli parents be able to buy their farm from its medieval masters.

Dinners at the farmhouse were populous affairs, with some thirty sitting down to their polenta each afternoon—Giovanni Battista and Marianna, their children (twelve in all, of which Angelo was fourth and the first male), a family of cousins, and an imposing great-uncle named Zaverio. What little they had they shared generously. The occasional beggar at the door was quickly seated by Marianna among the children. "God," as Angelo would later put it, quoting a Lombardy proverb, "blesses big pots more than little ones." The house was also big, but between the Roncallis and their cows, kept in stalls on the ground floor, space was at a premium and privacy unknown. The world of the Roncallis and of peasants like them on the farmsteads around Bergamo has been captured for all time in Ermanno Olmi's evocative film of 1978 *L'albero degli zoccoli* (The Tree of Wooden Clogs), which seems to breathe with the slow movement, saturated colors, sly humor, and solid compassion of this lost world.

Like peasants everywhere, the Roncallis were undemonstrative, "a little gruff," as Angelo would later describe them, "but serious and good." They called their first son Angelino (Little Angel), and he was no doubt all the more treasured by them after the death of their first child, Caterina, two years after Angelo was born. His earliest memory was of his mother on a miniature pilgrimage to a shrine of the Madonna that lay about a kilometer from their farmhouse at the end of an uphill track. Angelo was four, accompanied by his surviving big sisters, Teresa, six, and Ancilla, five. His mother, urging them along, had barely turned thirty, pregnant once again and carrying Zaverio, two, in one arm and Maria Elisa, one, in the other. No wonder they arrived after Mass had begun and found the little chapel too crowded to enter. One by one Marianna, she of the "simple and lucid conscience," as her son would one day recall her, lifted her children to the grille of the window. "*Ecco*, Angelino," said she as she lifted up her son, "look how beautiful the Madonna is. I have consecrated you completely to her." The little boy blinked at the polished surfaces, the gold, the flowers, the scarlet mantle and mild face of the Virgin, the Christ Child folded comfortably in her lap. To both figures the artist had given the piercing dark eyes, broad face, and prominent nose of the local peasantry: but for their finery, they could themselves be Roncallis. The peasants came here, as Angelo would one day remember, "to recall the kindness of Mary and to renew their hope."

Angelo provides us with a similar memory of his father, who in August 1889 on the feast of Christ's Transfiguration took his then eight-year-old son to Ponte San Pietro (Saint Peter's Bridge), six kilometers distant from their village, for the celebration of the eleventh anniversary of Catholic Action, a lay social movement begun in Bergamo and approved by the Vatican. Because Angelo was too small to see the parade over the heads of the onlookers, Giovanni hoisted him onto his shoulders. Almost seventy years later, when Angelo, now himself the Fisherman's successor and Supreme Bridgebuilder, is carried into Saint Peter's Basilica for the first time on the *sedia gestatoria*, the ceremo-

THOMAS CAHILL

nial litter used till recently to transport popes, he will be greatly moved to recall that he was once carried by his father over the heads of the crowd at Ponte San Pietro. "The secret of everything," he will reflect, "is to let oneself be carried by the Lord and to carry the Lord [to others]."

Among so many with so little, there were of course tensions and misunderstandings. But for Angelo, his simple, generous mother and faithful, taciturn father pointed the way to his understanding of the adventure of faith. Profound religiosity begins not in moral strictures or political tenets but in the pleasures of a child's senses: *Ecco*, Angelino ... beauty, kindness, and hope. If we let God carry us, we will also be able to bring him to others. The gesture of Giovanni's, so natural and spontaneous to every good father, so thrilling to every small child, became for Angelo the symbol of his life, the image that would undergird his every thought, prayer, and movement till the day of his death. In this abandonment to the power of a loving Father, reality is transfigured and we are lifted up, made capable of vision beyond our ken and action beyond our strength.

In our strident, hopped-up society, we must block out most sensory phenomena—the sirens and the billboards, the junk mail and the ringing phone, the neighbor's TV and the e-mail memos—in order to think a rational thought, attend to priorities, or name our own deepest needs. In such a society, it is difficult to appreciate the slow-paced, meditative worldview that was possible for a nineteenth-century Italian farmboy, who lived in an environment saturated with meaning—in which everything counted for something and nothing had to be excluded from consideration. Meaning came with the seasons of the year and the feasts of the Church. But it was present in every sight and sound, taste and touch, because this was how God spoke—through the simplest experiences of daily life. The sacraments of the Church—the cleansing water of baptism, the spiritual food of the Eucharist, the anointing with oil—were great storehouses of meaning. But all of creation, since it came from the hand of a good God, had messages for us. We had only to look and listen. This view of the created world as fraught with the divine Word is called by theologians "sacramentality." But Angelo had the experience long before he knew the word; and the sacramental perception of reality became his accustomed response to life before he could be conscious of what he was doing. As he grew in consciousness, this sacramental orientation would serve as his favored method of sorting out the truth of his life and making his crucial decisions.

It would be easy for the contemporary reader to brush aside such an orientation as medieval and socially retrograde. But this would be to underestimate its capacity to give joy and peace and to inspire many happy lives down to our own day with an abiding sense of plenitude. Nor did it exist—at least in a subject as astute as Angelo—in isolation from a sense of social concern.

Uncle Zaverio, Angelo's godfather, took on the task of instructing his charge in social Catholicism. Zaverio, known as "Barba" (or Beard, that is, the head of the household), was as close as the Roncallis came to having an intellectual-in-residence. Barba read books and subscribed to journals, including the *Salesian Bulletin*, edited by a certain Don Bosco of Turin, who would one day be declared a saint. Though Barba's reading was confined to Catholic matters, it tended in the direction of social and international questions, and with occasional citations he brought his already studious godson in touch with the world beyond Sotto il Monte. He, more than Angelo's parents, was involved in Catholic Action, the movement that originated in northern Italy to fill the void left by the papal proscription of Catholic participation in the secular state. Catholic Action looked to the social well-being of ordinary people, initiating, for instance, local cooperatives and credit banks, the very institutions that would eventually enable the Roncallis to buy their farm. The social interventions of Catholic Action thus often seemed to farmers like the Roncallis of more worth than anything the state had done for them.

Like many Italians, Barba also followed closely the doings of the papacy. Leo XIII, the pope of Angelo's early years, took the first tentative steps to mend the breach between the Church and modern society that his predecessor had found impassable. Coming to the papal throne after the establishment of the Italian state, Leo did not need to dwell obsessively on the loss of the Papal States as on a personal failure. Though fully aware of the anticlericalism that seethed through secular society, he preferred to emphasize peace and reconciliation whenever he saw an opening. In his encyclical *Immortale Dei* of 1885, he moved his Church away from imprecations against the "Satanic" state and asserted that any form of government may be legitimate if it serves the common good. Thus was democracy for the first time given tentative approbation by the Vatican. A subsequent encyclical, *Libertas praestantissimum*, enshrined freedom as a legitimate value and dared claim the Church as its custodian. Leo opened the Vatican archives to scholars, even non-Catholics, insisting that "the Church has nothing to fear from the truth." He was the first pope to speak of Protestant and Orthodox Christians as "separated brethren," rather than as heretics and schismatics.

Not all of Leo's initiatives were as magnanimous as they might have been. He continued to forbid Italian Catholics to vote; and though very many ignored the directive, the pope still stood effectively in the way of the formation of a party to represent the interests of Catholic voters. He condemned something he fuzzily called "Americanism" (for being too accommodating to democracy), and he declared Anglican priestly and episcopal orders "absolutely null and utterly void." These excesses aside, he was a temperate gentleman who wished to lead the way to a more just and merciful human society and who took particular interest in the plight of the urban workingman. In his most lasting contribution—the 1891 encyclical *Rerum novarum* (Of New Things)—he gave arresting evidence of his unease with capitalism as then practiced, asserting that wealth brought with it profound and unalterable social obligations—far above the whims of personal "charity"—and that workers had inherent rights to be paid a "living wage" and to form unions to ensure that their rights not be trampled. Leo's aristocratic prose was capable of memorable flourishes, as in his high-minded contempt for "a small number of very rich men who have been able to lay upon the teeming masses of the laboring poor a yoke that is very little better than slavery itself." If this gave pause to many anticlerical secularists who had long since concluded that the Vatican would always come down on the side of established power, it came as a terrible shock to laissez-faire industrialists, who ever after suspected that the papacy was secretly in league with the Socialists. And indeed, it is impossible to imagine Pio Nono stretching his mind so far as to think about the needs of the proletariat or even calling a document *"Rerum novarum"* without tacking on something like *"et horribilium."*

Because Leo spent more than twenty-five years on the papal throne (not dying till 1903 when Angelo was twenty-one), his moderation and sense of sympathy succeeded in softening the militancy of modern Catholicism, gave hope to liberal Catholics everywhere, particularly those engaged in ministries of social regeneration, and had a lasting influence on the Bergamasque farmboy who would become one of his successors. The pope, for families like the Roncallis, represented continuity between past and present, the living incarnation of Italian history and civilization.

But how could papal culture, so self-assertive and unyielding over so many centuries, have brought about the gentle social ambience found in the Roncalli family? Since the Roncallis were traditional Catholics (and therefore pro-papal), it is not surprising to find them in agreement with the policies of the reigning pontiff. But the policies of a given pope—or of the sum of his predecessors, for that matter—can hardly explain how the actors in this particular family, this particular community, relate to others. For this we must look to the social history of Lombardy and Italy, a history yet to be written.

Still, we may venture some hint of an explanation. Catholic culture often takes two forms, official and popular. The official version is the one sponsored by pope and higher clergy and usually has to do with "holding the line" (whatever that might mean at a given moment) in doctrinal and political matters. Popular Catholicism is devotional, sacramental, generous, affectionate, pleasure-seeking, and unconcerned with norms and strictures. Nowhere is this more true than in Italy, where the Vatican regularly fulminates and ordinary people regularly pay no heed. To understand the dichotomy, one has only to remember that through all the "no's" of Pio Nono, Italians were enjoying their bread, love, and dreams as they had always done, praying to their favorite saints, hiding dissidents from papal authorities, and engaging in revolution—as is the case in Puccini's *Tosca*, set in the repressive papal Rome of 1800 and first performed a hundred years later in the Rome of the Republic. This is a country of oppositions, cheerfully accepted, where one uncle may be a bishop and another a Socialist member of parliament, where seemingly mortal enemies—like the priest and the Communist mayor of the "Don Camillo" stories—may be secret friends.

This is not to say that Italians live schizophrenic lives: they are sincerely religious and sincerely rebellious. For them, this implies continuity rather than contradiction and is resolved in what might best be called "instinctive Christianity." And yet it is an instinct fashioned by centuries of Christian tradition, the longest Christian social tradition in the world. For me, the Italian attitude is best summed up in the incomparable aria Puccini gave his florid heroine Floria Tosca:

> *Vissi d'arte, vissi d'amore.*
> *Non feci mai male ad anima viva!*
> I've lived for art, I've lived for love.
> I've never hurt a living soul!

To make the world more beautiful, to make my loved ones happy, to do no harm to anyone: this is the Italian ideal, at once religious and secular. It explains the best (and sometimes even the worst) of Italian culture. And it is the strain that runs through the Roncalli family that cannot be explained by recourse to papal history. More important to an interpretation of this strain is the lively sense of sanctity as a local presence. The pope may be a faraway father, but Saint Francis once walked the streets of Assisi as Don Bosco now walks the streets of Turin. The saints are our uncles, brothers, and sisters; they are people like us, excitable, loving, full of expressive hand gestures—and the Madonna lives kindly up the lane. The Catholic domestication of God that seventeenth-century Calvinists found so objectionable saved religion in Italy from the severities of papal extremism.

One local "saint" was Sotto il Monte's parish priest, Francesco Rebuzzini, like many Bergamasque clergy a man able to absorb the discipline of Trent without losing his humanity. Don

Rebuzzini was highly regarded both for his manifest sympathy toward his parishioners and the aura of calm that surrounded him. Angelo observed him closely and learned by heart the sententious wisdom, attributed to Saint Bernard of Clairvaux, that the priest had hung in his study:

> Peace within the cell; fierce warfare without.
> Hear all; believe a few; honor all.
> Don't believe everything you hear;
> Don't judge everything you see;
> Don't do everything you can;
> Don't give everything you have;
> Don't say everything you know.
> Pray, read, withdraw, be silent, be at peace . . .

Good practical advice, of which any bachelor-pastor might wish to remind himself as he faced the daily storms of his profession. What is remarkable is that Angelo, at the age of ten or eleven when Don Rebuzzini was tutoring him in Latin (having already absorbed everything the local schoolmaster could give him), would find this dry meditation on tranquility something to commit to memory.

But Angelo, as he would later confess, "could never remember the time when [he] didn't want to be a priest" and was already schooling himself in the discipline of pastoral equanimity that he admired in Rebuzzini. He must have seemed a very grown-up sort of child. And, indeed, his childhood was drawing precipitately to its close, for just before his twelfth birthday Angelo set off for the seminary of Bergamo. He was about to wed himself to the Catholic Church and would never again be able to spend more than holidays in his family home. In later years, he would write to comfort others who were suffering "the pain of separation," referring to his early parting from his loving family: "It is right that [we should feel this way]. We are made to love each other eternally. It goes without saying that this feeling should find expression and be a cause of sorrow." But then, Angelo, ever the optimist and believer, would conclude: "So do we merit the sweetness of final reconciliation."

Angelo would need all his optimism and good humor once he was locked inside the forbidding fortress of the Bergamo seminary. Seminary training was a direct result of the decrees of Trent. Never again would the Catholic Church allow into the ranks of its clergy the human variety—from scandalous scamps to innovative thinkers and leaders—that had bloomed during the Middle Ages. The seminaries were meant to manufacture a uniform product that would neither scandalize the laity nor make waves that could disturb the sleep of the episcopate.

At the top of the seminary agenda was outward show: the priest-in-training was at all times to display himself as an angelic ideal. Angelo's initial entry in the journal he would keep till the end of his life was a fervent transcription of Trent's first canon on the reformation of the clergy:

> It is in every way fitting that clergy who have been called to the service of the Lord should so order their lives and habits that in their dress, gestures, gait, and conversation and all other matters they show nothing that is not grave, controlled, and full of religious feeling; let them also avoid minor faults, which in them would be very great, so that their actions may win the respect of all.

Though the text is an understandable response to the scandals that had plagued the Church, it became—as a guide to the conduct of adolescent boys—an invitation to mindless conformity, psychological stunting, and interior duplicity. That Angelo the seminarian did not always evade these traps is not so surprising as that he soldiered through his "formation" without becoming permanently deformed. He was taught to lower his eyes as he passed through Bergamo (always in the company of another seminarian) and never to look directly at a woman. He was to sleep on his back with a rosary around his neck and his arms folded across his chest, lest an "involuntary" erection in the course of sleep encourage active masturbation, which was considered mortally sinful and therefore predictive of damnation if one were to die without being shriven. In recent times, Catholic seminaries have been distinguished by an early morning flurry of seminarians seeking quicky absolutions from their priestly faculty, so they could then be seen to receive Communion—impermissible to those in a "state of mortal sin"—at the obligatory daily Mass. Since in Angelo's day it was customary to receive Communion but once a week at most, the seeking of absolution for such one-hand activity could be dealt with more discreetly.

Angelo's discretion is absolute. His diary contains no confessions of adolescent angst over his budding sexuality. The closest he comes to acknowledging the changes taking place in his body is a fleeting reference to "these movements, however innocent"—he means nocturnal emissions—and a resolution to "observe the greatest modesty with regard to my own body." But we cannot expect more of him than this. If his diary were a long howl of teenage complaint (like Portnoy's), he would have been out of the seminary and back on the street in no time. The humble child of uncomplaining nineteenth-century peasants, the fruit of generations of industrious patience, does not indulge himself as would a middle-class American of the 1950s. Even if he were not trapped in a seminary, he could not have permitted himself such candid self-regard. In truth, he has but two choices if he wishes to proceed toward ordination, which he already knows as his deepest desire. He can become a professional hypocrite, a priest who speaks publicly of purity and satisfies himself privately—an option taken by not a few post-Tridentine clerics—or he can master his natural impulses like an athlete training himself for a lifetime of disciplined abnegation. Angelo chose the latter course. As with all teenage athletes, how much this ascesis would cost him lay hidden in the future.

The year 1900, the year *Tosca* was first performed, brought with it some small distinctions to repay Angelo's native discretion. Whatever secret trials the onset of puberty had burdened him with, it had also given him a robustly beautiful tenor voice. He was made chant master, in charge of preparing the seminarians to sing the liturgy, and prefect of the seminary—something like class president, but an appointed position that brought its occupant into administration. He saw Rome for the first time, participating in a Holy Year pilgrimage and getting a glimpse of his hero, the ninety-year-old Leo XIII. Finally, he was informed by his bishop that he had been accepted for studies at the Roman College. There are few Italian bishops who did not begin their ascent to the hierarchy by being accepted for study in Rome, just as there are few bishops throughout the world who did not attend one of the colleges maintained at Rome by national episcopates as training grounds for their successors; and rare is the graduate of one of these colleges who does not become a bishop. Angelo was on his way.

There was, however, to be an interruption. He was just settling into his life in Rome, beguiled by its sumptuous ceremony, the theater he was allowed to attend, the lectures by the seminary faculty (more lively and challenging than those of Bergamo), when, soon after winning a prize for a paper in Hebrew, he was abruptly called up for military service. Since the popes had refused recognition of the Italian state (or any agreements with it), the state was in no mood to offer military exemptions to seminarians. If the Church acted as if the state did not exist, the state could act as if the Church did not exist. Private Roncalli reported for duty on November 30, 1901, to the Umberto I barracks at . . . Bergamo—an indication of how the nonrelationship between Church and state worked in practice, mediated in real life by tenderhearted Italians, who saw to it that Angelo could go home on weekend and holiday leaves and that the delicate little seminarian did not have his nose rubbed in military life any more than necessary. Angelo, more earnest and disciplined than most of his peers, made corporal, then sergeant, and even did well on the rifle range. He was, however, arrested at one point and confined to barracks because of the "insubordination" of his men. For all the attempts at mitigation, Angelino could hardly be turned into a leader of his fellow farmboy-soldiers, who spent *their* leaves in the local bordellos and returned to boast in a can-you-top-this spirit.

Angelo was disgusted: "The army is a running fountain of pollution, enough to submerge whole cities. Who can hope to escape from this flood of slime, unless God comes to his aid? . . . I did not think a rational man could fall so low. . . . Now, after my brief experience, I think it is true that more than half of all mankind [he can only mean males], at some time in their lives, become animals, without any shame." You'd think he was talking about battlefield atrocities rather than getting laid. Here is Angelo at his defensive worst, a twenty-year-old with no exploits to boast of, humiliated as "the laughing stock of the whole world." But he will improve—even on this subject—as time goes by. As his time in the army draws to its close, he feels he has had a narrow escape. He has seen both seminarians and priests fall by the wayside during their military service: "I might, like so many

other poor wretches, have lost my vocation . . . I might have lost
holy purity and the grace of God, but . . . I passed through the
mire and by His grace was kept unpolluted." In Angelo's mind,
just one sexual lapse would be irreparable. In his milieu, the loss
of virginity carried for the male an irreversibility similar to what
it carried for the female. Once you had tasted the apple, there was
no going back to Eden.

A relieved Angelo returned to the seminary full of new
vigor—"a passionate desire to study . . . a restless longing to
know everything, to study all the great authors, to familiarize
myself with the scientific movement in all its manifestations."
These phrases suggest that Angelo, despite his sexual puri-
tanism, is already breaking away from the restricted confines of
his seminary training and entering the broader bay of thinking
for himself. A more timorous soul would have been more careful
in his declarations: "To know *everything*" is more than a little
Faustian. "*All* the great authors" would include not a few pro-
scribed by the Index of Forbidden Books. Though many of his
professors would have been ignorant or contemptuous of anything labeled "the scientific movement"—which in Italian refers
not just to the physical sciences but to the whole spectrum of
scholarship as then practiced—Angelo is full of enthusiasm not
only for contemporary scholarship but for something that he
sees as allied to it and calls "the forward, upward movement of
Catholic culture." Angelo is already aware of the stirrings just
under the placid surface of the great city whose bishop refuses to
set foot within its precincts.

Winds of intellectual change are blowing across the Catholic
world, emanating mostly from France but quickly affecting Italy.
Men like Alfred Loisy, Marc Sangier, and Louis Marie Olivier
Duchesne are founding journals and movements, giving lectures, and writing books that are having a galvanizing effect on

Catholic intellectuals. For these new *philosophes*, Christianity and democracy have already been reconciled—at least at the notional level—and what is required are reinterpretations of history, theology, and biblical studies and new political models that will display that there is no need to oppose religion and modernity. They are building on the work of the previous generation of liberal Catholic historians, especially the German Ignaz von Döllinger and the Englishmen Lord Acton and John Henry Newman (whom Leo made a cardinal in Newman's old age). These three, who had to operate under the long shadow of Pio Nono, were nonetheless absorbed in the spirit of their time and took what may be described as a Darwinian approach to their subjects: political and ecclesiastical history, dogma, even the construction of the New Testament, must be seen as *developments*. Nothing arrives on the human scene fully formed. Whether we are talking about the truths of science or of Jesus and the Church, human understanding evolves over time—usually over a considerable time.

Angelo belongs instinctively to this camp, though to its most considered and catholic branch. Never willing to throw out the baby with the bathwater, he prefers to save whatever he can from the past, especially—as we shall see—from those historic churchmen whom he takes as his models and whom he can admire for their intellectual and affective amplitude. It is in this spirit that Angelo finishes his studies, receives his doctorate in theology and, on the morning of August 10, 1904, is ordained a priest in the exquisite Church of Santa Maria in Monte Santo on the Piazza del Popolo. But scarcely a year earlier, Angelo's beloved Leo XIII had died and been succeeded by a very different man, Giuseppe Sarto, who took the ominous name of Pius. It will not be long before this new Pio leaves his mark on Angelo's life.

From Secretary to Historian

PIUS X, the son of a seamstress and a village postman, had roots as humble as Angelo's. But whereas Angelo, almost from his first schoolday, was excited by ideas, especially as embodied in historical lives, Pius X was suspicious of all intellectual activity, which he thought could only confuse the faithful. There was one sure standard amid the strident intellectual confusion of the modern world—the pope, who had all the answers anyone needed. Pius thought these thoughts long before he became pope. When he was patriarch of Venice, the post he held before his election to the papacy, he had stated clearly in his first pastoral letter that when it came to the Vicar of Christ "there should be no questions, no subtleties, no opposing of personal rights to his rights, but only obedience."

A handsome figure, who had the placid, even-featured face of a pope from central casting, Pius was actually full of fear, alarmed by anything he had never heard of, and distrustful of all but a small cadre of flunkies. He may have been clinically paranoid. He had not been the electing cardinals' first choice; Cardinal Rampolla, secretary of state in the previous reign and the most prominent liberal in Leo's Curia, had been that, but the Austro-Hungarian emperor Franz Josef had exercised his veto against Rampolla—the last time such princely interference would be allowed in a papal election. The new pope lost no time in getting rid of Rampolla and replacing him with Rafael Merry del Val, a worldly but exceedingly reactionary Spaniard in his mid-forties. (Merry del Val soon banished Giacomo Della Chiesa from the Secretariat of State because he dared remain friends with Rampolla. As punishment, Della Chiesa was exiled to Bologna to be the lonely archbishop of Italy's most emphatically secular city; but he would become Pius X's successor.)

Leo had done all he could to encourage French Catholics to cooperate with their Republic and be good citizens. Pius twitted the French at every opportunity till he succeeded in returning their state—from which he saw so many corruptions flowing—to its previous hostility. Pius's "success" may be measured in the French Republic's expulsion of all religious orders and the seizure of their property. Having set the papacy on a collision course with all things French, Pius turned his attention to the universal Church. Then did the papal reign of terror begin.

In 1907, Pius issued—through his Holy Office, the renamed Inquisition—the decree *Lamentabili sane exitu* (A Lamentable Departure Indeed), condemning sixty-five propositions, most of them culled from *L'Évangile et l'Église* (The Gospel and the Church), a book of historical studies by Loisy that was enjoying phenomenal popularity. The conclusions of historians and Scripture scholars—conclusions accepted today by the majority of even moderate Catholic scholars—were ruled out of court: that there is a distinction to be made between the Jesus of history and the Christ of faith, that Jesus only gradually became aware of his Messianic destiny, that his knowledge was limited and that he could be mistaken, that he did not found the Church and institute its sacraments or hierarchy (including the papacy), that his resurrection is not a historical fact but an object of faith.

On the heels of *Lamentabili* came *Pascendi Dominici gregis* (Pasturing the Lord's Flock), an encyclical full of mean-spirited sarcasm, which set out to eradicate from the Roman communion the "poisonous doctrines" and "boundless effrontery" of "the Modernists." This newly coined term was used to describe a varied collection of scholars, many of them in sharp disagreement with one another, perceived by the Vatican as engaged in a diabolical conspiracy to ruin the Church by forcing on it all the dubious standards of modern scholarship and the modern world.

The target was evanescent and amorphous, but *Pascendi* intended to shoot it down.

The destruction of the newly discovered "heresy" of Modernism became almost the whole *raison d'être* of the papacy of Pius X. Committees of Vigilance (read "spies") were set up in every diocese to sniff out any taint of local Modernism, and diocesan censorship boards were established to oversee all literary output. These bodies were to operate in complete secrecy and allow none of their proceedings to be published. Priests and teachers were required to take a public oath against Modernism, which henceforth limited faculties in seminaries and other Catholic educational institutions to the strict formulas of an ahistorical and discredited scholasticism, a medieval system full of answers to questions no longer posed and with scant relevance to the contemporary world. Angelo was lucky to have completed his studies before the imposition of the oath.

The anti-Modernist crusade resembled in many ways the later anti-Communist crusade of the American senator Joseph McCarthy. It too left countless innocents harmed; but as it was directed by the Church's chief executive officer, there were few shelters secure from the storm. (Imagine had McCarthy been president.) Loisy was excommunicated, as were many writers. Brilliant teachers were silenced, pious priests defrocked, distinguished ecclesiastical careers shattered. As this tsunami overwhelmed the Church, even bishops and cardinals found they could be drowned. In the end, orthodoxy was not enough to keep one safe, as old scores were settled and small vindictive men set out to destroy whomever they envied. The campaign ranged far and wide. In New York, then (believe it or not) a hotbed of liberal Catholic theology, a journal called the *New York Review*, published from the diocesan seminary, had long been a thorn in the side of those for whom authority answered all questions. Its adventurous, personable young editor, Francis Duffy, escaped certain condemnation by signing up as a military chaplain and becoming the courageous and much loved "Father Duffy of the Fighting Sixty-Ninth," whose statue stands in Times Square. Not everyone was fortunate enough to find a hiding place as impervious to curial retribution as the U.S. Army.

An early casualty of Pius's paranoia was Giacomo Maria Radini-Tedeschi, a confidant of Leo XIII who had been expected to succeed Rampolla as secretary of state and was even viewed as an eventual candidate for pope. Radini-Tedeschi was the dynamic chaplain of Opera dei Congressi, the umbrella organization for Italian lay movements of social concern—of which Catholic Action was one. Pius had no use for lay movements like Catholic Action, in which he discerned less than total obedience to the hierarchy, a damnable enthusiasm for democracy, and other forms of sympathy for Modernism, and thought their effectiveness could best be thwarted if they had no national direction. He therefore suppressed Opera dei Congressi and got Radini-Tedeschi out of the way by making him bishop of Bergamo. Before setting out for his diocese, the new bishop consulted his old friend Vincenzo Bugarini, the rector of the Roman College, about finding a suitable secretary. Angelo, who was still at the college and just beginning his study of canon law, soon found himself on his way back to Bergamo, at twenty-four secretary to an assured, aristocratic bishop who had no intention of letting Pius X put an end to his dedication to the social Gospel.

The two must have seemed an odd pair. The refined bishop, whose impressive figure and demanding countenance brooked no dissent, moved in the manner of one born to nobility. (No one bears a double surname in Italy unless there is an appropriately ancient lineage behind it.) His secretary, with the broad features, stocky build, and plodding gait of a peasant, was even then beginning to put on weight and looked like a farmer masquerading in clerical dress. But Angelo already knew Radini-Tedeschi and was part of his circle—"that valiant band of Romans," as Angelo would call them, who met regularly for "pleasant and cheerful conversation" and who also helped staff Radini-Tedeschi's many Roman projects: soup kitchens, hostels for the poor, recreation centers for soldiers. Though Angelo knew his own limitations and never essayed the dryly august style of the elder man, he would go from his initial admiration to deep reverence and love for this father figure whom he ever after referred to in capital letters—even after he reached the papacy—as *il Mio Vescovo*, My Bishop.

Radini-Tedeschi took possession of his cathedral church on April 9, 1905, and soon began what Angelo called "his innumerable projects"—of modernization (at least, that's what they would have been called but for the Vatican's opinion of the word). He restored the cathedral, built a new residence to replace an impossible and smelly old palazzo, installed running water and central heating in the seminary, and introduced the novelties of science labs and physical education. He took it on himself to visit every parish in his diocese and encourage everyone to spiritual renewal. He stood by striking workers and made a very public and handsome contribution to their strike fund, outraging conservatives. His first pastoral letter took as its subject Catholic Action, which, wrote the bishop, "must be particularly active wherever justice and charity are most obviously neglected. . . . It must harmonize authority and freedom, find its unity in the cooperation of all men for the common good and in the mutual trust between all men and social classes." In the context of Catholic Italy, this was as close to dissent from the Vatican as a bishop dared come.

Radini-Tedeschi paid a price for his independence. His diocese was repeatedly the object of "apostolic visitations," diocese-wide investigations by snooping papal delegates with no announced agenda (and which Radini-Tedeschi dubbed "apostolic vexations"). He found himself surrounded by informers always sending off some bit of news about the latest "unorthodoxy" to the Vatican. "Gradually," Angelo knew, "he came to suspect that with the Pope he no longer enjoyed the esteem of former years, and so he feared that more credit was given to informers' reports than to his own concerning the true state of the diocese."

But Angelo was enthralled. He particularly admired his bishop's vocal—and monetary—support for the Workers' League, the union that in 1909 struck the immense Ranica textile factory just outside Bergamo. "The bishop's alms," whined *Perseveranza*, a local right-wing paper, "is a consecration of the strike, a blessing given to a frankly Socialist cause." Angelo countered eloquently with an article in the diocesan paper, *La Vita Diocesana*: "The priest who lives in the light of the teachings of the Gospel could not pass by on the other side of the road." This is a reference to Jesus's most powerful parable, in which a heretic Samaritan performs the essential "Christian" task of helping someone in need—in this case, a man whom robbers have left for dead—while more officially religious types "pass by on the other side of the road." A bishop has "a duty in charity toward the weak who [are] suffering for the triumph of justice." To claim that "a bishop should not embrace the cause of the oppressed" was to overlook that in the gospels "Christ's *preference* goes to the disinherited, the weak, and the oppressed." Here is Angelo in the first decade of the new century already anticipating the core insight of the Latin American liberation theologians of the 1970s and even advancing what would become their central term, "a preference for the poor."

The article was clipped, by whose bony hands we can't be absolutely sure, and sent off to Cardinal Gaetano De Lai at the all-powerful Consistorial Congregation, the Vatican department that oversees seminaries and the appointment and (when necessary) deposition of bishops. It will remain in the growing file marked "Roncalli," next to the file marked "Radini-Tedeschi." There John XXIII will find it when, soon after his accession and much to the consternation of the Curia, he will demand to see the "Roncalli" file.

The flame of Pius's hatreds was now stoked so high that even Angelo would soon feel the heat. In the year of his ordination, he had attended a lecture by Marc Sangier, the leader of the French movement for Christian democracy, which Pius was preparing to condemn. Angelo's assistant at his ordination ceremony was his brilliant friend Ernesto Buonaiuti, who had been ordained the year before but was already under suspicion and on his way to triple excommunication for his open espousal of Modernism. (All those who took exception to *Pascendi* would be likewise cut off.) The next year, soon after his arrival in Bergamo, Angelo had met Andrea Carlo Ferrari, cardinal archbishop of Milan, who became his friend and spiritual advisor. Ferrari was the most important religious figure in northern Italy; he was also on the pope's enemies list and a frequent subject of his crude humor. Ferrari had the courage to issue a pastoral letter condemning the "anti-Modernist zealots" who were discovering Modernists in every cupboard. All such "evidence" of Angelo's Modernist tendencies were making their way into the "Roncalli" file.

Angelo was, at least in his own mind, setting himself apart from the zealots. Pius loved to read newspapers and often planted pointed, if pseudonymous, pieces in his favorite intransigent journals. He was especially fond of Milan's *Riscossa*, which was the bane of Cardinal Ferrari's existence and which bore the Latin motto *Frangar, non flectar* (I will break rather than bend).

Angelo took the motto as his own but reversed the word order: *Flectar, non frangar* (I will bend rather than break). Not long before his ordination, he had written in his journal a reflection on the man he wished to become, a reflection that combines spiritual and intellectual goals.

> I do not despise criticism, and I shall be most careful not to think badly of critics or treat them with disrespect. On the contrary, I shall love it. I shall study new systems of thought, their continual evolution, and their trends; criticism for me is light, is truth, and there is only one truth [i.e., the supreme truth of Christ cannot ultimately be in conflict with other truths].
>
> But I shall always try to introduce into these discussions, in which too often ill-considered enthusiasms and deceptive appearances have a part to play, a great moderation, harmony, balance, and serenity of judgment, allied to a prudent and cautious broad-mindedness.

Don Rebuzzini of Sotto il Monte, his first model in spiritual equanimity, has not been forgotten. But now the words "moderation, harmony, balance, and serenity" have taken on broader meanings to encompass not only the personal composure of the priest but a way of peace through the intellectual controversies that were stirring up the Church and the world. They are words that could never have escaped from Pius's pen.

In the fall of 1906, Angelo accompanied a diocesan pilgrimage to the Holy Land and was enchanted especially by the Sea of Galilee, where he imagined Jesus in Peter's boat sailing to meet him and his fellow pilgrims. He was scandalized, however, by the scene he witnessed at the site of Jesus's death and resurrection, "the confused disorder of people, objects, languages, rites, and beliefs that surround the Holy Sepulchre." It remains a place of painful disunion, with clergy of various Christian traditions sharing the same space and refusing to speak to one another. Here Angelo prayed for the reunion of "the separated brethren." More and more, he saw for himself a mission of union and harmony, a part he could play in a world in disrepair.

Angelo's growing consciousness of this personal mission could only have been set in bold relief when he considered the disposition of the reigning pontiff, whom he had first seen close up at his coronation in Saint Peter's: "The pope came in to a hurricane of applause and *vivas*. For a moment he lowered his head a little, and when he looked up again his eyes were filled with tears. And the crowd fell silent." Angelo makes no further comment, but the silence of a young man who wants nothing more than to see the pope in the most favorable light indicates— like the silence of the crowd—that he saw something amiss in Pius's response to his great office.

In 1908, he was part of a delegation from Bergamo come to congratulate Pius on the fiftieth anniversary of his priestly ordination: "After the address of homage, Pius X spoke with such anxiety about the perilous times we were living through and of the insidious traps that the evil one lays for the good faith of Catholics that he completely forgot to thank us for our gift," a tray of 25,100 lire in gold coins carried by Angelo, who was completely bewildered by this papal performance, knowing he had already schooled himself in more heightened consciousness and self-control than the pope displayed. In the privacy of his own thoughts, he reproved the pope for "let[ting] himself be overwhelmed by anxiety and show[ing] himself so anguished." This was no way for a pope to behave. Angelo much preferred the model of Radini-Tedeschi, who kept private his suffering over the pope's low opinion of him and "knew how to hide his grief in public."

Angelo would have been even more bewildered if he could have heard the rough talk the pope allowed himself among his cronies. "Kindness is for fools," snapped Pius when begged to show compassion for an alleged Modernist. The Modernists, sneered the pope on another occasion, "want to be treated with oil, soap, and caresses, but they should be beaten with fists. In a duel, you don't count or measure the blows, you strike as you can. You don't wage war with charity." This is a pope who seems never to have read the Sermon on the Mount; his language in private is as shocking as the aggressive nastiness of the Nixon White House. It is no wonder that, as pope, Angelo will ask to see not only his own file but the *Disquisitio* on Pius X, the historical study prepared in advance of Pius's beatification. By the time Angelo was able to read through this, Pius had been not only beatified (that is, declared to be in heaven) but canonized as an official Catholic saint (that is, held up as a heroic model) by Angelo's immediate predecessor, Pius XII. If there was natural curiosity behind Angelo's request to see his own file, behind his need to see for himself the evidence by which this peculiar man was raised to the altars lay years of bafflement.

In 1906, Angelo had begun to lecture on Church history at the seminary and was soon asked to give talks on history to lay audiences at Bergamo's Casa del Popolo. His friendship with Ferrari had enabled him to browse at leisure through the ancient library of the bishops of Milan, where he discovered "thirty-nine parchment bound volumes which bore the title: *Archivio Spiri-tuale—Bergamo*. I explored them: I read them through on successive visits. What a pleasant surprise for my spirit! To come across such rich and fascinating documents concerning the Church of Bergamo at the most characteristic period of its religious renewal, just after the Council of Trent, in the most ardent period of the Counter-Reformation." At the same time that Pius X was attempting to reform dioceses by the imposition of "apostolic visitors," Angelo had unearthed a shining historical precedent for the kind of reform he was naturally drawn to.

At the time of the Counter-Reformation, Bergamo was still in the charge of the bishops of Milan. The bishop whose conscientious visits to the parishes of Bergamo were recorded in detail in the *Archivio* was none other than Charles Borromeo, the great saint of the Catholic Reformation, whose indefatigable persistence had roused to action the bishops who reluctantly attended the third and final session of the Council of Trent. Indeed, it is hard to see how Trent would ever have been finished or have accomplished anything much without Borromeo's ceaseless prodding. He cut a sensational figure through his time, for he was both noble and good. His uncle was the Medici pope Pius IV; and Borromeo spent his family's wealth and that of the bishop's office in a vast welfare program for the poor. He saw to it that his priests were morally upright, conscientious in their duties to their parishioners, and well informed in theological matters. He built three seminaries for their education, one of these the Bergamo seminary that was Angelo's alma mater. He created the Confraternity of Christian Doctrine, the driving force behind the reform of catechetical teaching—the weekly instruction of the faithful, especially children, in doctrine and morals—which had fallen so low. He insisted that vowed religious live in accordance with their vow of poverty—which meant in some cases the liquidation of prodigious possessions. One very rich and recalcitrant order, the Humiliati, became so opposed to the bishop that they decided to do away with him during vespers, a plot that succeeded only in knocking Charles down, as the bullet that was meant to end his life bounced off his clothing and fell to the floor. The Humiliati were doubly humiliated.

But if bullets did not harm him, the Milanese famine of the early 1570s and the plague of 1575 shortened Charles's life, as did his personal penances. The people of Milan, who were (and are) a worldly lot, admired him especially for his faithfulness to them. As the nobles, the politicians (including the governor), and not a few clergymen escaped the city, Charles remained, inspiring many ordinary people to come down from the Alps to assist the sick and the dying. As all commerce fled before the plague and severe malnutrition set in, the bishop managed to find food to feed some sixty to seventy thousand persons daily, exhausting all his resources and incurring large debts in the process. He nursed the sick, ministered personally to the dying, and wept openly—for others, not for himself as Pius X had done. When he died on a November night in 1584, at the end of a life full of incident, he was only forty-six years old.

This was Angelo's kind of saint, a priest concerned for the orderly functioning of the Church, an encourager of holiness in others who knew that, as bishop, he must be the model that others could be inspired to follow, a Christian who saw the blessedness of poverty of spirit, of mercy, meekness, and peace—the beatitudes preached by Jesus—as the lofty pinnacles of genuine holiness. Charles Borromeo did not expect the reformation of his diocese through the medium of apostolic visitors sent from the pope but through his own care and especially through his meetings with his people. As Angelo followed Radini-Tedeschi through his pastoral visits to every corner of Bergamo, observing his warm personal encounters, he felt they were following in the footsteps of the great saint who had trod these paths before them. He was a privileged witness to a bishop's care and concern for other human beings, the humble interpersonal techniques of holiness in action.

The Bergamo Archive that Angelo had discovered would become his scholarly life's work, as he edited Charles Borromeo's thirty-nine parchment volumes into five annotated volumes, published seriatim in 1936, 1937, 1938, 1946, and 1957, the year prior to his election to the papacy. As Borromeo became his historically hallowed—but local—model of priesthood and episcopacy, Angelo was also on the lookout in his wide-ranging reading for a nearby model of scholarship that he could wholeheartedly embrace.

He found what he was looking for in Cesare Baronius, an Italian priest whose life bridged the sixteenth and seventeenth centuries and who was a member of Saint Philip Neri's Oratorians. Baronius was created cardinal by Pope Clement VIII (1592–1605) and would have been elected pope at Clement's death had he not begged the electors to choose someone else. These items of Baronius's curriculum vitae, as well as his championing of papal prerogative, gave him the unchallengeable aura of Catholic orthodoxy. But Baronius is also the father of ecclesiastical history in its critical modern form and, if justice were done, should probably be acknowledged the father of all history written in the modern spirit of critical analysis. As Arnaldo Momigliano, the unparalleled twentieth-century historiographer, says: "From the sixteenth to the eighteenth century ecclesiastical history (especially of the early Church) was treated with a much greater display of erudition, with much more care for minute analysis of the evidence than any other type of history. There is no work in profane history comparable with the Madgeburg Centuriators and the *Annales* of Baronius." From this priest-cardinal, then, friend of Robert Bellarmine—a sacred pillar of Counter-Reformation orthodoxy—stem the exacting methods of rational inquiry, of "minute analysis of the evidence," that Pius X had placed under suspicion. Here was a patron who could serve as an intellectual harbor from the anti-Modernist storm.

For Baronius was also a historian who believed passionately, as Angelo did, that history had a "supernatural dimension," however elusive the attempt to limn it accurately. "Considering facts in the light of ideas," wrote Angelo, "Baronius was able to weave into a unity all the scattered threads even of secular history, and to bring out its wonderful ordering toward the triumph of the sovereign idea which dominates the history of the world, that is, the action of Divine Providence through which human actions converge toward the victory of the City of God." How quickly Angelo had gone from simple farmer to imitative seminarian to tentative cleric to substantive intellectual, finding in his own researches, meditations, and judgments a balanced personal solution to the seemingly intractable crisis that the anti-Modernist campaign had provoked. And it was a solution that mixed sacred with secular history and embraced the need for an evolutionary paradigm—the gradual convergence of "human actions" toward an outcome—if one were to interpret successfully the past and the present and to look to the future with hope.

In early December 1907—at the beginning of Advent, the Church's yearly contemplation of salvation history—Don Roncalli gave a lecture at the Bergamo seminary to commemorate the third centenary of Baronius's death. His announced topic was "Faith and Scientific Research." As *Pascendi* had been issued just four months earlier, he was entering treacherous waters—and he knew it—but he was, however humbly, opposed to the final victory of those who would throw out critical science in the name of faith. He had found a solution, and he would share it. As his more worldly and knowing listeners trembled for him, he spoke of the "wonderful progress that has been made in scientific history in the last few years" and praised "historical criticism." He called his dear Baronius "the founder of historical criticism"—even though "some scholars, especially in Germany [Bultmann and others who were detaching the Bible as a historical document from all subsequent theological interpretation], believe that they have a monopoly of truth . . . as though the Church feared the light that might come from the results of such criticism." This was precisely what "the Church"—at least in the person of Pius X—did fear. But Angelo's "Church" is the Church of Leo XIII, of Baronius and Borromeo, of his mother and Uncle Zaverio. It is broader and deeper, more mysterious and abiding, than the contentious organization centered in the Vatican.

Angelo went on to describe what might be called "the state of religious thought": "The remarkable historical period which, prepared by the pagan renaissance, started with the German Reformation is still unfinished at the dawn of the twentieth century." The problems that began then have not been laid to rest and have only been exacerbated by positivism, the materialist philosophy claiming that nothing exists that cannot be inspected scientifically. But the solution was not to hide but to confront these intellectual challenges with faith and the "general renewal of Catholic scholarship."

It was, in the circumstances, a breathtaking performance by a man of no provenance, just turned twenty-six. He had evaded the rock of medieval obscurantism and the whirlpool of scientific positivism and had steered his calm course between them. But how would the papal spies, who were present in every audience, delate him? What spin would they put on his words? The following June a new apostolic visitation descended on the seminary and Giuseppe Moioli, the professor of New Testament, was removed. Though Angelo and the other instructors survived, they could almost feel the breath of spies surrounding them. But nothing further happened; and by the time something did happen, Moioli's sacking was almost forgotten and the professors had somewhat relaxed their vigilance.

One of the canons of the Bergamo cathedral, however, a certain Monsignor Giovanni Mazzoleni, was hungry for more victims. It was probably this man's "information" that had been responsible for the removal of Moioli and for much of the paper that filled the "Roncalli" and "Radini-Tedeschi" files. In the fall of 1911, he wrote once more to his friend Cardinal De Lai a letter full of insubstantial insinuations about the bishop and the seminary faculty. One "fact," however, stood out for De Lai: some of the faculty, including professor Roncalli, were using Duchesne's *History of the Early Church* in their lectures. A few months later, the work would be placed on the Index of Forbidden Books, but Roncalli and the others could hardly have known of the coming condemnation. The book, after all, had originally been praised by some of the most prominent—and papally approved—*intransigenti*. By this point, the signals for what was and was not orthodox had become so arbitrary that the possession of almost any book or the thoughtless utterance of almost any word might lead one into trouble. But De Lai did not pounce till the victim had been lured into his lair.

On June 1, 1914, Angelo came to Rome with his rector for a discussion of seminary finances with Cardinal De Lai. As the two were leaving at the end of the meeting, De Lai called Angelo back. With the frozen smile and dead eyes that the higher clergy reserve for such occasions, De Lai said only, "*Professore*, please be careful in the teaching of Scripture" and then fell silent, continuing to stare at the young man before him with a cordially vacant expression. Angelo, long familiar with Italianate indirection, was too overwhelmed to respond and had to take his leave in silence. He spent the rest of the day praying in the Church of the Gesù.

When he regained his wits, he wrote to De Lai to say that he had never even taught Scripture and was, in any case, faithful to "the directives of the Church and the Pope always and in everything." De Lai answered, beginning with a deliberately vague but chilling phrase: "*According to information that has come my way,* I knew that you had been a reader of Duchesne and other unbridled authors, and that on certain occasions you had shown yourself inclined to that school of thought which tends to empty out the value of tradition and the authority of the past, a dangerous current which leads to fatal consequences." Fatal, indeed, for, as Angelo knew, De Lai had the power to remove, defrock, excommunicate. Angelo's whole life was on the line.

His second response was a little craven, minimizing his library, his circle of intellectual contacts, and his reading of Duchesne (without which no one of his day could have been called a legitimate teacher of Church history), though he did enclose a copy of his lecture on Baronius—in De Lai's eyes hardly adequate assurance of the author's orthodoxy. It didn't matter, for the gaunt spectre of Death had arrived on the scene. Two years earlier it had taken Uncle Zaverio, dear old Barba, the Roncalli family's own embodiment of history, at the age of eighty-eight. Now on August 20, 1914, less than three weeks after the outbreak of World War I, it came for Pius X, on the day Belgium fell to Germany. Two days later, it carried off Radini-Tedeschi at the age of fifty-seven. With Pius gone, the Church could leave behind the destructive purge he had unleashed and look at last beyond the Modernism controversy to a larger world. But the world Angelo had grown up in was about to change forever.

From Orderly to Archbishop

DESPITE THE ETERNAL sameness of life in Sotto il Monte, the Bergamo seminary, and papal Rome, the larger world into which Angelo had been born had proved unpredictable enough. Italy, for all its glorious past, had from the end of the eighteenth century to its unification been squeezed by greater powers, first by Napoleonic France, then, after the apportionments of the Congress of Vienna, by Austria, which through its sovereignty over much of the Po valley, stretching across northern Italy from Turin to the Adriatic, controlled access to the peninsula. In the course of the nineteenth century, the small states that made up Italy had run through a quick succession of political models, from autocratic Napoleonic republics to more liberal constitutional governments to the reimposition of monarchies, some constitutional, others medieval and feudal.

Not all Italians welcomed Italy's unification. The Napoleonic version of Republicanism had disappointed landowners, who had been effectively excluded from power and who lost most of their ancestral privileges; its confiscation of ecclesiastical estates had permanently alienated most of the clergy; and its reform of the feudal system—which had previously granted peasants many rights over common land and even over the estates of their landlords—had impoverished tenant farmers and left them more monarchist than ever. The confiscation of ecclesiastical and common property and its subsequent resale to the highest bidder became the usual method by which the little republics, and afterward united Italy, financed government operations, causing inevitable power shifts in society.

From the time of its unification to the aftermath of the Second World War, "Republican" Italy was actually an ill-defined constitutional monarchy, ruled by the princes of the House of

Savoy, whose rule had previously been limited to the backward Kingdom of Piedmont and who kept significant powers, such as the powers to form international alliances and make war, out of the hands of the Italian parliament. Many republicans found the situation insufferable and continued to conspire for more radical reforms, often gathering in secret societies such as the Freemasons. Initially, only the tiny minority of substantial landowners (about two percent of the population) profited from Italy's transformation from a patchwork of medieval kingdoms into a "modern" state, because only these landowners were given suffrage—and a free hand in evicting their tenants.

Slowly, the most important of the landowners—the old noble families—faded in importance as an educated, professional class began to emerge from the ranks of urban artisans and smaller landowners. But everywhere, subsistence farmers were made desperate by these political changes, and the poor became much poorer. Many, whether monarchists or republicans, noblemen or peasants, felt that their "country"—not Italy, but Sicily or Sardinia, Mantua or Modena—had been stolen from them. Given the confusion of national purpose, one can appreciate that the ordinary Italian Catholic, who had yet to experience any of the benefits of what we think of as "democracy," would tend to trust an institution of constant authority like the papacy or a supportive local institution like Catholic Action, rather than a state that appeared uncaring, anti-religious, unstable, and without precedent.

Into this volatile mix there would soon be injected the two opposed utopian "solutions" that would all but wreck Europe in the twentieth century: Communism and Fascism. Italian society, which had always been instinctively paternalistic in its structures and craftily conservative in its politics, was in flux as it had never been before; and Italy's political destiny seemed so unpredictable as to unsettle many minds. Early in the twentieth century, liberal electoral reforms extended the vote to all adult males who could read and write, but this included less than a fifth of the adult male population; and the paternalistic conservatism that was so natural to Italy was already devising its own twist on democracy: *trasformismo*, the antithesis of two-party politics, a form of permanent coalition government in which every constituency—from right to left, from the Mafia to the Camorra—got a piece of the action, a hand in the pork barrel, encouraging and even institutionalizing system-wide corruption.

The interplay of opposing forces became increasingly complicated, as movements like Socialism and anarchism, labor unions and farming cooperatives, intransigent Republicanism and intransigent monarchism asserted their power to bring ordinary life to a standstill in localities where their numbers were decisive. Northern Lombardy and the Veneto were Catholic, Emilia-Romagna was Socialist, bourgeois Tuscany was radical and would one day go Communist, the south was hopelessly feudal and resentful. Each region was in the process of developing the political character it retains to this day. For a time—from 1900 to 1914—the Piedmontese statesman Giovanni Giolitti was able to diffuse tension and encourage political stability by creating a broad coalition in favor of free speech, universal manhood suffrage, and laws that protected workers' rights. But Italy's now rising economy (thanks, in part, to Giolitti's practical politics), its residual inferiority complex (over its unimportant place in the world and the ill treatment of its poor immigrants in Europe and America), and the gathering European storm at last overwhelmed Giolitti's strategies. In 1911, Italy attempted for the second time to become a colonial power, this time over Libya, its earlier adventure in Abyssinia having proved an embarrassing disaster. In 1915, after much behind-the-scenes plotting by the king and his ministers and without the consent of parliament, Italy entered the First World War on the side of the Russo-Anglo-French Entente, having renounced both its previous commitment to the Triple Alliance with Germany and Austria-Hungary and its subsequent neutrality. Those who wanted the war knew that ordinary Italians would never side with Austria, which still held the Italian-speaking cities of Trent and Trieste, and that if they wished Italy to cut a dashing figure on the world's stage it would have to be on the side of Austria's enemies.

Though the vast majority of Italians—an amorphous, pacifist agglomeration of Catholics and moderate Socialists—were opposed to the war, a campaign of effective rhetoric had brought Italy to this point, a campaign whose organizers didn't much care which side Italy went with as long as it became a belligerent. These men were a disparate bunch but well positioned in urban centers and united as much in their unquestioning belief in the positive value of violence as in their oft-proclaimed "nationalism," the word that seemed now to be on every patriot's lips. Among them, the Futurists were artists, pro-French, anticlerical, leaning toward anarchism, opposed to conventional morality and middle-class dullness, who called war "the world's only hygiene." The mannered, macho poet Gabriele D'Annunzio attracted a crowd of 100,000 in Rome and, speaking from the steps of the Capitol, ridiculed "the stench of peace" and denounced Giolitti as a "neutralist" and therefore a "traitor." Radical republicans and Freemasons heard the call to war as a return to the heady days of *Risorgimento* that would lead to a purer Italian democracy. One man, an accomplished journalist who scorned all reformers and attempts at moderate progress, had recently broken with the Socialist Party and founded a much-read newspaper, *Il Popolo d'Italia*, financed by leading Italian industrialists as part of their war campaign and destined to become the mouthpiece of a new movement. This jaw-jutting warmonger imagined that the war would bring an end to the contemptible "cowardice" of political compromise. His name was Benito Mussolini and his movement would become known as Fascism.

The Catholic opposition to war—this war and all wars—had been articulated unforgettably for Angelo by Radini-Tedeschi. As Angelo, to whom fell the grim task of bringing the old man the information that he had reached his last hour, knelt at his bedside, the bishop uttered his final prayer: "O my crucified Jesus, I offer you willingly—yes, willingly, O Lord—the sacrifices of my life in union with your sacrifice on the cross . . . in expiation for my own sins and those of my people, for holy Church, for the new pope you will give to her, for my priests, my city and my diocese, all religious everywhere, all who suffer, all who loved me as well as those who felt no love for me, for all those dearest to my heart, for my relations and friends near and far—for my country . . ." "At this point," recalls Angelo, "he opened his eyes and seemed to be gazing far away as he added, with a strong and clear voice, 'and for peace, and for peace.'" Radini-Tedeschi died with the word *peace* on his lips. Ever after, Angelo would treasure the memory of this model bishop's model death—a man whose inner sight, even in his last moments, never strayed from its attention to Christ crucified and whose final sentiment was sympathy with the sufferings of others.

Despite the machinations of Cardinal De Lai, the College of Cardinals, as if hearing the bishop of Bergamo's prayer, elected a moderate progressive, Benedict XV, who had been a friend and admirer of Radini-Tedeschi. In his first encyclical, *Ad beatissimi Apostolorum* (At [the Threshold of] the Most Blessed of the Apostles), issued less than two months after his election, Benedict called a halt to the anti-Modernist persecution and dissolved the abominable network of spies that had been brought into being by his predecessor. These loathsome creatures, who were called "integralists" because they were always insisting that one's Catholicism be *integral* (rather than eclectic or adaptive), were left in the lurch by Benedict's admonition: "There is no need to add epithets to the profession of Catholicism. It is enough for each one to say, 'My given name is Christian; my family name is Catholic.' To live up to these names in one's life is what matters." One needn't be an integralist; to be a Catholic Christian of any variety could suffice.

In May 1915, in the midst of military mobilization and just days before Italy declared war on Austria-Hungary, Angelo was drafted as a hospital orderly, once again conveniently stationed at Bergamo. Italy was hardly prepared for the war that its eager politicians had made, and the casualties began to arrive in ever larger and more sickening waves. Angelo, older and wiser than in his first encounter with the military, grows a formidable mustache, intending this time to take no chance of being dismissed as a prig. But he is no longer a soldier but a comforter, a role he can play with sincerity and effectiveness. He goes about the hospital wards, hearing confessions, offering what services he can to those in pain, again and again anointing the bodies of dying men in their final agony—as much chaplain as nurse. The toll of the dying and the dead is often overwhelming. As Angelo will recall soon after the war: "It often happened . . . that I had to fall on my knees and cry like a baby, alone in my room, unable to contain the emotion that I felt at the simple and holy deaths of so many poor sons of our people—modest peasants from the Marche, Garfagnana, the Abruzzo or Calabria."

There is no longer any tsk-tsking over the soldiers' sexual peccadilloes, just genuine admiration for these abused men in "the flower of their youth," the poor and unprotected "sons of our people," the ones always used as cannon fodder. Some of

Angelo's diaries from this period may have been lost, but there is one surviving page, dated March 8, 1917, which gives us a sense of Angelo the orderly. He describes a certain Domenico Orazi, a nineteen-year-old from Ascoli Piceno, struggling with "a violent case of bronchial pneumonia." Angelo calls him "a humble peasant with a soul as limpid as an angel's. It smiles out from his intelligent eyes and his good and ingenuous smile. This morning and evening, as I listened to him murmuring in my ear, I was deeply moved: 'For me, Father, to die now would be a blessing: I would willingly die because I feel that by the grace of God my soul still remains innocent. If I died when I was older, who knows how disfigured I'd become. And then, when you die older, the separation is more painful: it costs a lot to give up wife, children, home. But what does it cost me to die now?'"

If it is all a little too romantic, it is not because the young orderly is in love with death, for Angelo adds a moment later: "But I on the other hand, dear Menicuccio [extremely affectionate diminutive for Domenico], pray the Lord that he may grant you many years of life. The world needs such chosen, simple souls who are a fragrance of faith, of purity, of fresh and holy poetry. And we priests need them too to feel encouraged to virtue and zeal."

Domenico would die a month later while undergoing surgery. Angelo's surviving references to young men like him, as well as his tributes to priests like himself who "lean over our dying younger brothers and listen to the anguished breathing of the nation expressed in their passion and agony," are remarkably reminiscent of passages in the writings of Walt Whitman, who lovingly nursed casualties from both sides of the conflict during the American Civil War half a century earlier. One cannot but wonder if there may be gaps in the diaries because an eye less naive than their author's saw that the four-year accumulation of

Angelo's heartfelt descriptions of the plight of young soldiers could lead to psychological interpretations unthinkable in the milieu of early-twentieth-century Bergamo. After all, the adult Angelo, now in his mid-thirties, was experiencing the only intimate physical contact he would ever have with the bodies of other human beings. The Vatican, scared to death of any whiff of homosexuality in its ranks, would never approve for sainthood a man whose own words might appear to convict him of such a tendency. If my hunch is well founded, the saving of the description of Domenico would make sense, since it can be interpreted as simply denoting Angelo's admiration for the boy's piety and desire for his recovery.

At any rate, Angelo's admiration for his soldiers and their stoical acceptance of their fate hardly persuades him of the righteousness of their cause. Though Catholic theology had long ago made room for the "just" war, any theologian not unbalanced by nationalism or, like Julius II, by his own intemperance knew that, immediate self-defense aside, the requirements for such a war had seldom, if ever, been met by either side in any of history's conflicts. "War is and remains the greatest evil," said Angelo unequivocally in a speech soon after the war's end, "and he who understands the meaning of Christ and his Gospel of human and Christian brotherhood can never detest it enough."

This conviction will only deepen over the course of Angelo's life; and though he will need nothing more than his own experiences to reinforce it, Benedict XV, the pope of the First World War, already stood out for him as a model peacemaker. The pope was uncompromising in his refusal to be taken in by the rhetoric of the warmongers. For his anguish at what he called "the useless slaughter" and his attempts to broker peace, Benedict was called "the Kraut pope" by the English, the similarly pejorative *"pape boche"* by the French, *"der französische Papst"* by the Germans, and *"Maledetto"* (Damned, rather than *Benedetto,* Blessed, his name in Italian) by his own countrymen. The pope's fear of the consequences of the breakup of Austria-Hungary would prove prophetic. Soon after the guns fell silent, Angelo shaved his mustache, destroyed his uniform, and slipped back to the seminary.

The war had exacted even greater suffering from the Italians than from other belligerents. Of the 600,000 Italian soldiers who became prisoners of war, more than 100,000 died in captivity, largely because the inhumane Italian government, suspecting them of being deserters, refused to send food and clothing as stipulated by the 1907 Hague Convention. Peasants and poor urban workers knew perfectly well that they and their comrades had been used repeatedly in senseless frontal assaults by well-born officers who cared nothing for their safety. These and other officially perpetrated injustices inflamed many ordinary Italians with a profound hatred of the class system and of their own government, a hatred that would have dire political consequences.

At opposite ends of the already multicolored Italian political spectrum, two new political forces were gaining in prominence, both dissatisfied with the status quo. Benedict, realizing the importance of allowing Catholics to participate fully in a state that was not about to vanish, permitted what the Vatican had long prohibited: the establishment of a Catholic party. It was called the Popular Party and was the brainchild of a man who would one day be acknowledged as one of Italy's most influential twentieth-century thinkers, Luigi Sturzo, a Sicilian priest-sociologist who was passionately and intelligently committed to democracy, land reform, and the social Gospel. At the other end of the spectrum, the example of the Russian Revolution, defeating czarist Russia in the midst of the Great War, gave hope to many secularists disappointed in the secular state; and as labor strife gained momentum throughout the country, these newly minted Communists began to imagine that Italy had already reached its "pre-revolutionary" phase.

Angelo's attention lay elsewhere. No longer secretary to a bishop (since new bishops inevitably show the door to their predecessor's confidants), he was devoting himself to teaching at the seminary, where he had been appointed spiritual director to the seminarians, and to building residences for communities of students at Bergamo, where he planned to "love my students as a mother her sons." He was also achieving a small reputation as an inspiring and sought-after speaker.

These modest enterprises were enough to bring him to the notice of Cardinal William van Rossum, the Dutchman who headed Propaganda Fide, or Propagation of the Faith, the Vatican congregation (or department) that oversees missionaries throughout the world. Angelo was invited to become national director for Italy, which, aside from the Veneto and his native Lombardy, had a spotty reputation of supporting foreign missions. He had already met Benedict, who would remain his favorite among twentieth-century popes. Still, he did not like "the Roman atmosphere" and had admitted in his journal during a visit to Rome that "I wouldn't want to live here." He tried to escape by confessing to van Rossum that he was "someone who doesn't get much done; by nature lazy, I write very slowly and am easily distracted"—all true, no doubt, if a little exaggerated. But in the end, he accepted a post that he could hardly have refused and became a member of the Curia, a minor papal bureaucrat. He was also named "domestic prelate," a vacuous honor that meant he could now wear red piping on his cassock and be addressed as *"monsignore."*

When his friend and mentor Cardinal Ferrari died in February 1921, Angelo traveled to Milan for the cardinal's impressive funeral, attended by every sector of the Milanese populace. All of Angelo's old advisors were now gone; and in January of the following year, Benedict XV died of influenza. He had lasted but eight years, a tiny, frail, strange-looking man of blue complexion and noticeably asymmetrical physiognomy. (Because of an injury at birth, one eye, one ear, and one shoulder were markedly lower than their counterparts, and he walked with a limp.) He had suffered years of contempt from the world because of his unswerving devotion to international peace and from crusade-loving churchmen because of his unremitting insistence on peace within the Church. He worked mightily to make missionaries drop their colonial prejudices and encourage freestanding indigenous Churches, a reform that had a direct effect on the work Angelo was now doing. Benedict came close to bankrupting the Holy See because of his outpourings of generosity on behalf of the victims of war, especially in Soviet Russia—where he even dared hope that the new political situation would encourage a healing of the breach between Eastern and Western versions of Christianity! He has still to be acknowledged as one of the most humane, courageous, and far-seeing men ever to occupy the chair of Peter. But Angelo knew him as a great spirit, full of the milk of human kindness and always approachable.

Benedict's successor was Achille Ratti, the papal librarian who had just taken Ferrari's place as archbishop of Milan. Angelo knew him slightly but found him distant and impossible to assess. Ratti's enigmatic presentation of himself may have helped his electability among the cardinals of the conclave, for he triumphed as the "dark horse" compromise, once the old right of Pius X and the newer left of Benedict XV found that neither of their favored candidates could prevail. The old right, however, must have allowed themselves some grunts of satisfaction when the new pope took the name Pius XI.

In this case, the name chosen by the pope was somewhat misleading, for this new Pius intended, above all, to bring about the reconciliation between the Vatican and the Italian state that Benedict had initiated. Unfortunately, the longed-for reconciliation would now have to be effected with a Fascist state, for late in 1922, the year of Pius XI's election, Victor Emmanuel III, king of Italy, invited the Fascist deputy Benito Mussolini to form a government. Fascism had risen among the same people who had seen the war as the mystical instrument that would cleanse Italy of its impurities and give it heroic purpose. Now, amid the political confusion of the war's aftermath, they took their opportunity, recruiting bitter war veterans into black-shirted *squadristi*, who, encouraged by Italy's grasping *petite bourgeoisie* and financed by large landowners and major industrialists, set out to intimidate Socialists, progressive Catholics, union organizers, and landless farmworkers.

The favorite method of these (mostly middle-class) thugs, who had no program beyond their own resentments, was violence, which proved exceedingly effective in a country so fragmented. Anti-Fascists were threatened, brutalized, force-fed quantities of castor oil, sometimes murdered outright. Those who had previously been outspoken began to watch their words. The Socialist Party, champion of the masses of workers, was roundly criticized for not having succeeded in bettering the lot of the poor and began to lose its way, no longer certain of its constituency. Labor leaders received ominous late-night visits and found in the daylight that their unions had been co-opted by Fascist-inspired organizing committees. Local government officials found they had to cede their decision-making powers to some resident blackshirt. Newspapers were shut down. By the time the massive and threatening Fascist March on Rome took place in October 1922, most political parties seemed in disarray, and Mussolini appeared the man of the moment, the only one with broad enough popular support to form a stable government.

It was a grave moment for the Vatican, which allowed itself to be sedated by Mussolini's soft words. Though a well-orchestrated Popular Party–Socialist alliance would have defeated the Fascist movement, which could never have stood up to such overwhelming numbers, an alliance of that sort was still unthinkable to the little men of the Vatican, who had only just begun to contemplate the possibility of granting the secular state a measure of legitimacy. Mussolini, known to be atheist and anticlerical, now offered a secret deal: Catholicism as the state religion and an end to anti-papal propaganda. In return, it was suggested that the Vatican turn over a list of "unreliable and mistaken men" who were supporters of the Popular Party. This was the beginning of the negotiation that would end in the Lateran Accords of 1929, by which the Vatican was established as a 108-acre sovereign state and financially compensated in the spectacular amount of $105,000,000 for the loss of its former territories, the Vatican in its turn recognizing the Kingdom of Italy with Rome as its capital.

Angelo, though he worked for the papal bureaucracy, knew nothing of these negotiations. His office was well outside the Vatican in Piazza di Spagna and he lived in nearby via Lata in a flat he called "my crow's nest" above the Church of Santa Maria. With him were his maiden sisters Ancilla and Maria, who served him attentively as cook-housekeepers, and the retired rector of the Roman seminary, Bugarini, whom he took in, for the old man had found himself with nowhere to live. Angelo's job was going nicely: he managed with dispatch to double the donations Italians made to the work of the missions; he was able to travel to many parts of the country he had never seen before, meeting a variety of people and savoring local cuisines; and, thanks to detailed reports from missionaries, he was gaining insight into far-away cultures very different from anything he had ever known.

But Angelo was also aware of the headway the Fascists were making and the concomitant decline of the Popular Party, of which he was an ardent supporter. In July 1923, Luigi Sturzo was ordered by the Vatican to resign from the Popular Party, after which he went into exile. The Popular Party had to make its last stand in the elections of April 1924 without Sturzo. Angelo urged his family to "remain faithful to the Popular Party," despite the fact that *L'Osservatore Romano,* the Vatican newspaper, had fallen suddenly silent about the Catholic party, while beginning to speak positively of Mussolini. The threat of election violence was so present that Angelo advised his family to stay at home "if there is danger of trouble, and let the world go its own way."

If this advice appears to cede the battle in advance of its being waged, it is of a piece with the mentality that many Catholics assumed unquestioningly, even Catholics as instinctively left-leaning as Angelo. The Church was the eternally dependable Good Place, always on the side of justice and kindness; the State, whatever its form, was less than reliable, since it was based on nothing deeper than the words of men. Kingdoms come and go, but "the word of the Lord endureth for ever." This bit of mental gymnastics allowed people like Angelo, whose sentiments were magnanimous and pacifist but whose political understanding was somewhat underdeveloped, to exempt themselves from the political fray whenever the going got rough or the issues seemed beclouded. Still, he concludes, "In my conscience as a priest and a Christian, I feel I cannot vote for the Fascists. . . . Of one thing I am certain: the salvation of Italy cannot come from Mussolini even though he may be a man of talent. His goals may perhaps be good and correct, but the means he takes to realize them are wicked and contrary to the law of the Gospel." Sadly, this was a great deal more than the temporizing Holy See was willing to say.

Two of Angelo's activities in this period put him on a collision course with Fascism. He became the friend of Giovanni Battista Montini, who as Paul VI would succeed Angelo in the papacy. The young Montini, who was working in the Vatican Secretariat of State, came from a politically prominent family far more connected and cultivated than Angelo's own. Montini's father, Giorgio, was a newspaper editor and Popular Party member of parliament from Brescia. After the Fascists in June 1924 offed the Socialist Giacomo Matteotti, Giorgio Montini's fellow deputy who had written a famous exposé of Fascism, Montini and the other opposition deputies—who had already been illegally reduced to a minority—found the only protest left to them was to withdraw from public life and thus refuse to engage in further parliamentary charades. In Angelo, his son sensed a kindred soul.

On September 1 of the same year, Angelo preached in Bergamo cathedral on the tenth anniversary of the death of Radini-Tedeschi. His theme was true patriotism, which he said was "a form of brotherly love." A country's greatness could shine forth only in "justice embodied in law," not in "military enterprises, diplomatic agreements, or economic successes." The "fundamental laws of civilization" are to be found not in the madness of the moment but in "the Ten Commandments and the Gospels." To our ears, this may seem pretty tepid stuff, but to his listeners it was clear that Angelo was dissociating himself and his Church from Fascism.

A week later Pius XI denounced the Popular Party's attempt to form an alliance with the Socialists, which removed the last obstacle from Mussolini's path. The pope wanted no interference with his goal of establishing normal relations with the Italian state. Angelo's associations and his public discourse had made him one of the "unreliable and mistaken men" whose names the Fascists had wanted the Vatican to turn over to them. But Angelo was let off easy. Early in the new year—on February 17, 1925—Monsignor Roncalli was informed that the pope had appointed him apostolic visitor to Bulgaria.

Angelo was not cut out for heroism or adventure. He was devastated. He had to confront the "groans, tears, endless lamentations" of Ancilla and Maria, whom he would have to leave behind. Where would they go? What would become of them? In the night, Angelo shed his own tears quietly, and in the day his eyes would fill up whenever he thought of his impending banishment. An Italian homebody like Angelo, who loved sacrament-soaked Lombardy with a pride born of centuries, might come to appreciate the splendor of Rome, might enjoy a trip to Sicily, find the Sicilians curious and charming, their customs fascinating, their scenery Edenic, their food sublime—but *Bulgaria*? It sounded like the moon.

He tried to find out what lay behind this unwished-for honor, but no one would give him so much as a hint. The secretary of state, Cardinal Gasparri, told him only that "the situation in Bulgaria is very confused. . . . Could you go there and find out what is really happening?" He met with the imperious Pius, who said unhelpfully: "Your name was suggested to me for this visitation." (Ah, the Italian passive voice, which can conceal mountains!) But the pope also told him of his own humiliation when, while not yet a bishop, he had served briefly as apostolic visitor to Poland and been outranked by the Polish bishops. He would not let such a thing happen to Angelo. *He* would go to Bulgaria as an *arch*bishop, outranking anyone he might meet—which frightened Angelo even more.

Angelo spoke with his new friend Montini, who had no inside knowledge but could offer consolation. In Bulgaria Angelo would learn directly about the ancient Church of the East, for Bulgarians were mostly Orthodox. There were also many Muslims, so there would be opportunity for interfaith encounters such as never occurred in Italy. All this may have sounded more exciting to Montini than to Angelo, but, painfully aware of saying good-bye to *il bel paese,* home of all good things, and to everything he knew, he began to reconcile himself to his coming mission—which everyone assured him would be over in no time, after which he would be given a more pleasing diplomatic assignment, such as Argentina, which was full of Italians. Had he known the Bulgarian assignment would last ten years and that twenty-eight years would pass before he would return permanently to his native land, he might never have brought himself to leave Italy.

He rented half a house, perched grandly on a hill in Sotto il Monte, from Baron Scotti. It was called Ca'Maitino, dialect for Casa di Martino, after an ancestor, Martino Roncalli, the first Roncalli to settle in Sotto il Monte. He installed his two sisters at his expense—they would continue as his housekeepers though the householder was *in absentia*—and sent there the books and personal belongings he could not transport to Bulgaria. The house would remain his summer home till his election to the papacy. Then, with a heavy heart, he prepared for his episcopal ordination by making a retreat.

It has been the custom of serious post-Tridentine priests to make a yearly retreat, a custom Angelo followed faithfully. Each year he ended his retreat with a series of resolutions and *sententiae* to help him on his way. He was now forty-three, losing his hair and growing fat. When he says of the elaborate robes in which he will be clothed as bishop that these "will always remind me of the 'splendor of souls' which they signify and which is the Bishop's real glory—God forbid they should ever become a motive for vanity!" there is every reason to take him at his word. He was not vain.

He puts before himself a prayer from the liturgy for the consecration of a bishop: "May he be tireless in doing good, fervent in spirit; may he hate pride, love humility and truth, and never forsake them under the influence of flattery or fear. . . . May he learn from wise men and fools, so that he may profit from all." This was pretty much what Angelo hoped to accomplish. He had no specific program, except to be a good bishop. He admits to being terrified "for I feel and know myself to be very helpless and incapable." Again, there is no reason to doubt him; he does not think highly of himself or his talents. His most important thought is placed at the head of his list: "I have not sought or desired this new ministry." Again, we know he is telling himself the truth. He goes on painfully: "The Lord has chosen me, making it so clear that it is his will that it would be a grave sin for me to refuse. So it will be for him to cover up my failings and supply my insufficiencies. This comforts me and gives me tranquility and confidence."

Angelo has placed his life at the service of the Church, so whatever ecclesiastical officials ask of him (short of sin) he feels he must do, though he has hardly given up his own judgment. At the end of his reflections, he chooses his episcopal motto, which will one day appear on his papal coat of arms. It is the same motto that Cesare Baronius repeated daily as he kissed the foot of Saint Peter's statue in the great basilica: *Obedientia et Pax*, Obedience and Peace. It is no small irony that, while Angelo was recording his motto, the Fascists were draping Rome's public buildings with their own pseudo-religious motto, *Credere, obbedire, combattere* (Believe, obey, fight). Angelo, who could only have been repelled by *combattere*, would have understood the awful parody of *credere* and *obbedire*. He believed deeply, not in

Mussolini, but in Jesus and his Gospel, and was seeking peace, not combat, through obedience to a posting that had no appeal for him.

He was ordained archbishop on March 19, 1925, the feast of Saint Joseph, in San Carlo al Corso, the church dedicated to Saint Charles Borromeo. His "see" was far away, the uninhabited ancient Roman ruin of Areopolis, which lay between the Red Sea and the Dead Sea. Because a bishop must be bishop of a particular place, the Vatican uses such fanciful designations to lend prestige to the "bishops" of its bureaucracy and its diplomatic corps. In actuality, they are bishops of nowhere.

"Now, forever, I assume also the name of Joseph," he wrote in his diary, "one of the names given me at my baptism, in honor of the dear Patriarch who will always be my chief protector, after Jesus and Mary, and my model." All we know of Joseph is that he *was* a protector who stayed in the background, letting his wife and son take center stage. Angelo hoped to do the same. Wearing his long black coat and soup-plate hat, he boarded the Orient Express at Milan, sat himself down in one of the plush green compartments, and headed for Sofia.

From Diplomat to Patriarch

MONTINI WAS RIGHT. Contact with the Church of the East would be one of the pluses of Angelo's out-of-the-way assignment, though not an unmitigated pleasure. The new archbishop was the first papal representative resident in Bulgaria in more than five centuries, and he was initially seen by the Orthodox as part of an insidious papal plot to convert Orthodox believers to Catholicism. Orthodoxy was intimately entwined with Bulgarian identity and patriotism; and Angelo's position was made more difficult when, in 1930, Boris III, the Orthodox Bulgarian king, took the daughter of Victor Emmanuel III of the nominally Catholic House of Savoy as his wife. Their marriage was celebrated in a Catholic rite at Assisi, Angelo in attendance, after the couple had signed the usual promises to bring up the children of their union as Catholics and the pope had granted the usual dispensation. A few days later, King Boris and the now-queen Giovanna were married again in a grand and widely publicized Orthodox ceremony in the cathedral of Alexander Nevski in Sofia. Three years later, their first child would be given an Orthodox baptism, as would their subsequent children.

Angelo, who was growing ever more worldly-wise and tender-hearted (at least in contrast to the majority of Vatican bureaucrats), found none of this surprising or reprehensible. What else was the king to do? He took the promises made to the Catholic Church as his part in an empty form. He ruled a country on the verge of explosion, was himself constantly subject to assassination attempts, and would have provoked revolution and needless bloodshed had he done anything else. Pius XI, however, who felt cheated, was furious and wasted no chance to issue thunderbolts in the direction of the Bulgarian royal family. (In this period, Pius, who easily became unhinged when he thought the sanctity of marriage was at issue, was also hurling thunderbolts at the Lambeth Conference of the Anglican Communion for its tentative approval of contraception.) Angelo, in consequence, was banished from court for a year, though the king explained himself clearly to his apostolic visitor:

You know perfectly well, your excellency, that by family and baptism I was a Catholic [Boris was a Bourbon-Parma]. If I have acted as I have twice over, it was solely out of concern for the interests of my country. The Holy Synod [the ruling body of the Bulgarian Orthodox Church] was beginning to doubt my loyalty. . . . The Communists seize upon anything that can turn the people against me. I have to do all I can for this torn and divided country.

In his thinking Angelo was already light-years ahead of Pius XI, and in any case his instinct was to embrace rather than to confront. He was a careful historian and a friend of many Catholic thinkers, like Montini, who were keen to mend the breach between Catholicism and Orthodoxy. Angelo knew that the differences between the two were virtually all historical and linguistic rather than substantive and that the Orthodox had, in some respects, the greater claim to antiquity of origin. What was the point of creating needless additional divisions? Of course, Angelo was the pope's man on the scene and had to mouth the party line. But Boris and Giovanna came to understand where his heart lay, and the Catholic "interloper" grew ever closer to the royal couple. He would keep their photograph by him all his life, long after Boris's suspicious death in 1943 while returning home by plane from an unpleasant meeting with Hitler—though it is also true that Angelo would maintain an ever-growing photograph collection of all the places he lived and all the people with whom he developed a relationship.

To us, reading history backward, the rise of Fascism in Europe has all the goosestepping inevitability of Leni Riefenstahl's *Triumph of the Will*. But through the twenties and thirties many Europeans refused to acknowledge the direction in which events were heading. The blindness of the Vatican is well expressed in *L'Osservatore Romano*'s embarrassing ecstasy over the newly concluded Lateran Treaty and Concordat. "Italy has been given back to God, God to Italy," pealed the editors on February 12, 1929. By this point, Italy was already a repressive dictatorship. Angelo came to view his Bulgarian exile in a new light: "It seems to me a great Providence that I am out of Italian affairs. I follow all the papers and find the whole thing painful," he wrote to a friend.

His main role in Bulgaria, however, was not as liaison to the monarchy or to the Orthodox Church but as encourager and protector of the Catholic minority, a role he played with dogged faithfulness. Most of the Catholics (about 48,000) were resident foreigners—businessmen, diplomats, and their families who belonged to the Latin rite. These were clustered in Sofia and a few other urban centers; they were guided by two bishops, one in the northern city of Rustchuk, the other in Sofia, and required little protection from Angelo. But there were also 14,000 Uniates, mostly poor refugees from Thrace and Macedonia, who lived precariously in rural areas and had no bishop. Uniate Churches follow Orthodox liturgy and customs (such as allowing married priests) but are in union with the Holy See. Except for Ukraine, where they are a substantial minority, Uniates constitute marginal, detested subcultures in Orthodox lands. They have symbolic value to the papacy because of its claim to universal jurisdiction. Their value to Angelo was rather more as flesh-and-blood human beings.

He began a Radini-Tedeschi-like visitation that took him by mule, cart, and raft to outlying areas where roads were bad or nonexistent. "I became their neighbor," he would say later. The people he visited were touched by his interest and began to call him *"Diado,"* or Good Father. He was touched by their liturgies, especially by the tragic plangency of their Slav music, so much earthier than the disembodied swoops of Gregorian chant: "As I joined with them in singing their grieving lamentations, which were the echo of centuries of political and religious slavery, I began to feel myself more catholic, more truly universal." He proposed to the Vatican that it appoint his impressive guide, the

Uniate priest Stefan Kurtev, as bishop for the Bulgarian Uniates, who often had to endure, in addition to humiliation at the hands of the Orthodox, the condescension of their bourgeois brothers of the Latin rite. But Kurtev was only thirty-four, and the Vatican took its time in agreeing to the appointment.

Angelo's second goal was to give the Uniates their own seminary. He bought the land with the Vatican's permission, but permission was never given to go ahead with construction. "Rome has changed its mind once again," he wrote to his family. He felt himself more and more Slav, less and less Roman. To one friend he wrote, "My heart breaks when I think that you in Rome can devise no further ways of making more spectacular the triumph of Jesus in the Eucharist, while here we don't even have oil to light the lamps in the chicken-coops we use as chapels." In another letter of this period, he was struck by the "strange fact" that his difficulties were "not caused by the Bulgarians for whom I work but by the central organs of ecclesiastical administration." Pius XI was not an easy boss, since "he almost always went against the advice that was given him," according to Ludwig von Pastor, then Austrian ambassador to the Holy See and a leading historian of the papacy. According to an unconfirmable story, Pius once kept the visiting Angelo on his knees before him for forty-five minutes in penance for "permitting" the Orthodox baptism of Prince Simeon, heir to the Bulgarian throne (the same man who in 2001 was elected prime minister of post-Communist Bulgaria).

But Angelo had found in Pastor's forty-volume *History of the Popes* an anecdote that cheered him. It concerned Cardinal Morone, "one of the greatest servants of the Church in the sixteenth century, a great diplomat, a man of exquisite courtesy, upright, pious, etc.," who was imprisoned in Castel Sant'Angelo on a whim of Paul IV, a man of truly poisonous temperament, whom

Angelo termed "no doubt a holy but an impetuous man." This had become Angelo's preferred style: find a venerable historical precedent, damn the villain of the piece with faint praise (especially if he is a pope), but make one's desired point—in this case, that it is not the pope but Morone, who "had to put up with the most humiliating trials until the death of Paul," who is to serve as Angelo's model of action and that even popes can be overcome with patience.

Angelo's name was much bruited about in Vatican circles when, in early 1929, the see of Milan fell vacant. But Mussolini, who had already silenced all opposition, was unlikely to have allowed such an appointment. In the event, the appointment went to Ildefonso Schuster, who soon declared that "right from the start Catholic Italy and the Pope have blessed Fascism," a statement that even *L'Osservatore Romano* had to take exception to. Angelo's post was upgraded to that of "apostolic delegate," but as the years slipped by no further mention was made of Argentina or of any other posting, and it was coming to seem as if Angelo might finish out his career in Bulgaria.

"As for me," he wrote to his family at Easter 1930, "I continue to be well and to live peacefully and happily, without any thought other than to do the will of the Lord. In part I owe this tranquil disposition and ability to let myself go in the arms of Providence and obedience to being born in the countryside, into a family that is poor in material goods but rich in faith and the fear of the Lord, and that is used to the simple realities of nature coming round day by day and year by year"—Lombardy transported to Bulgaria. At the same time, he complained in his journal of "the uncertainty . . . about the exact purpose of my mission in this country; my frustrations and disappointments at not being able to do more, the enforced restrictions of my life . . . in contrast to my longing to work directly ministering to souls; my interior discontent with what is left of my natural inclinations, even if so far until now I have succeeded in keeping them under control." On balance, his easygoing temperament had made it easier for him to accept the possibility that he had been permanently misplaced by the Holy See, but it did not wipe away all anguish.

Toward the end of 1934, Angelo was at last awarded a new assignment. He was to be transferred to Istanbul as apostolic delegate to Turkey and Greece, which would also allow him to act as bishop to the small Catholic community of Istanbul. This was a promotion, all right, though not quite what he might have hoped for. On January 5, 1935, he arrived in Istanbul, a city he had visited many times in the previous ten years, seat of the ecumenical patriarch, the most important figure in the Orthodox world. Turkey's Christian history, especially as site of the early ecumenical councils of Nicea, Ephesus, Chalcedon, and Constantinople, stirred Angelo's imagination; and he would over the course of his tenure become known as a sure guide to Christian antiquities. But Istanbul—or Constantinople, as Angelo preferred to call it—was now an Islamic city, and though it was for Angelo achingly full of historic resonances and "by its situation . . . the finest city in the world," the diminution of the patriarch's status in the new secular state of Atatürk was pitiable. Angelo called the city "this central but now almost spent heart of Orthodoxy."

In Turkey, Angelo would soon find himself deprived of his soutane and soup-plate hat and dressed up in business suit and bowler under Atatürk's relentless secularization. Most Italian clerics of the period, who were never seen without the distinctive costumes that set them apart from ordinary humanity, would have found this change of dress a rankling imposition. "What does it matter," confided Angelo to his secretary, "whether we wear the soutane or trousers as long as we proclaim the Word of

God?" Other moves by the Atatürk government—the closing of many Christian schools and of Angelo's own diocesan newspaper—were more onerous. It is considerably more difficult to proclaim the Word of God if one can no longer teach or publish. The situation, however, gave Angelo some sense of the far more terrifying constraints borne by believers in Soviet Russia.

In his new job, Angelo set about making friends of the many people his tactless and forbidding predecessor, Carlo Margotti, had alienated. When he called on the city governor, Vali Muhidden Ustundag, he got an icy welcome, but the visit ended with repeated toasts of raki on a terrace overlooking the Bosporus. Angelo was careful to befriend all the diplomats he met in Turkey, no matter which country they represented, and these friendships would soon prove essential to his mission.

Increasingly pained by what he was coming to see as the needless division between Catholicism and Orthodoxy, he was particularly careful to cultivate a strong relationship with the patriarch. The wall between East and West was formidable, but, said Angelo sportively, "I try to pull out a brick here and there." With this in mind, he insisted that in his little cathedral the parts of the liturgy not required to be said in Latin—the Gospel, the Litany, the "Blessed be God"—be read in Turkish. These shocking innovations got him denounced to the Vatican and he had to defend himself: "The Gospel . . . does not admit national monopolies, is not fossilized, and looks to the future." The friendships with everyone, the ecumenism (then a dirty word in the Vatican), the modest inculturation: these were gentle hints of an unusual papacy to come—had anybody been watching for such signs (which nobody was).

On October 2, 1935, Italy invaded Abyssinia, a senseless adventure that Pius XI appeared to approve. From now on, the international crisis would spin so quickly out of control that each week news of raw events would be flung at diplomats like Angelo. Angelo's task—to be the eyes and ears of the Holy See—was full of obscurities as event was piled on event and prediction of future outcomes grew steadily less confident. Angelo was no prophet; he passed on whatever "information" he came by, even when it was crude propaganda slipped him by Franz von Papen, a duplicitous leftover from the Weimar Republic who had been made Germany's ambassador to Turkey—and thus earned a dismissive comment from the imperious Domenico Tardini at the Vatican Secretariat of State: *Questo non ha capito niente* ("This chap understands nothing").

Indeed, Angelo could be gullible and was capable of foolish opinions. "General Pétain put it very well yesterday," he wrote home in 1940. "One of the causes of the French defeat was their unbridled enjoyment of material pleasures after the Great War. The Germans on the other hand began to impose limitations and sacrifice on themselves, and so were prepared and strong." Though his heart lay with the outlawed Popular Party, he would also occasionally—in these private letters to his simple family—express the kind of patriotic sentiment that could easily be misinterpreted as support for Mussolini, but he was just trying to paint a rosy picture to help them keep up their spirits.

The rapidly aging Pius at last roused himself against Nazism and Soviet Communism in two encyclicals—*Mit Brennender Sorge* (With Searing Anxiety) and *Divini Redemptoris* (Of the Divine Redeemer)—issued in March 1937. His objections to both systems were similar—the suspension of the rule of law, the subordination of the individual to an omnipotent state, the cult of the "heroic" figures of Hitler and Stalin as national saviors—but the pope's eyes had now been opened to the essential racism of the Nazi worldview, which he condemned as fundamentally anti-Christian, even calling Hitler a "mad prophet possessed of repulsive arrogance."

The Fascists' adoption of the same racist doctrines in 1938 occasioned a decisive break between the Vatican and the Italian regime, and Pius set in motion the writing of an encyclical condemning anti-Semitism, an encyclical unfinished at his death and left unpublished by his successor (not, in itself, a reason for comment, since there is no precedent for a pope to publish his predecessor's unfinished documents). Pius XI's appreciation of Western civilization's debt to the Jews—"Spiritually, we are all Semites" was his unforgettable formulation—would become the foundation stone for the first serious Jewish-Catholic dialogues in the postwar period. As Hitler arrived in Rome to great hoopla in May 1938, the old man—who never seemed to realize that he had once helped to legitimize the tactics of Fascism, which then served as a model for Hitler's program—pointedly left for his summer residence at Castel Gandolfo in the hills south of the city, having ridiculed the swastika as "a cross not of Christ" and shut the Vatican museums against the infamous "tourist."

Pius XI died in February 1939 and was succeeded by his secretary of state, Eugenio Pacelli, Angelo's immediate predecessor as pope, who took the name Pius XII. He would fail to address the issue of anti-Semitism altogether, even though he was receiving some of the best diplomatic information in the world and was early made aware of Hitler's impending "Final Solution," which his predecessor could not have known about. There is no question that Pius XII saw the protection of Catholics as his most basic duty and that he was fearful of inciting the Nazis to additional violence were he to speak out. When the Dutch Catholic bishops *did* speak out in favor of the Jews, their outspokenness only provoked additional roundups.

133

Pius XII used his personal resources to ransom Jews; and Italian churches, monasteries, and convents, prompted by the directive (and example) of the Vatican, gave asylum to many more. Italy's record of saving Europe's Jews from their would-be executioners comes close to being the best in the world. In Rome alone, more than five thousand Jews were hidden in rectories and religious communities; and throughout Italy, with its highly assimilated Jewish population of some seventy thousand, fewer than twenty percent were lost. The distinctive Italian combination of religiosity and rebelliousness no doubt played a part in this saving mission. And, in any case, the resourcefulness on which every Italian prides himself was pricked by the challenge.

Being himself a skillful diplomat, Pius XII may have put too much reliance on silent diplomacy and not enough on the power of his position as a mouthpiece for morality. But the charges hanging over this pope of being personally anti-Semitic and excessively pro-German amount to hunches lacking sufficient proof. What is undeniable and inexplicable, however, is that, though Pius lasted to 1958, he never in the fourteen years left to him after Italy's liberation by the Allies brought himself to refer clearly and publicly to the Holocaust, let alone to condemn it. This fact alone, I submit, puts Pius XII in the category of moral pygmy.

In the same month that saw the interregnum between Pius XI and Pius XII, Angelo's mother, now eighty-five, lay dying and hoping to see her Angelino once more. As chaos descended on the world, Angelo was required to stay at his post and could not attend his mother's deathbed, anymore than he had been able to attend that of his father, who had died four years earlier at the age of eighty-one, the same age Angelo would reach. He could not even attend their funerals, and was left alone in his chapel "*a piangere come un bambino*" (to cry like a baby). On Good Friday

1939, Italy invaded Albania, subduing it in a week and stationing troops along the Greek border, which hardly endeared Angelo to Greece, where he was a frequent visitor on the Holy See's behalf (though he could never warm to the suspicious Greeks as he did to the Turks). A month later Hitler and Mussolini signed their "Pact of Steel," making it inevitable that Italy would enter the war against the Allies. Germany and the Soviet Union were soon busy destroying Poland, executing its priests and intellectuals. In May 1940, Germany invaded neutral Holland, Luxembourg, and Belgium; on June 10, Italy entered the war; on June 14, Paris fell.

Angelo was first alerted to the fate of Jews in occupied Poland by a party of Jewish refugees he met in Istanbul on September 5, 1940. He helped them on their way to the Holy Land and from that time stood ready to facilitate the escape of Jews in whatever way he could—with clothes, money, documents, and a quiet sense of common humanity that many never forgot. Whatever was in the heart of the reigning pope, Angelo was in no doubt about what his heart was telling him. "We are dealing with one of the great mysteries in the history of humanity," he wrote to a concerned nun in Bucharest. "Poor children of Israel. Daily I hear their groans around me. They are relatives and fellow-countrymen of Jesus."

In the sacred work of smuggling human beings, the apostolic delegate relied on the many friendships he had forged over his years in the East: with Raymond Courvoisier, Ankara director of the Red Cross (despite the fact that some in the Vatican viewed the Red Cross with suspicion as rivals in international charity); with von Papen, the strutting German ambassador, whom Angelo rightly judged had a soft spot and would be willing to be used; with King Boris of Bulgaria, whom Angelo believed to be a man of conscience. (Boris was actually a far more ambiguous figure—see Tzvetan Todorov, *The Fragility of Goodness: Why Bulgaria's Jews Survived the Holocaust* [2001]—but such ambiguities lie outside our narrative.) For the first time in his life, Angelo was in a key position, and he played every card in his hand. Turkey was still neutral, and for many European Jews the only remaining escape route lay through the Balkan countries and Istanbul to Palestine, then under British mandate. Among the people Angelo helped escape were Slovakian Jews who had been herded to Hungary, then to Bulgaria. For these, Angelo's friendship with Boris proved decisive.

He met twice with Isaac Herzog, grand rabbi of Jerusalem, concerning 55,000 Jews stranded in Transnistria, a Romanian-administered territory seized from the Soviet Union. Could Angelo move the Vatican to intercede with the Romanian government? He did, and the intercession was successful. Herzog sent him a glowing letter, praising "the noble feeling of your own heart" and promising that "the people of Israel will never forget the help brought to its unfortunate brothers and sisters by the Holy See and its highest representatives at this the saddest moment of our history."

To smuggle more people out of Eastern Europe, Angelo sent stacks of peculiar documents by diplomatic pouch to Vatican representatives in Hungary and Romania. These were "Immigration Certificates," issued by the Palestinian Jewish Agency for distribution among fleeing Jews. Even though they conferred no rights on the bearer, they could often spell the difference between death and life. When one stack of certificates was exhausted, Angelo would send another. "Since the 'Immigration Certificates' we sent you in May contributed to the saving of the lives of the Jews they were intended for," Angelo wrote to Angelo Rotta, the apostolic nuncio in Budapest in August 1944, "I have accepted from the Jewish Agency in Palestine three more bundles, begging your excellency to pass them on to the person they are intended for, Mr. Milos Krausz"—actually Moshe Kraus, Budapest secretary for the Jewish Agency, but Angelo was never good at non-Italian names. Out of interventions like these the legend may have arisen that Angelo actually issued baptismal certificates to save Jews; and though he may have done so, it is far more likely that these were Vatican visas, which announced that the individual named was under the protection of the Holy See—and which Angelo certainly issued to fleeing Jews in large quantities.

The letter to Rotta gives a hint, however, of Angelo's willingness (so imitative of Saint Paul's Epistle to Philemon) to wheedle and beg, which he probably had to do in order to secure von Papen's complicity in his smuggling operations. Later, when von Papen would stand trial for Nazi war crimes before the International Tribunal at Nuremburg, a letter from Angelo would save his life. "I do not wish to interfere with any political judgment on Franz von Papen," wrote Angelo to the president of the Tribunal. "I can only say one thing: he gave me the chance to save the lives of 24,000 Jews." This number would one day be repeated under oath by von Papen to the postulator of the cause for the beatification of John XXIII. Whatever the cumulative number of those saved by Angelo Roncalli—since no adequate record survives and Angelo, despite his fastidious record keeping, was not one to keep count of such an achievement—it was surely in the scores of thousands and may have been much greater.

Angelo was now in his sixties and, if anything, seemed older, a little grave, but full of evident tenderness toward his fellow human beings. It was a tenderness often reciprocated. On a visit to Greece, now partly occupied by Italy, as he visited the troops of the Italian Eighth Army, one corporal broke ranks and knelt before the apostolic delegate. "What is it, my son?" asked Angelo.

"Monsignore," responded the soldier. "May I embrace you in the name of all of us?" As he stood and hugged the fat, lovable little bishop, his fellow soldiers broke out in applause. This sort of incident, which became more and more common as Angelo aged, was possible only because of the aura of goodness that emanated from him.

Angelo dieted but to little avail: for breakfast, coffee and fruit; for supper, soup and fruit; though for the midday meal, the usual Italian three courses with wine, dining as he said "like a good Christian"—that is, in his parlance, like a normal human being. He acquired an Irish secretary, Thomas Ryan, who tried to teach him English, which he learned to read but never to speak. He reflected on war ("War is desired by men, deliberately, in defiance of the most sacred laws. That is what makes it so evil"), on nationalism ("The world is poisoned by morbid nationalism, built up on the basis of race and blood, in contradiction to the Gospel"), and on the holiness of human beings ("The Spirit is poured out on the whole Church—and even the simplest faithful and the humblest souls share in the Spirit, sometimes super-abundantly and to the point of heroism and holiness"). This last reflection, from a Pentecost sermon delivered in his little cathedral of the Holy Spirit, is copied from the language of the prophet Joel, of Peter's first sermon in the Acts of the Apostles, and of the Eastern Church. It anticipates Angelo's inspiration for the great Council of the 1960s.

The events of the early 1940s often took Angelo by surprise: Germany's attack on Russia, its defeat there, and Italy's switching of sides in the war. He was, however, impressed by Italy's occupation of famine-wracked Greece, which Primo Levi called "the most compassionate military occupation that history records." Attempts by the Vatican to trace prisoners of war brought Angelo in contact with the Russian consul in Istanbul, Nicholas

Ivanov. Though their worldviews could not have been further apart, they had a long, amiable conversation, and Angelo discovered that it was possible to converse humanely even with an agent of Soviet Communism.

On the night of July 9, 1943, the Allied liberation of Italy began. Within weeks, Mussolini was arrested, after which Fascism quickly crumbled. "In all human persons and institutions," wrote Angelo to his brother Giovanni, "there is a mixture of good and bad, high and low. . . . The fact that Italy could pass without disturbance in a couple of days from one political constitution to another means that common sense and dignity count for more than the mere victory of brutal and overwhelming power. So there's no need to speak about anyone with bitterness." If Angelo's picture of Italy passing "without disturbance" to a new era hardly does justice to the partisans fighting in the territory still under Nazi occupation, it may nonetheless be noted that his political vision is gaining somewhat in complexity, that he is aware of the moral ambiguities of all political positions (even, it would seem, of the official Catholic position on Communism), and that he is already looking forward to national reconciliation.

In his next Pentecost sermon, he speaks again of the Spirit, so necessary to humane life. Left to itself, the human race resembles "one of those iron-age villages, in which every house was an impenetrable fortress, and people lived among their fortifications." It is so easy to stay within one's group, especially for Catholics, cutting ourselves off from "our Orthodox brothers, Protestants, Jews, Muslims, believers or non-believers in other religions." But "I have to tell you that in the light of the Gospel and Catholic principle, this logic of division makes no sense. Jesus came to break down the barriers; he died to proclaim universal brotherhood; the central point of his teaching is charity—

that is, the love that binds all human beings to him as the elder brother and binds us all with him to the Father." He hoped for "an explosion of charity," in which the word *Catholic* would no longer carry any exclusive connotation but would signify universal unity. Here, in Istanbul in 1944, the breath that would animate the council was already blowing.

On December 6, Angelo received a coded telegram from the Vatican, containing an announcement that struck Angelo "like a thunderbolt": he was appointed nuncio to France, the grandest diplomatic assignment in the pope's gift. He hurried to Rome, in confusion over such an unexpected honor. At the Secretariat of State, Tardini was brusque. It was all the pope's doing; he had nothing more to say. In his audience with Pius, the pope told Angelo only: "I want to make it clear that I was the one who acted in this nomination, thought of it, and arranged everything. For this reason you may be sure that the will of God could not be more manifest or encouraging." That was the way popes talked, and Angelo was quite used to it and even capable himself of employing such exalted language, which hid more than it revealed.

Behind the scenes, a great pissing match was in progress between Pius and General Charles de Gaulle, leader of newly liberated France, who was resolved to rid his country of all officials who had collaborated with the Nazi puppets of the Vichy regime. To his mind, this included all French bishops who had cooperated in any way with their oppressors, a rather large number. It also included the papal nuncio, Valerio Valeri, who had been cozy with Pétain. De Gaulle and Pius were physically and psychologically similar: tall, thin, austere, humorless, solitary, possessed of an unwavering sense of their personal dignity, incapable of taking advice. The more de Gaulle insisted, the more stubborn Pius became in upholding principle: the secular state had no business proposing or disposing of bishops; the purpose of any ambassador was to form a relationship with the regime, however oppressive, of the state he was assigned to. De Gaulle was a faithful Catholic, but he could not abide Pius's finicky insistence on diplomatic niceties in the aftermath of Nazi atrocities. They soon reached an impasse.

Then Russia became the first country to recognize the new French government, and its ambassador was confirmed. It was a tradition for the head of the French state to be greeted at the New Year by the diplomatic corps and addressed by their dean, who was always the papal nuncio. But de Gaulle would not have Valeri, so the honor of the New Year's address to the provisional president of the Republic would fall, by default, to the senior ambassador—who would be a godless Communist. This would prove more humiliating to Pius than to give way on the appointment of the nuncio. So he pulled Angelo out of his hat, a man uncompromised by any stain of Nazism, a man no one could criticize since no one in Western Europe knew anything about him. Angelo was, in fact, Pius's second choice; his first—Joseph Fietta, the nuncio to Argentina, a job once promised to Angelo—had to decline because of ill health. A French journalist who tried to find out something about the new nuncio was informed by a cruel curialist that he was *"une vieille baderne,"* an old fogey.

The old fogey was facing an uphill assignment. His New Year's address—in which he congratulated de Gaulle on his "political wisdom" by which "this beloved country has recovered her liberty and . . . her faith in her own destiny"—had been written by Valeri as a kindness to Angelo, whose French was a bit shaky. But it impressed de Gaulle by making the right noises. Before delivering it, Angelo turned to the Russian ambassador, apologized for upstaging him, and promised to make his first diplomatic call to the Soviet embassy the very next day. As he won points for diplomatic refinement, his mind was on the continuing diplomatic impasse between pope and president over the collaborationist bishops.

De Gaulle also meant to appoint the famous philosopher Jacques Maritain his ambassador to the Holy See. Maritain, a convert from Protestantism, was impeccably anti-Nazi and a fervent, if discerning, Catholic. A little too discerning for the Vatican. Maritain was finishing a lecture tour in Latin America, where he had been passionate about human rights in the face of some of the world's most repressive regimes. Though it is hard, more than fifty years later, to imagine what the Vatican could have found objectionable in the faithfully orthodox Maritain, there was nervousness about the language of "rights," reminiscent of revolution—and to be a *French* intellectual still merited automatic suspicion in Italian clerical circles. The Holy See would have been more comfortable with a less fervent, more worldly career diplomat. Angelo set about securing the Vatican's acceptance of Maritain. Once this was accomplished, Maritain himself was able, within weeks of Germany's unconditional surrender on May 8, 1945, to dispose of the matter of the collaborationist bishops. Though the Gaullists had wanted to replace twenty-five bishops, they settled in the end for seven, admitting by their acquiescence that their original demand had been overzealous.

The second item on Angelo's list of difficulties was to prove less tractable. Amid the pressures of the war, the formidable archbishop of Paris, Cardinal Emmanuel Suhard, had begun a bold experiment. In 1942, the Germans had sent 800,000 Frenchmen off to forced labor camps in Germany but had refused to allow chaplains to accompany them. So Suhard secretly sent along twenty-five young priests, who, attired like the other deportees, were not identifiable as such. To the Vatican—and indeed to most post-Tridentine Catholics, who did not expect to see a priest out of clerical clothes unless he was up to no good— this was an innovation that could result only in scandal. Many of the priests were discovered and repatriated; two died in the camps. But for some of the priests, the labor camps were a transforming experience, and, on their return at the war's end, they petitioned Suhard for permission to remain "worker priests" who would not, like other priests, live carefully apart from their people but share their work, their poverty, their lives. Suhard gave his support, and other young priests began to join in the experiment.

In this, as in many other things, Suhard was a visionary, who saw that the Europe that had existed and even thrived before the war—the Europe of neat class divisions and moral predictability—was now in its death throes. The horrors perpetrated by the Nazis (and, to a lesser extent, by the Fascists) had brought into question all comfortable certainties about the legitimacy of the state and its powers, the goodness of human beings, the value of traditional morality, even the purpose of life. After the deaths of millions of innocent victims, how could the survivors return to the convenient assumptions of conventional bourgeois life, whether in its religious or its secular guise?

Of course, many did. But Suhard, in his resolve to engage his own time, was percipient in realizing that for some young people there would be no going back to the ways of their fathers and that, in this new and less predictable world, the mission of the Church—which had not always spoken with courage during the Nazi horrors—was in mortal peril. A radical questioning of all authority and a subsequent relativizing of all philosophical systems would be among the lasting results of the Second World War. In such a world, as Suhard saw, Christianity—arrayed in any of the costumes from its traditional wardrobe—could easily end up looking foolish and irrelevant.

The new worker priests were dedicated to living with the pain of their people. This involved everything from sharing insalubrious living quarters, working in factories and dockyards like ordinary laborers, befriending anarchists and Communists, and supporting radical labor demands to spending long nights in smoky cafés while discussing "life" with the alienated young, who took their cue not from preachers and theologians but from Sartre and Camus. Discovering that the rites of the Church meant nothing to the workers, some priests began to say Mass while wearing their factory uniforms, the eucharistic bread and wine laid out not on a gold-encrusted marble altar but on whatever surface was available, the *"Dominus vobiscum"* (The Lord be with you) transformed into *"Salut, copains!"* (Hello, mates!). Not a few worker priests became gradually indistinguishable from the people they meant to help, more Communist or existentialist than Catholic; some lived openly with women, not only casting aside priestly celibacy but despising the bourgeois institution of matrimony. The nuncio's ears burned with the shocked complaints he had to listen to from more traditional Catholics; and it is hard, even now, to distinguish the facts from the malicious rumors that swirled around this experiment.

Some, not satisfied with the nuncio's mild and equivocal responses, took their outrage to the Vatican, where they gained an eager audience in the archconservative Alfredo Ottaviani, who had been appointed Pius's Grand Inquisitor. (We will meet Ottaviani again as the chief obstacle to the success of the Second Vatican Council.) At the Secretariat of State, however, Angelo's old friend Montini saw the matter differently: "When so much is at stake, risks must be taken, lest one should be guilty of failing to do all that is possible for the salvation of the world." But

Montini was a Francophile and a longtime friend of Maritain. (One day, Montini, as Angelo's successor, Paul VI, would even offer to make Maritain the first lay cardinal since the unification of Italy, an offer declined by the proposed honorand.)

A diplomat is supposed to have no opinions of his own, just those of the state he represents, so it is difficult to gauge what Angelo may really have felt about the intellectual stirrings in postwar France or even, to judge by his sparse comments, whether he grasped the permanent transformation in culture and religion that was under way. He was known as "a very lively talker"—in the words of André Latreille, the government's *directeur des cultes,* who met with him often. "Stout, friendly, words tumble forth from him so that it is hard to get a word in edgewise." No one could tell for sure whether Angelo's demeanor flowed from simplicity or calculation. Angelo knew himself to be Pius's second choice: *"Ubi deficiunt equi, trottant aselli"* (When horses are unavailable, asses come in handy) was how he summed up his appointment. And Angelo knew that Pius wished to have no innovators or thinkers in his employ: *"Io non voglio collaboratori, ma esecutori"* (I want no collaborators, only implementers) was Pius's oft-repeated expression.

It is difficult even to assess Angelo's relationship to Suhard, though there is no doubt that Pius viewed the archbishop of Paris with mounting suspicion. There was never a question of sacking Suhard. Cardinals don't get sacked, nor do archbishops of capital cities, especially one like Suhard, who was treasured by Parisians, by the French nation, and, more and more, by well-informed Catholics everywhere. Such a move would signal to the world that there was conflict at the highest levels of the Church, something a modern pope can ill afford. But Pius had no doubt that Suhard was not one of his meek *esecutori,* and he watched his activities like a hawk. In February 1947, Suhard published his famous pastoral letter *Essor ou déclin de l'Église* (Development or Decline of the Church), a milestone of modern intellectual Catholicism. Who was the archbishop of Paris to dare to pontificate on whether or not the Church was in decline and to call for the Church's adaptation to the needs of the present day? In Pius's eyes, Suhard was attempting to play pope.

In his open questioning and innovative responses, Suhard was relying not only on his own insights but on those of leading French Catholic intellectuals who were rising to the challenges of secular society and even rethinking the meaning of the Church. These were laymen like Étienne Gilson, who showed that the theology of Thomas Aquinas was a medieval form of existentialism, and Emmanuel Mounier, who in his periodical *Esprit* had revivified the French Catholic tradition of *engagement* with politics; priests like the Jesuit Henri de Lubac, who wrote *Catholicism* to show that his faith was diametrically opposed to the suffocation of the individual in any collectivist system and who saw "natural" and "supernatural" not as discrete realms but as a description of the continuity of human experience, and the Dominican Yves Congar, who stressed the Church's constant obligation to reform itself and who explored the nature of the Church, which could be expressed in the Church of any locality, in non-Catholic Churches, and even in communities not expressly Christian.

Angelo was familiar with French fiction, old and new, and had read some Bernanos and Mauriac. He knew Claudel personally, he underlined Péguy's poetry, and he was good friends with the historian Daniel-Rops. Any of these sources might have led him to Gilson or Mounier, de Lubac or Congar, but what Angelo understood at the time of this *nouvelle théologie* we can't be sure. What we do know is that de Lubac and especially Congar would become the leading theologians of Vatican II and that the French influence on John's council would have far greater impact than that of any other national Church. In the tireless determination of the bishop of Paris that Christianity be seen as relevant to the times in which we live, Angelo found a model from which he would borrow when he became bishop of Rome. Angelo, who had no need to be viewed as an oracle, would also welcome warmly just the sort of collaboration with committed, outspoken bishops that Pius despised.

There is no record that Angelo ever met the worker priests or gave them his blessing; on the other hand, there is no record of his condemning the experiment. His own, exceedingly simple *engagement* with Parisians took the form of strolls around his *beau quartier* and animated conversation with those he met, such as Yvette Morin, the Holocaust survivor who ran his local newspaper stand. For this he was upbraided by Pius, who judged it undignified for a papal nuncio to be seen walking the Paris streets and rubbing shoulders with the unclean masses as if they were all on the same level.

But the nuncio, now nearing seventy, was becoming ever more easygoing and, in his own playful way, fearless. The fight against his weight was decisively lost, his earlier severities were relaxed, he was known as a delightful host with a superb kitchen (his chef would go on to open La Grenouille), and he was not infrequently seen at diplomatic receptions with a glass of champagne in one hand, sometimes with a cigarette in the other. At one of these gatherings, so the story goes, he was approached by a woman of considerable *décolletage*, who wore a large crucifix between her mountainous breasts. *"Quelle Golgotha!"* (What a Calvary!) exclaimed the nuncio merrily. On another occasion, in the course of the Roncalli-inspired redecoration of the nunciature, a carpenter who accidentally hit his thumb with a hammer began to blaspheme vigorously. The nuncio, stern-faced, rose from his desk, walked to the room where the carpenter was working, and demanded. *"Alors, qu'est-ce que c'est ça? Vous ne pouvez pas dire 'merde' comme tout le monde?"* (So, what's this? Can't you say "shit" like everybody else?) Though neither of these stories can be unassailably documented, they are one with a cloud of anecdotes that begin to appear in this period, all testifying to the freedom that came to Angelo as he approached old age.

During the course of his tenure as nuncio, the intellectual life of the French Church became more and more exciting. In 1948, the Paris Dominicans invited Camus to address them, which he did with unforgettable passion, urging the priests to even greater involvement in their times by seeking Christ "in the blood-stained face of the history of our own age." Suhard, roundly criticized by *L'Osservatore Romano* as soft on Communism, plunged ahead, heedless of his critics. "The first task is to save the souls of the people of Paris," he proclaimed in the storied cathedral of Notre Dame on the fiftieth anniversary of his ordination to the priesthood, the papal nuncio in attendance.

It is for these masses that I will have to answer on the day of judgment. This is the thought that weighs me down day and night. When I see these crowds of people [the same ones Pius instructed Angelo to stay away from] my heart is wrung. I constantly meditate on how to break down the barrier which separates the Church from the masses—for unless it is broken down, Christ cannot be given back to the people who have lost him. That is why we have entrusted the Paris mission to specially chosen priests [the worker priests, now seen as missionaries to their own city], who are in the vanguard of the Church's progress.

The Vatican, aware of the ardor between Suhard and his people, continued to hold its fire. In April 1949, Suhard issued his last pastoral, *Le Prêtre dans la cité* (The Priest in the City): "The Christianization of this new world, the modern urban world, calls for a complete intellectual renewal; it will perhaps be a long time before we are able to outgrow the methods of medieval Christianity." In the cardinal's public scorn for Catholicism's medieval methods and his call for its complete intellectual transformation, the gap between the bishop of Rome and the archbishop of Paris opened so wide as to become nearly unbridgeable.

But Suhard's death some weeks later put an end to his bravery and emboldened the Vatican, which immediately issued a decree, excommunicating anyone who defended Communism or collaborated "in any way" in actions that could lead to the establishment of a Communist regime. A year later, Pius issued *Humani generis* (Of the Human Race), solemnly condemning every theological development of postwar France. De Lubac was silenced, forbidden even to live in a Jesuit house where there were students whom he might corrupt with his "historical" theology—that is, theology dependent on accurate texts of newly recovered ancient Christian sources, rather than on the ahistorical "eternal truths" of medieval scholasticism. Congar was sent into exile in England, forbidden to converse with non-Catholics or even with his fellow Dominicans, because of his "false irenicism"—Vatican-speak for Congar's openness to other religious traditions. The followers of the Jesuit paleontologist Pierre Teilhard de Chardin (who had been silenced on all but strictly scientific matters for more than twenty-five years) were banned for their "immanentism" (associating God too closely with humanity) and "polygenism" (the scientific hypothesis that the human race may have evolved from several sources, rather than from one couple as implied by the Book of Genesis). The Dominican Marie-Dominique Chenu, an advisor to the worker priests who was also largely responsible for the monumental editing of the ancient Christian writings on which so much of the new theology was based, found his unremarkable study of Thomas Aquinas placed on the Index.

In the end, it was a clean sweep: not one of France's new theologians was left standing. Perhaps more important, Pius XII's *Humani generis* succeeded in doing for the 1950s what Pius X's *Pascendi* had done for the decade prior to the First World War: it created a climate of fear and recrimination throughout the Church. The antic definition of Mary's "assumption," a dogma based on pious legends and proclaimed in 1950 with the same heedlessness with which Pius IX had proclaimed Mary's immaculate conception, was interpreted by the French as Pius's deliberately retrograde challenge to their despicable modernity, a sort of ecclesiastical "Fuck you." In 1953, after Angelo was gone from Paris, Pius would shut down the worker priest movement entirely.

Meanwhile, Angelo kept his own counsel. *His* favorite Frenchman was known to be Saint Francis de Sales, certainly a safe choice, whose sensibly cheerful advice he read over and over. He made friends with anyone willing to have him, finding his way into the hearts of many non-Catholics, militant secularists, Socialists, and (despite the Vatican's warnings) Communists. He was especially fond of his many Jewish friends, both religious and secular, though he was vigorously supportive when one of these returned to the religious observance of his forebears—and he formed a close connection with the father of Simone Weil, whose writings he was much taken by. Never forgetting he was a diplomat, he left French religious matters to the French bishops, making what he described as "a half-turn to the left followed by a half-turn to the right"—the diplomatic ballet of never committing oneself unnecessarily.

Still, there were indications of what was in his heart. From 1951, as official Vatican observer to UNESCO, he was impressed by this international project, which seemed to him to embody many of the aims of Christianity without its official vocabulary. He encouraged Catholics working for UNESCO to enter into dialogue with both unbelievers and other kinds of believers. "Meet without mistrust, draw close together without fear, come to one another's aid without compromise" was his advice. He became good friends with Suhard's successor, Maurice Feltin, who as president of Pax Christi, the international Catholic peace organization, introduced Angelo to the idea that war, in an age of nuclear weapons, presumed the moral suicide of the human race—a line of thinking that would one day find expression in John's great encyclical, *Pacem in terris* (Peace on Earth).

Feltin is on record as appreciating Angelo's unusual qualities: "He was always friendly, understanding, and sought to smooth out difficult problems; but when action was needed, he did not lack decisiveness and firmness of character. His goodness was strong, not soft. He could, moreover, be subtle, perspicacious, and farsighted; and I could give plenty of examples of the way he slipped through the grasp of those who sought to exploit him." Here at last is a portrait of Angelo not as gregarious simpleton but as a good and subtle priest, employing peasant craftiness and his own hard-won worldliness to achieve humane results—a just judgment. But Angelo preferred anonymity, never drawing attention to his accomplishments, happy when good could be effected without his being credited as its author. When he could have no influence on events or when his presence might be misinterpreted as approval, he would simply absent himself. For instance, after *Humani generis* was published in 1950—in the dead of August when no one was in Paris—Angelo stole away for a two-month vacation in his native province. On his return, he had not a word to say about Pius's thunderbolt; even his diary remains blank till year's end. "Above all," Pius would admonish Angelo's successor, Paolo Marella, "don't be like your predecessor, Roncalli: he was never there."

Pius, despite his dismissiveness of subordinates (who were expected to kneel not only in his presence but whenever they heard the nasal Pacelli voice at the other end of the telephone), came to require new cardinals. He had made thirty-two men cardinals in 1946, but cardinalatial numbers were dwindling again and Pius had now to think about the composition of the college that would choose his successor. His new list of twenty-four represented a considerable internationalization of the College of Cardinals and Pius's tacit acknowledgment of the growing internationalization of his Church. The Italian contingent was reduced to a third of the College; and among that third was the reliable Angelo Giuseppe Roncalli, who on January 15, 1953, received his red hat—and the *Légion d'honneur*—from the hand of Vincent Auriol, an agnostic and one of Angelo's best friends, now president of France. By this point, everyone had come to realize the immense importance of the nuncio's years of quiet peacemaking between Church and state, so the ceremony turned into one of those must-attend events packed with dignitaries. "Your experience enabled you," said Auriol, "to appreciate the role of France in the world and made you understand, long ago, the traditions of justice and tolerance which have always been the honor of our nation and which were to unite, in answer to Pope Leo XIII's solemn appeal, all the spiritual families of France around the Republic."

Despite the confrontational tradition of the Piuses, Angelo

had succeeded in resurrecting his beloved Leo's project of reconciliation. He was leaving a France in which the Catholic-secular
clash was more muted than it had ever been. He *was* leaving;
everyone knew that. Angelo was morose. He had learned—on
the same day he had been informed by Montini of his impending
elevation "to the sacred purple"—that his sister Ancilla, "the most
precious treasure of my household," was dying of cancer. He
made a quick trip to her bedside. On returning to Paris, he confided to Feltin his fear that he was marked out for a post inside the
Roman Curia but "wanted to stay in France. I love France and I
love Paris, and I hoped to stay a little longer. I can't really see myself in Rome, going along day after day to meeting after meeting
and concerned with administration. That's not what I'm good at.
I'm really a pastor"—the role he had originally fashioned himself
for and the one thing he had never been allowed to be.

However cursorily Angelo may have dabbled in the new theologians, his most reliable literary companions were a compact
shelf of books to which he returned again and again. Chief among
these were of course the Bible, especially the gospels, the books of
the Church's liturgies and rites, and *The Imitation of Christ*. His
work as a historian had brought him to a deeper understanding of
the Church's history of holiness, which was to be found in the
lives of its saints—those who had been notably successful at imi-
tating Christ—especially, for Angelo, those who had occupied
difficult posts in difficult periods. To these he had added, during
his time in the East, the holy books of Orthodoxy, especially the
liturgies and the sayings of the saints of the Eastern Church. With
this background, he was quite ready for the French Church's rediscovery of the ancient texts of the Greek and Latin fathers (and
even a few mothers)—*Sources chrétiennes*—and could unre-
servedly welcome this development as the right way to prepare for
the future by a more profound appreciation of the past.

But there was one book he particularly cherished, a nineteenth-century novel of his native Lombardy, *I promessi sposi* (The Betrothed) by Alessandro Manzoni. Set in the seventeenth century, Manzoni's great work has an unparalleled place in Italian literature, for it definitively established the Tuscan dialect as the national language. *The* novel of nineteenth-century Italy, it is for Italians Fielding, Scott, Thackeray, and Dickens rolled into one. Manzoni does not shrink from criticism of ecclesiastical figures, and in fact the first character presented to us is a spineless priest whose overriding concern for his own interest endangers the lives of the poor hero and heroine and sets the story in motion. But the story is suffused, like Lombardy itself, with a resonant sense of God's Providence. Angelo's well-thumbed copy was full of underlined passages that helped him over the rough moments of his life. He turned now, as he had so often in the past, to prayerful acceptance and to the words of Manzoni's heroine, Lucia, as she prepares to fly into the unknown: "He who gave you so much joy is everywhere; and he never disturbs the happiness of his children, except to prepare for them a surer and greater happiness."

As Auriol was honoring Angelo, the Vatican was announcing a further honor. The new cardinal was also to be the new patriarch of Venice. Like Renzo, the fugitive hero of *I promessi sposi*, Angelo, now seventy-one, had somehow outwitted the vile fate prepared for him, escaping his would-be captors—in Angelo's case, the dreary Vatican bureaucracy—in the nick of time. He was going home at last—as pastor to that fantastic city where the plain of Lombardy meets the Adriatic. It was, he was quite certain, his final appointment.

PART III

RONCALLI THE PASTOR, JOHN THE POPE

✠ ✠ ✠

Venice

THE WORLD is divided into two kinds of people: those who say Venice is the most beautiful city on earth and those who claim another, usually Florence. But if Florence, Rome, Paris, Prague, Kyoto, and Capetown all have their devotees, none are so effortlessly certain as those who love canal-cut Venice, known to her admirers as La Serenissima.

On March 15, 1953, the people of Venice, who delight in pageantry, turned out in force to welcome their new patriarch, the central figure in a colorful procession of freshly painted gondolas, their distinctive flags aflutter, sailing up the Grand Canal past fairy-tale palazzos hung with brightly striped and checkered cloths. The Venetians were getting a patriarch ready-made for them, a serene old man who himself delighted in pageantry. "I want to speak to you with complete frankness," he said on reaching land.

Things have been said about me that greatly exaggerate my merits. I humbly introduce myself. Like every other man on earth, I come from a particular family and place. I have been blessed with good physical health and enough common sense to grasp things quickly and clearly. I also have an inclination to love people, which keeps me faithful to the law of the Gospel and respectful of my own rights and the rights of others. It stops me from doing harm to anyone; it encourages me to do good to all.

He went on to describe his modest origins "in contented and blessed poverty, a poverty that has few needs, builds up the highest virtues, and prepares one for the great adventure of life." He had traveled "the roads of East and West"—giving him something in common with Venice, the storied Western merchant city that faces East—and had "come close to people of different religions and ideologies." But always, he said, "I have been more concerned with what unites than with what separates and causes differences." He went on to cite Petrarch, who loved Venice, and Marco Polo, the city's favorite son. His own ties were no less strong, for he came from the hills "beyond Somasca and the cave of Saint Jerome Emilian" that had once been part of the Venetian Republic. Without doubt, he concluded,

the great position entrusted to me exceeds all my capacities. But, above all, I commend to your kindness someone who simply wants to be your brother, kind, approachable, and understanding. . . . This is the man, this is the new citizen whom Venice has been so good as to welcome today with such festive demonstrations.

If only all bishops could begin their tenure with such sentiments (which Pius XII would doubtless have labeled "false irenicism"). At any rate, the Venetians fell in love with Roncalli immediately. A patriarch who wanted to be their brother! The word *patriarch* means, of course, father-ruler. Within Christianity, there were originally four—the patriarchal bishops of Jerusalem, Antioch, Alexandria, and Rome, all of which sees were thought to have been founded by Peter, the great pastor (or shepherd) whom Jesus had commissioned to "feed my sheep." To these four was added Constantinople at the time of its founding in the fourth century, since it was unthinkable that the emperor's principal residence should lack a patriarch all its own. Over the centuries, additional cities of the East were named patriarchal sees, especially as new nations, such as Bulgaria and Russia, became Christian. Just a half-step down in importance from the patriarchs are the metropolitans (or archbishops of major metropolitan centers), who have certain responsibilities over the mere bishops who govern the smaller outlying cities. In the West, however, the title of patriarch is jealously guarded by the pope, who has permitted the honorific to be conferred beyond himself only twice—on the metropolitans of Venice (since 1451) and Lisbon (since 1716).

The facade of Saint Mark's, the patriarch's cathedral, beckoned him with all the extravagant imagination of Byzantium and medieval Europe combined, an airy fantasy of domes and arches, turrets and steeples, birds and fishes, lions and horses, gargoyles and men, a delicate, dancing latticework that seems more lace than stone. The many golden apses of the facade are but a hint of what lies within, where the visitor is stunned to find himself in a vast and blazing cave of gold, its endless, ever-receding walls and lofty, circling heights covered in ancient tesserae of gold before which emerge in stately procession all the figures of the Old and New Testaments. "Never," whispered Ruskin in amazement, "had city a more glorious Bible." If Saint Peter's is religion as reason and power, Saint Mark's is religion as dream and hope.

But if the new patriarch could only be happy to find himself master of such a domain, he was not long in learning that beyond the fantasy lay harsh realities. "Despite the ecclesiastical splendor that surrounds me and the veneration shown me as cardinal and patriarch," he wrote in his journal, "I already have two painful problems: lack of funds and the throng of poor people who want work and financial help." Seldom in Christian history has a new bishop not found his treasury insufficient to his plans. But good Italian bishops, like Charles Borromeo and Angelo Roncalli, have always known that a deeper obligation than raising funds for their pet projects is finding adequate employment for the poor and miserable. For beyond fairy-tale Venice lay rough working-class suburbs like Mestre and the port of Marghera, full of dissolution and despair. Though he loved the priceless beauties that had been placed in his care, he would often find cause to repeat that "we are not on earth as museum keepers but to cultivate a flourishing garden of life and to prepare a glorious future."

He bent himself to the task of creating employment, which meant ingratiating himself with local moneybags and suggesting how splendid it would be if they would sponsor some restoration project or other. One of his most successful collaborations was with Count Vittorio Cini, who restored the ancient Benedictine abbey on the isle of San Giorgio, just across the lagoon from Saint Mark's Square. San Giorgio came to house not only the abbey but a cultural center, an open-air theater, a technical school, and an orphanage, all restored or constructed anew with local labor and all necessitating the development of permanent new staff positions. For the patriarch, San Giorgio functioned as a metaphor of the Church at its best, creating a more humane present by cherishing the treasures of its past and allowing these treasures to prompt the people of the present to build a better future. He called it "a miracle of resurrection, an island rising up to new and glorious life."

Long ago in the seminary, Roncalli had been taught to steer clear of what was delicately termed "particular friendship," that is, friendship between two boys intense enough to exclude others. Two boys seen too often in one another's company were a source of suspicion and, if they persisted, a cause of scandal. Though the word *homosexuality* was never spoken, the fear was that an adolescent crush would lead eventually to open defiance of the Church's rules. "The rule of three"—three or more taking their recreation together—was the standard held up for imitation. But there is also an assumption in Italian society that a man in his seventies is beyond temptation.

Roncalli, now officially exempt, could at last allow himself the sort of human intimacy the absence of which he had suffered so long. The object of his affection was Loris Capovilla, a seasoned priest in his late thirties whom Roncalli had met previously and whom he now appointed his secretary. Capovilla had grown up nearby in the province of Padua, was intelligent, discreet, even meek, but energetic, lean, more boyish-looking than his years, and possessed of a capacity for devotion that only someone as impressive and affectionate as Roncalli could satisfy. Years before their first meeting, he had seen a photograph of Roncalli and felt mysteriously drawn to him. Capovilla was of a height with Roncalli (a little over five and a half feet), fashion-conscious enough to wear his hair in an American-style crewcut, and had the well-scrubbed, clean-cut features that would have marked an American boy as "cute." He would become for the patriarch amanuensis, companion, wife, and child. I do not mean to suggest that their intimacy ever included any sexual manifestation. But it was more ardent than father-son companionships commonly are and unalloyed by the occasional tensions and reservations that can attend the relationship of a father and his grown son. Capovilla himself, now a retired archbishop in his mid-eighties, told me that he never characterized himself as Roncalli's "friend"; he would not so presume. Roncalli was his bishop, his father, his patriarch, Capovilla simply playing the same role to him that Roncalli had once played to Radini-Tedeschi. They never even called one another by their first names, a form of address unknown to the Italian clergy of their day. (An ancient curial cardinal once told me that no one had called him "Agostino" since his childhood and that the Italian episcopate was stupefied when, at the Second Vatican Council, American bishops were overheard addressing one another as "Frank" and "Jack.") Roncalli was always "Your Eminence" (and later "Holy Father"), Capovilla always "Don Loris." But the depth of their attachment to each other was beyond question. Capovilla would remain with Roncalli till the older man's death ten years later within the walls of the Vatican.

Roncalli permitted Capovilla to be witness to an emotion he never expressed to another living soul. His sister Ancilla, who had been slowly dying for a year, gave up the ghost on November 11, 1953. Her brother the patriarch was absent from the scene, though he had promised to be there, had visited as often as he could, and had sent her many messages of encouragement. But he came to see her in her coffin at Sotto il Monte and to kiss her good-bye on her cold forehead—"the second time I've done that," he told Capovilla. "The first was when I knew she was dying." (Such were the affective constraints under which Catholic priests then operated. Nowadays, a popular Italian television series, *Un prete tra noi* [A Priest Among Us], shows its main character embracing just about everyone in sight—a measure of how much effect the Roncalli pontificate would have on the unblocking of emotion in Catholic contexts.) After the burial, Roncalli and Capovilla returned to Venice by train. It was a cold, rainy night, conducive in any case to thoughts of death, and perhaps the patriarch had a premonition of deaths soon to come—his sisters Teresa in 1954 and Maria in 1955, leaving only Assunta and three surviving brothers. *"Guai a noi se fosse tutta un'illusione,"* he said to himself but loud enough for Capovilla to hear. "Woe betide us if it all turns out to be an illusion." Faith is not the same thing as knowledge, and to be a man of faith is not to be without the occasional shudder of doubt.

On his return to Venice, the patriarch threw himself into his work, blessing oil tankers and football teams, telling the city council—which contained a number of anti-religious secularists—that what made a man "Christian" was not a word but good deeds, visiting all the parishes of his diocese in the Radini-Tedeschi manner, calling in 1957 a diocesan synod of priests on the model of the synod of Charles Borromeo, and even, earlier in the same year, having the nerve to welcome to Venice the thirty-second congress of the Italian Socialist Party. The patriarch prayed publicly that the congress might help bridge the gap between Catholic and secular culture, expressing his belief that the party was "inspired . . . by the desire to bring about the mutual understanding that is needed to improve living conditions and social prosperity." *L'Unità*, the Communist newspaper, praised this "opening to the left," which could provide the basis for innovative cooperation between all those with a social conscience, whether believers or nonbelievers. No praise was heard from the Vatican, however, and the "naive" patriarch was rebuked privately. Roncalli felt done in by "the malignant scissors of my enemies" that tore his phrases from their context. "Isn't courtesy," he asked, "the first aim of charity?" What could be wrong with welcoming anyone, and shouldn't all welcomes be warm?

In similar manner, he gave a splendid reception to the artists and other participants of the Biennale, the famous exhibition of contemporary art held in Venice every other year. His predecessors had all denounced the show as indecent, no doubt increasing its popularity, and had forbidden the clergy from going anywhere near it. Roncalli lifted this ban and opened the hall of the patriarchal palace to the artists and their admirers. As pope, in *Pacem in terris,* his great encyclical on the rights and obligations of the human race, he would defend "the pursuit of art" as an inherent human right.

He prayed daily for all the places he'd lived: for France, when he said the office of Prime; for Turkey, at Terce; for Greece, at Sext; and at Nones, "for my beloved Bulgaria." He brought to a dramatic halt the populous festivities planned at Sotto il Monte to celebrate the fiftieth anniversary of his ordination to the priesthood, upbraiding his young nephew Battista Roncalli, now a priest, in no uncertain terms: "I want to be *alone, alone,* with my family and the dear parishioners of Sotto il Monte. Have you got that? . . . I've had enough public celebrations in my life already." He was harassed by a seer, Gaston Bardet, who predicted his election to the papacy in a pontificate that would be characterized by "doctrinal interventions and disciplinary reforms." "Some mad Frenchman," he called the man in a letter home.

There were, however, many satisfactions, such as his friendships with such local stars as the art historian Bernard Berenson and the composer Igor Stravinsky (with whom he was sometimes seen strolling the quays in animated conversation) and with such foreign churchmen as Cardinal Francis Spellman of New York (always one to make the acquaintance of even the remotest *papabile,* or papal candidate) and Cardinal Stefan Wyszynski of Warsaw. At the same time, the patriarch retained the common touch, insisting on taking the public *vaporetto* (or water bus), jostled by all the other commuters, and giving strict instructions to his staff to admit *anyone* who asked to see him day or night. Such a style is easier to adopt in a diocese of some 400,000 than it would be in one of many millions, but word of the open door made the patriarch still more beloved, as if he were truly father to all Venetians. He even had the Latin words *Pastor et Pater* (Shepherd and Father) inscribed over his doorway. All the same, he was conscious of the limits of his role and spoke candidly to his clergy of the evils of authoritarianism (which "represses legitimate initiatives, is unable to listen, confuses harshness with firmness, inflexibility with dignity") and paternalism ("a caricature of paternity" that "keeps people immature in order to maintain its own superior position," "speaks protectively, and does not accept true collaboration"—the word despised by Pius XII).

Pius had been dying for years now—he had been thought to be mortally ill at least since early 1954—but had somehow managed to live on, making speeches in which he offered himself as an expert on every form of human knowledge, beatifying and canonizing his personal favorites (such as his predecessor—and Roncalli's, in the see of Venice—Pius X), and exiling Angelo's able friend Montini from the Curia to the see of Milan but refusing to name him cardinal because he had briefly hesitated in relaying a piece of information to the pope. Gradually, however, the work of the Holy See ground almost to a complete halt, as the Curia attended with bated breath to Pius's dying agonies. As he concerned himself less and less with what went on around him, he came to rely almost exclusively on Sister Pascalina Lehnert, the rigid and domineering German nun who ran the papal household and who came to be known around Rome as *Virgo Potens* (Virgin of Power, one of the titles of Mary) and *La Papessa*. It was said that in his last days Pius was vouchsafed a portion of the sufferings of Christ and visions of the Mother of God, to whom he had always been unswervingly devoted.

Certainly, his last days were made more difficult by his Swiss gerontologist, Paul Niehaus, who injected him with lamb's tissue intended to restore the vigor of the old man, who had a hypochondriacal tendency to grasp at "cures." Another treatment, meant to prevent the softening of his gums, hardened his palate and gullet to such an extent that he became the victim of constant hiccups. Pius was certainly not infallible in his choice of doctors. After his death—on October 9, 1958, at Castel Gandolfo—his embalming was botched by the official papal physician, Riccardo Galeazzi-Lisi. In the Roman heat, the corpse began to explode inside its coffin with firecracker-like salvos. Lisi labored through the night to improve his work prior to the exhibition of the body in Saint Peter's. But as the faithful filed past Pius's bier the next morning, the face of the dead pope turned green, a foul odor issued from the corpse, and his nose nearly fell off. Angelo Roncalli, viewing the defenseless body of the dead pope—Pius for the first time without his severe, rimless spectacles—saw only "the great lesson of death."

Galeazzi-Lisi called a press conference to describe in ghoulish detail his special Egyptian-style embalming methods and sold his photographs of the papal corpse to news agencies. He was sent on his way by the curial cardinals. The patriarch of Venice, about to disappear into the conclave that would elect Pius's successor, sent a stark warning to his importunate nephew, Don Battista, not to come anywhere near Rome, where the nephews of Pius XII were visible and prominent. At this point, anything that looked like the assembling of a new papal administration by one of the cardinal electors would doom such a candidate's chances—so Roncalli knew he was *papabile*.

A conclave is so called from the medieval Latin *con clave* (with a key), because the cardinal electors—in this case, a mere fifty-one, since Pius XII had made so few appointments—are literally locked inside the Vatican palace, given none-too-comfortable accommodation in temporary quarters, and not allowed to leave before they have elected a new pope. Once locked in, they are forbidden under pain of excommunication ever to reveal anything that transpired there. There is to be no politicking, which in the circumstances is like telling a dog there is to be no barking. But the rules under which the cardinals operate derive from a post-Renaissance desire to free the electors from insider machinations and outside pressure. Just before lockup, Roncalli wrote a letter to the bishop of Bergamo, stating that "my soul finds comfort in the confidence that a new Pentecost can blow through the Church."

Despite the threat of excommunication, details of papal conclaves inevitably leak out, so it is possible to construct a fairly accurate account of this election. After a long pontificate such as Pius's, there is always sentiment for a pope who will be unlike the one that has just passed on. The voice of authority becomes more grating the longer it is heard; and even conservative cardinals can come to long for a change of direction. In short order, the conclave broke down into two groups, the liberals, who were backing the saintly, innovative Giacomo Lercaro, archbishop of Bologna—a man who was known to favor a simplified liturgy in local languages and who had turned his episcopal palace into an orphanage—and a conservative party clustered around the aggressively sententious Giuseppe Siri, archbishop of Genoa, who stood to the right of Pius XII. But Siri, at age fifty-two, quickly lost ground, since no one wanted another interminable pontificate; and Lercaro, too far to the left and too well defined, could not muster the two-thirds plus one necessary for election. At this point, the cardinals began to consider seriously a compromise candidate, one who would not last too long but could serve as "a bridge between all levels of society, between all nations—even those that reject and persecute the Christian religion," as Cardinal Antonio Bacci had urged them in his official address just before the doors were locked. In other words, an unPius.

They hit on two possibilities, Cardinal Gregory Agagianian, patriarch of the Armenian Uniates and a non-Italian, and the patriarch of Venice. (There was some consideration of Montini, the archbishop of Milan; but Pius had denied him a cardinal's hat, and the cardinals preferred to stay within their own ranks.) For several votes, Agagianian and Roncalli "went up and down like two chickpeas in boiling water," as Roncalli would later describe it. After each inconclusive vote, black smoke wafted up above Saint Peter's Square to alert the world that a pope had still not been chosen. The smoke came from a little stove kept in the Sistine Chapel, where the electors meet for their rounds of votes. After the tenth vote, at 11:10 A.M. on October 28, black smoke billowed up once more from the flue of the Sistine Chapel to the disappointment of the waiting throng. But Agagianian, who now had all the conservative votes he could get, had peaked, as a steady majority of Italians and Frenchmen, led by Roncalli's old confidant Cardinal Feltin, the archbishop of Paris, continued to attract new electors to their chosen candidate. Roncalli left the chapel and returned to his cell, where he waited for Capovilla to bring him lunch. He preferred not to eat with the others in the grand Sala Regia, the papal throne room. The two men took their modest meal—a bowl of soup, a slice of meat, a glass of wine, and an apple—in embarrassed silence, and then the older man asked to be left alone to compose himself. At 4:00 P.M., the electors returned to the chapel to drop their eleventh ballot one by one into the waiting chalice under Michelangelo's terrifying image of Christ in Judgment. At 4:50 P.M., the slow process having been completed and a tally having been made, Angelo Giuseppe Roncalli, Bergamasque peasant and patriarch of Venice, was elected by thirty-eight votes of his fellow cardinals pope of the Roman Catholic Church, 258th successor, by Vatican reckoning, to the apostle Peter.

"Vocabor Johannes," said the new pope in his strong, melodious voice, so different from the chickenlike cawing of his tone-deaf predecessor. "I will be called John." John? The electors who knew their history were confounded. The last John had been an anti-pope, a former pirate, and a murderer, the last valid John had been an Avignon pope, a wealthy fool, and a heretic. As with the name Henry in the British royal family, the last bearer of the name was thought to have rendered it unusable. What was Roncalli thinking of? For one thing, he had a better grasp of ecclesiastical history than anyone else in the room, and he knew that even bad popes had served divine purposes and that a new life in a new time could redeem an old name. But he was thinking more of familial history—of his father Giovanni, who like the Good Shepherd had once borne Angelino on his shoulders and whose name he would now bear. He was thinking also of biblical history—of John the Baptist, who had prepared the way for Jesus, and of John the apostle, who had leaned on Jesus's breast at the Last Supper and had become the "evangelist of love"—God's love for us, our love for one another.

Wisps of white smoke went up over Saint Peter's and the huge crowd cheered. The news would soon speed out over the airwaves and around the world. In Sotto il Monte, at the foot of the purple hills he loved and would never see again, Assunta Roncalli, the new pope's youngest sister, who was listening to her radio, clapped her hands to her head and screamed, "My God, they picked Angelino!"

The Vatican

THE PRESENTATION of a new pope is wrapped in layers of ancient tradition. The cardinals are seated in conclave, each on a miniature throne shaded by a crimson parasol. At the announcement that one of their number has received the necessary votes, they wait to hear his acceptance, after which the cardinals fold their parasols, leaving but one still open above the head of the new pope. Each in turn approaches the throne of the winner to make his obeisance, as the stupendous figures of Michelangelo's frescoes look down on them. The new pope is then whisked off to the sacristy to be vested in his new robes. In the case of Roncalli, a short man who weighed as much as 220 pounds, there was a momentary quandary as none of the white cassocks prepared in advance by the papal tailor would quite fit around him. Safety pins were drafted to hold one cassock together in the middle where the buttons could not reach, and a tentlike surplice concealed the result. The pope was led to the central *loggia*, or balcony, overlooking the main entrance to Saint Peter's but told to wait out of view. Cardinal Nicola Canali preceded the pope onto the balcony to chant the time-hallowed greeting to the waiting crowd, who knew from the white smoke that there was a new pope but did not yet know his identity: *"Nuntio vobis gaudium magnum: habemus papam!"* (I announce to you a great joy: we have a pope!) He gave the name of the cardinal chosen and his new papal name. Then Angelo Giuseppe Roncalli came forward and, raising his right hand over the wildly enthusiastic throng and making a triple sign of the cross, gave his first papal blessing *urbi et orbi,* to the city and the world.

The lights of the television cameras that beamed Roncalli's image around the world dazzled the new pope: "I blessed Rome and the world as though I were a blind man. As I came away, I thought of all the cameras and lights that from now on, at every moment, would be directed on me. And I said to myself: if you don't remain a disciple of the gentle and humble Master, you'll understand nothing even of temporal realities. Then you'll really be blind."

Because papal conclaves are sealed off from the outside world, even telephone lines are cut and need to be reconnected afterward. While the new pope waited for a repairman to finish the work of reconnection so that he could make a call, he fell into conversation with the man. *"Come va?"* (How's it going?) asked the pope. The man, unaware of the identity of the robed figure he was addressing, took the informal question as an invitation to complain about his life: he was father of a large family and his Vatican salary was insufficient to make ends meet. His listener encouraged him to be specific and listened with interest to each detail the man provided. John would soon see to it that the salaries of Vatican lay employees were doubled, over the sputtering objections of clerics who thought this an extravagant expenditure that might necessitate a cutback in contributions to charity. "Too bad," the pope would reply. "Justice comes before charity." But this reform lay some months in the future. On the night of his election, he simply thanked the repairman, who had been addressing him as "Your Eminence," and whispered conspiratorially, "Just between us, I'm not 'Your Eminence' anymore. I'm the pope."

The pope, not yet ready to occupy the living quarters of Pius XII, asked to spend the night in the apartment of the secretary of state, which had not been lived in for years, since Pius, not wanting collaborators, had acted as his own secretary of state. But before retiring, he told Capovilla that he wanted to see Domenico Tardini, the man who, since Montini's departure, had run the Vatican Secretariat of State as best he could, given the difficulties of implementing the will of the testy, ailing Pius. Tardini, who was not an especially gracious man, had always been brusque and unhelpful to the liberal friends of his rival Montini, and he was known to have scant esteem for the insights and intelligence of Roncalli.

When Tardini arrived, he knelt before the pope as had been customary in all meetings between Pius and his staff. But the new pope drew him to his feet and invited him to sit down. He asked Tardini to remain on at the Secretariat and to take the official title of pro-secretary—in other words, to be the Church's prime minister. (He could not be named secretary because he was not yet a cardinal.) Tardini objected that he was not the man for the job, that they had never seen eye-to-eye, and that he was, in any case, *"stufo"* (sick and tired). "Now," said John, "the roles are reversed; tonight I can ask obedience of you." He alluded to Tardini's forty years of labor in the papal service and said that he required his experience. "I'll be loyal to you and you'll be loyal to me. The Lord will guide us." Tardini knelt again and accepted.

This appointment was a signal: the new pope would not replace Pius's Curia. For one thing, he knew little about the workings of the papal bureaucracy and needed the men already in place if he was to proceed. But, more important, John did not believe that new men were needed in order to implement some vast program of change that he was cooking up. The Church could manage just fine with the old men. What he had in mind was not ideological but methodological and so did not require the sort of change of staff that becomes imperative when, for instance, a Republican president is replaced by a Democratic one. Beyond these considerations, John had no intention of precipitating a clash of ideologies within the Church; he had lived under clashes that favored the right wing and hardly saw value in a clash that would favor the left. John took with high seriousness Jesus's prayer to the Father on the night before his crucifixion, as reported in John's Gospel—"That all may be one"—and understood the weighty obligation it imposed on all Christians to work for reunion. How much more so was it incumbent on the pope to work for unity among Catholics and never to provoke unnecessary dissension.

But he did create a raft of new cardinals almost immediately, including the first cardinals ever appointed for Japan, the Philippines, Africa, and Mexico. He was especially happy to be able to appoint the first black cardinal in history, Laurean Rugambwa, archbishop of Dar-es-Salaam, Tanzania, and of course he made Tardini a cardinal, but topping the list was his old friend Montini, the much-abused archbishop of Milan. John enjoyed his papal coronation at Saint Peter's and, soon thereafter, his taking possession of his Cathedral of Saint John Lateran. Each ceremony took about five hours, but the new pope was a sucker for ceremony. His relatives all showed up for the festivities, breaking down in tears at every turn. "Come on now," pleaded His Holiness at one point, "what they've done to me isn't so bad." Would his niece, Sister Angela, become his housekeeper? "One Sister Pascalina was enough," he countered. He would not be inviting any of his relatives to take up residence in Rome, though in the night he mourned the absence of an earlier generation of Roncallis: "O mother, O my father and grandfather Angelo, O Uncle Zaverio, where are you? . . . Keep praying for me."

He took some trouble over the look and sound of his pontificate, asking that the lion of Saint Mark on his new coat of arms be made to look less fierce and Germanic, "more human," and that *L'Osservatore Romano* drop its flowery phrases, such as "we received the following illumination from the august lips of the most Supreme Pontiff." From now on, just say "the Pope said," please. He gave the first papal press conference in history; and what the reporters found most startling was not anything the pope said but that he spoke without notes, said whatever came into his head, and clearly enjoyed himself. "His face," marveled Silvio Negro in *Corriere della Sera*, "is constantly illuminated by a confident and humorous smile. The listener feels that he is gradually caught up in a family atmosphere and that he is taking part in a conversation." John completely confused the Vatican gardeners by stopping to chat with them. Under Pius they had been instructed to disappear whenever the pope walked in the garden and never to look at him. "Why shouldn't they look?" asked the new pope. "I'm not doing anything scandalous." Finding the Vatican chilly, John revived the *camauro*, the red velvet hat, lined with white fur, that the Renaissance popes had worn: it didn't slip off his bald pate as the white skullcap did, and it kept him warm. It also made him look a little like Santa Claus.

The speech he gave over Vatican radio on the first full day of his pontificate stressed two things, Christian reunion—"That all may be one"—and world peace, neither of which was high on the list of his predecessor, who had eschewed non-Catholic Christians and been so vocally anti-Communist that he was known as "the pope of the Atlantic Alliance." John offered his good wishes to "all those who are separated from this Apostolic See," and he bemoaned the wealth that was wasted on "pernicious instruments of death and destruction" instead of being used to lighten the burdens "of all classes of society, especially the least lucky." He spoke positively of "the rights of man," an old bugbear of the Vatican. But the pope spoke in Latin, and even in translation his thoughts were disguised by conventional papalese. He had already acquired speechwriters, one for Latin, another for Italian, and throughout his pontificate he would have to struggle against them to say what he meant—and in a down-to-earth manner they inevitably considered unpapal. The world press ignored the speech. But one man, at least, heard what the pope intended:

Luigi Sturzo, founder of the socially progressive Popular Party that was destroyed by Mussolini and the Vatican (and had been succeeded by the Christian Democrats of the postwar period), who was now in his late eighties and would be dead in less than a year. "Peace, justice, freedom, mutual understanding of rights and duties—all in the accents of love," wrote the old priest approvingly in *Avvenire*, a national Catholic newspaper.

On Christmas Day 1958, Pope John left the Vatican to visit children suffering from polio in the Bambin Gesù Hospital on the Janiculum Hill. Though the Janiculum is only the next hill over from the Vatican, this departure from custom caused astonishment. The pope was supposed to be "the prisoner of the Vatican," confined in his suffering by an uncaring secular state. Of course, since the Lateran Accords of 1929, the pope was actually free to go where he liked, but Pius XII had ventured an appearance beyond Vatican territory only once in his nineteen-year pontificate. The children were delighted with all the fuss but not unduly impressed by their visitor. *"Vieni qui, vieni qui, Papa"* (Come here, come here, Papa), they shouted at him. *Il Papa* shuffled over and embraced each one in turn. Some confused him with the Spirit of the Season and called him *Babbo Natale* (Father Christmas), which confusion the pope, with his bag of gifts, was happy to encourage. When he asked one little boy his name, the child told him earnestly that he had an awful lot of saints' names but that people usually just called him Giuseppe (or Joseph). "What's *your* name?" asked the boy. "Oh, my name's Giuseppe, too"—it was his second given name—"but now," he shrugged as if he, too, had been unaccountably given more names than he needed, "everybody calls me Giovanni." He was in his element.

The next day, he visited Regina Coeli Prison at the foot of the Janiculum, setting off an international orgy of press reporting. The film of this visit, made by RAI, the Italian television network, preserves much of the feeling that the event had for the original participants. The pope is, as he described it afterward, "hemmed in on all sides: officials, photographers, prisoners, guards—but the Lord was close." What we see on the film is a confident, cheerful old man, his soft brown eyes alight, completely at ease with himself and his audience, gesturing expressively with his big farmer's hands, and speaking with spontaneity, obviously making up his comments as he goes along. Since they couldn't come to see him, he tells them, he came to see them. He comes from poor people. There are only three ways of losing money in Italy: farming, gambling, and women. His father chose the least interesting way. One of his brothers had been caught poaching; an uncle had done time. These are the things that happen to poor people. But we are all children of God. "And I . . . I am Joseph, your brother."

It was a three-thousand-year-old line from the Book of Genesis, spoken originally by Joseph, son of Jacob, who breaks down in tears as he reveals to his many brothers his real identity. This was the second time that John had used the line; the first time had been at his coronation. But here, in these circumstances, it took on deeper reverberations. The audience—from priests to politicians, from convicts to jailers—wept openly, and in the film you can see copious tears coursing down hardened faces. A murderer dared approach the pope to ask: "Can there be forgiveness for me?" In answer, the pope just took the murderer in his arms and hugged him, heedless of all danger to his person, let alone to his dignity. The immaculate prisoner of the sterile Vatican had become the rumpled brother of sinful mankind, and John XXIII became an overnight sensation, a pope such as the world had never seen.

Soon enough, the pope was making other forays, even resurrecting the *passeggiata* of Benedict XIV. Though Rome had grown too large for a pope to take leisurely strolls through its precincts, John would get one of his fun-loving drivers—the Venetian brothers Paolo and Guido Gusso, both laymen—to drive him around and stop here and there, especially in poor districts, so the pope could emerge at street level to meet his people and converse with them. The people, if not Vatican security, were delighted and began to call John *"il papa buono,"* literally "the good pope." In Italian, an adjective follows rather than precedes a noun for special emphasis; and *buono,* which is richer in meaning than the English "good," is most commonly used of food in the sense of "tasty and wholesome" and of people in the sense of "good-hearted and kind." The phrase also implies a judgment on all Roncalli's predecessors, since no pope had ever before been awarded such a popular appellation. Here at last was a pope as a pope ought to be.

John's first Holy Week as pope proved no less precedent-shattering than his first Christmas. At the Good Friday liturgy in Saint Peter's Basilica, he changed forever the harsh prayer *"Oremus et pro perfidis Judaeis"* (Let us pray also for the faithless Jews). The rest of the invocation was no better: "God, you do not exclude even the faithless Jews from your mercy. Hear our prayers, which we bring before you because of the blinding of that people. . . ." John's new text read, "Let us pray also for the Jews to whom God our Lord first spoke. May he keep them in fidelity to his covenant and in the love of his Name, so that they may reach the goal to which his will wishes to lead them." By remaining faithful to the many Jewish friends he had made over the course of his life, John was helping his Church to turn a corner no one had thought it could turn.

But Good Pope John was not without cunning. It is true that he had not sought the papacy, and he considered the first grace of his pontificate to be that he accepted the office without seeking it. But it is also true that his humility was of the genial rather than the pathological kind: he welcomed his election and took up the burdens of the papacy with gusto. Nor was he foolishly demeaning of his own intelligence, which he now needed to employ to the full in the riskiest venture of his life. For he had in mind a program so unusual that he foresaw there would be opposition Machiavellian enough to kill his plans before they could be rightly launched. Whether or not the pope is infallible, he is certainly not omnipotent; and John knew perfectly well that the whole entrenched Vatican bureaucracy could be secretly and smilingly turned against him, reducing him to little more than a figurehead. He turned the matter over and over in his mind. It was a question of strategy: how to outmaneuver his opponents before they could marshal their forces against him, before they even knew what was happening. In the first steps of the tremendous venture he was about to undertake, we glimpse John at his most evasively political, the same man Cardinal Feltin knew when he described Roncalli the nuncio as "subtle, perspicacious, and farsighted; and I could give plenty of examples of the way he slipped through the grasp of those who sought to exploit him."

The project of his heart—and, in his mind, the second grace of his pontificate—was the calling of an ecumenical council. There had not been one since Vatican I had declared Pio Nono infallible and been abruptly shut down at the outbreak of the Franco-Prussian War. Pius XII had considered convening a council and had even formed secret commissions to advise him on the subject. The commissions had wanted fresh condemnations of heresies and of modern philosophies and restatements of the Church's eternal verities. Pius decided he could do all that on his own. By the end of 1958, John was already reading through the files of Vatican I, especially the accounts of its preparation, and the material spawned by Pius's commissions; and there even are indications that he was thinking of a council within a day or two of his election. For all his elaborate deference throughout his life to his ecclesiastical superiors, he left in journals and public statements sufficient evidence for us to conclude that he thought the leaders of his Church unnecessarily narrow-minded and insufficiently open to the world. I suspect he had been thinking about a council as the answer to the Church's airlessness for much of his adult life. Now that he had the reins of power in his hands, he would need to manage them with supernatural dexterity, if he were to avoid being overtaken by those who would do everything they could to stop him.

John was not only concerned about his strategy; he needed to be convinced that his idea of a council was prompted by the Holy Spirit. So he let the idea ferment slowly and waited to sniff what kind of vintage it would make. He told Capovilla, who was vehemently opposed. It could be a terrible failure, too much for an old man to handle. John thought about this and a few days later had his rejoinder. "The trouble is, Don Loris, that you're still not detached enough from self—you're still concerned with having a good reputation. Only when the ego has been trampled underfoot can one be fully and truly free. You're not yet free, Don Loris," teased the pope. John, putting his trust in Providence, was unconcerned about possible failure or even about the stress of a council.

He spoke of a council to his confessor, who told him that "those who are guided by the Spirit are the sons of God." Well, he had the idea and it would not go away, nor could he discover any reasons against it, beyond the reasons of self-protection proposed by Capovilla. He no longer had any superior to consult, only God himself. Was God prompting him with this idea? He knew well what self-deception was: one of his favorite characters in *I promessi sposi* was Donna Prassede, who "put all her efforts into seconding the will of Heaven but [who] often made the serious mistake of confusing her own whimsies with the divine intent." He continued to mull it over, I think, till he saw the way forward—of hoodwinking those who would be likely to form his opposition and luring them into working for his project.

On Tuesday, January 20, 1959, John met with Tardini and told him that, after much prayer and meditation, he had decided that the program of his pontificate would be made up of three things—a synod for the priests of the diocese of Rome, an ecumenical council, and an updating of the Code of Canon Law—and that he would announce these three things to the cardinals the following Sunday, January 25, at the Basilica of Saint Paul Outside the Walls. John wisely placed the council between two far less dramatic initiatives, thus giving it some camouflage. And, in his own words, "I was rather hesitant and uncertain." Tardini, whatever he may have felt, expressed only "the most gratifying surprise." He would have had little time to assemble opposition before the announcement hit the wire services—and John was giving no hint of what he expected from this council. Tardini was free to imagine that it would have all the boring predictability of Pius XII's aborted plan.

That Sunday at Saint Paul's in the chapter room of the abbey, John gave the cardinals a talk quite unlike any he had ever delivered. He spoke of the "two cities" of Saint Augustine—the City of God and the City of Man—and said that the latter was controlled by "the prince of darkness," Satan. He bemoaned "the lack of discipline and the loss of the old moral order." He condemned modern "errors," which had led to "fatal and unhappy divisions [in Vatican-speak, the Reformation], to spiritual and moral decadence [secularism], and to the ruin of nations [Communism]." He went on and on in this fashion, uttering one tired phrase after another, no doubt making the cardinals so comfortable that they stopped listening altogether. John's principal biographer, Peter Hebblethwaite, thinks that this was a ploy—more camouflage—to win over the conservatives to the announcement of John's "three things," which he made toward the end of his speech. At any rate, the audience received the announcement in impassive silence, seriously disappointing the pope. It was the first of many begrudging responses. Even Cardinal Lercaro, Catholic Italy's most outspoken liberal, was outraged: "How dare he summon a council after one hundred years, and only three months after his election?" He called John "rash and impulsive," inexperienced and lacking in culture—though only in private. Even John's friend Montini was skeptical, confiding to a friend, "This holy old boy doesn't seem to realize what a hornet's nest he's stirring up."

John gave a small indication of the kind of council he had in mind when at the very end of his speech, sounding at last like himself, he told the cardinals that his projects "will involve hard work for the enlightenment, the edification, and the joy of the Christian people, and a friendly and renewed invitation to our brothers of the separated Christian Churches to share with us in this banquet of grace and brotherhood, to which so many souls in every corner of the world aspire." But when the Vatican issued the official version of John's speech, the "friendly and renewed invitation" and everything that followed it was gone, replaced by "a renewed invitation to the faithful of separated communities likewise to follow Us, in good will, in this search for unity and peace." The pope may be infallible, but if he falls into indiscretion by putting himself on an equal plane with heretics and mistakenly calling their sorry communities "Churches," he needs to be edited.

John had trouble with the papal *We* and commonly slipped

into *I* and *me*. He was often engaged in trying to get visitors to stop kneeling in his presence. "One of the humiliations we have had to endure as the successor to Saint Peter," he claimed, solemn-faced, "is to see men kneel to us. Our attendants used to kneel three times on arriving and departing. We have now agreed that they will genuflect only once in the morning and once at night." After trying for his first week in office to eat alone, as protocol had prescribed since the days of Pius V, he invited Capovilla to eat with him. But he soon widened the circle of dinner guests, complaining that "I get no pleasure out of eating alone with Capovilla. He eats like a canary." He gave out that the best tip he had for weight reduction was to stand next to Cardinal Gaetano Cicognani, by far the largest of the cardinals. "Then I feel that I am thin as a rail." Catching a glimpse of himself in a full-length mirror, he murmured with a chuckle, "Lord, this man is going to be a disaster on television." Life in the Vatican was beginning to resemble a high-spirited Italian comedy, staged by Totò; and these anecdotes and many more like them filtered out into the international press, delighting the world at large but especially Catholics, who wondered why they had been content till now with humorless popes who had made the life of the spirit seem an oppression.

The conservatives might have been pleased with the soaring popularity of the old pope had he confined himself to genial *bons mots*. But his popularity was fueling extravagant expectations for the coming council. The world at large had paid no attention to the pope's two other initiatives, but the announced ecumenical council was encouraging, in the conservative view, a rash of irresponsible speculation and hopes that the Church couldn't meet in a million years. Even the word *ecumenical* was being misconstrued. It referred to a council of the world's Catholic bishops, as opposed to a national or regional council. But the press was using the word as Protestants used it—to refer to the world movement to reunite various types of Christians—as if the coming council would be a council of reunion. John was not helping matters, because he had given no clear signal as to the kind of council he had in mind and sometimes almost left the impression (surely unintended!) that he might be contemplating an ecumenical meeting in the Protestant sense. In their nervousness, the conservatives relied on their usual method: control the agenda and you control the outcome.

The first step in organizing an ecumenical council is to invite the world's bishops to propose items for the council's agenda. This was the very step that, in the view of the extreme papalists, could provoke chaos. In theory, a council should be free to deliberate as it sees fit. But the world was much larger than it had once been, and so was the number of bishops. Thousands of them would be showing up in Rome for the event itself, and who knows how many would send in recommendations for discussion? How could these recommendations—some contradictory of others, some sparked by local rather than universal considerations, some patently absurd—be dealt with in a sensible manner? Under cover of the evident need for order, and for producing a council that would not last interminably, the Roman Curia began to shape the agenda. But their great, and unvoiced, fear was not that too many unusable suggestions would flood into the Vatican but that the bishops, once assembled in council, might turn themselves into an ecclesiastical parliament, overruling the pope and, far worse, the Curia itself. A council on the horizon meant that the old fire-breathing monster of Conciliarism, previously slain or at least confined permanently to its cave, could rise once more to destructive life, terrorizing the papal bureaucracy—which, like any bureaucracy, tends to see itself as the abiding essence of the enterprise it is engaged in and all others, including its chief executive officer, as transitory phenomena that need only be endured for a time.

John's instinctive collegiality and welcoming of collaboration, so unusual in a modern pope, gave many the impression that "this holy old boy," as Montini called him, had turned the governance of the Church over to others. "Tardini reigns, Ottaviani [the Grand Inquisitor] governs, John blesses" was the tag that went the rounds. As the Curia's domineering tactics continued, even John was heard to sigh, "I'm only the pope around here." John nevertheless appointed Tardini head of the Ante-preparatory Commission, which was to receive episcopal suggestions from around the world. Tardini, in turn, appointed Pericle Felici, a canon lawyer, as his assistant and began to work closely with Ottaviani, who had long viewed Roncalli as naive and insufficiently anti-Communist. (It was he who had instigated Roncalli's chastisement for welcoming the Socialist Party to Venice.) Ottaviani, intolerant of any opinions but his own, was old, ailing, and half blind; Tardini seemed, in the words of Bernard Wall, an English observer, "like a pedant or a schoolmaster, dried up, almost sour," with a mouth that "was not expressive of human sympathy." Wall thought he knew what was happening: "Pope John in a flush of universal benevolence after his election . . . had a great project for reunion. He overlooked the detailed difficulties. . . . And of course he had not considered the Vatican offices enough." It was beginning to look to many as if John had overreached.

Ottaviani liked to remind everyone that his domain, the Holy Office—the name had been changed from "Roman Inquisition," but it was still the Vatican's doctrinal police force—was the Church's "supreme" congregation. The Ante-preparatory Commission was succeeded by the institution of several preparatory commissions, each led by a prominent curialist and mandated to prepare draft texts, or *schemata*, supposedly inspired by the suggestions of the world's bishops, that would be presented to all the bishops when they arrived for the council. Tardini and Ottaviani saw to it that the preparatory commissions were stacked with conservatives, drawn from the dreary theological faculties of Italian universities, and that they worked at a snail-like pace. There need be no fear, therefore, that any upsetting "foreign" ideas would be introduced into the preparations. For many months, John did not interfere. The synod for the diocese of Rome—the first in its history—proved a sadly innocuous affair. Everything seemed to be going well for the *intransigenti*.

On July 30, 1961, Tardini died, unexpectedly felled by a heart attack. John appointed a new secretary of state, Amleto Cicognani, younger brother of Gaetano Cicognani, the fattest of the cardinals, a blander and more neutral figure than Tardini and not so tied to Ottaviani. But now the old warhorse Ottaviani took charge of the conservative cause. Just as his Holy Office was the "supreme" congregation of the Roman Church, the preparatory commission of which he was master, the Central Preparatory Commission, was, he averred, the "supreme" commission and would judge the work of all the others. Ottaviani instigated the preparation of *schemata* condemning the modern world, affirming Mary's perpetual virginity, declaring that there was an essential difference between priests and the rest of the baptized, condemning those who dared speak of the sinfulness of the Church, and proposing a new "Profession of Faith," modeled on Pius X's anti-Modernist oath but even more restrictive. It was the whole warmed-over program of Pius's aborted council, which Ottaviani had once been instrumental in drawing up. John continued to treat Ottaviani as if he were an old uncle, difficult but lovable.

Others, however, were finding their voices. An informal consortium of Dutchmen, Germans, and Austrians, led by Cardinal

Bernard Alfrink of Utrecht, began to oppose Ottaviani in the meetings of the Central Preparatory Commission. It was a new experience for the Grand Inquisitor, who had never before known opposition. More than this, certain extra-curial cardinals were gaining the pope's ear: Léon-Joseph Suenens of Malines-Brussels, Alfred Bengsch of Berlin, and his old friends Wyszynski of Warsaw and Montini of Milan. Each of these informal advisors was bringing John news of the aspirations of the world beyond the Vatican and helping him privately to find language for his own, as yet unarticulated, aspirations. The council should meditate upon the Church not as a juridical institution but as a mystery unfolding in time, a mystery central to the healing of the world. The Church would have to face up honestly to the problems of the contemporary world, as it actually is, but only after rediscovering its own identity. To do this the bishops must see themselves not as some sort of ecclesiastical nobility left over from the Middle Ages but as the representatives of their (often suffering) people. "It is the whole Church that expresses itself in the Council," Montini told the Milanese in a letter called *Pensiamo al Concilio* (Let's Think about the Council), "and we [the people of Milan] are the Church." The reasoning was pure Congar, the most important intellectual in the French Church and a man silenced by Pius XII. But, then, one of the worst things the *intransigenti* could say of Montini was that he was a Francophile.

The pope, seeing at last that a new consensus was developing that could take the Church beyond the curial mentality, began to give indications of his approval. He broke a logjam in one of the preparatory bodies, the Biblical Commission, which was spending all its time preparing condemnations of Catholic Scripture scholars who had the gall to utilize the basic assumption of modern critical scholarship—that the Bible is not a single unified book but a library of diverse works written in different times and cultures and according to different literary conventions and forms. John sent his secretary of state one of the most trenchant messages he had ever composed: "The time has come to put a stop to this nonsense. Either the Biblical Commission will bestir itself, do some real work, and by its suggestions to the Holy Father make a useful contribution to the needs of the present time, or it would be better to abolish it and let the Supreme Authority replace it in the Lord with something else." It took a lot to provoke John, but he could be provoked. This was in late May of 1962, less than five months before the council was to open. In July, John went beyond his words of warning, replaced the secretary of the Biblical Commission, and gave it "foreign" consultors, distinguished biblical professors from France and Germany.

In June of the same year, John took his ruler to one of the *schemata* to measure its prose: "Seven inches of condemnations and one of praise: is that the way to talk to the modern world?" The pope sent Montini into the final meeting of the Central Commission to deliver a judgment (which all knew came from the pope) that condemnations and anathemas were not the way forward. Modern errors usually ended up by condemning themselves. All that was necessary to speak to the world was the true Christian witness of mercy and love. Here, just months before the council was to open, the ground was shifting under the conservatives. They knew it, and they also knew that there was now insufficient time to prepare an adequate counteroffensive. John had shown his hand late in the game. "I pray God," pronounced a furious Ottaviani after enduring Montini's admonition, "that I may die before the council's end. That way I can die a Catholic."

As early as 1960 John had been directing two other initiatives, both of them brilliant end runs around the Ottaviani team. The first of these was John's creation of a new curial department, the Secretariat for Christian Unity, under the leadership of Augustin Bea. Bea was a German biblical scholar, frail, stooped, six months' senior to the pope, and rector of the Biblicum, the Church's principal institution of biblical scholarship. Though highly regarded by his scholarly colleagues, he had escaped the usual condemnations because of his consummate discretion and political wiliness. He was a Jesuit who knew his way around papal Rome; he had even served as personal confessor to Pius XII—which helped put him off-limits to those who might wish to attack him. How would one go about criticizing Bea as a daffy Johannine leftist, destroying the legacy of Pius XII, when he was the man Pius was known to have trusted more than any other, to have trusted even with his soul? It left the usually outspoken *intransigenti* speechless.

Bea, now created cardinal, began to school the pope in ecumenical etiquette, something papal Rome knew little about. John stopped speaking of the "return" of other Christians to the fold of the Catholic Church, as if they were all errant sheep. "All are brothers" was a phrase John had often used, as he had often in different contexts introduced himself as "Joseph, your brother"—never more affectingly than when he received a delegation of Jews, who would appreciate immediately John's reference to the Hebrew Bible. Under Bea's tutelage, this vocabulary became more prominent. Word went out that the pope considered it unacceptable for non-Catholic Christians to be referred to as "schismatics," "heretics," or "dissidents." They were always to be spoken of lovingly as "the separated brethren."

Bea, who according to the English cardinal John Heenan "resembled Pope John in the serenity of soul shining in his face," set himself an ambitious program that would have exhausted a much younger man, flying everywhere, it seemed, to take the pulse of Protestant and Orthodox leaders. The then-current and widely disseminated advertising slogan of British European Airways was "See the world with BEA," which served as a gratuitous pinprick to the Ottaviani men. Bea's announced reverence for non-Catholic Christians, who "always bear not only the name of Christ on their foreheads but his actual image in their souls, deeply and indelibly imprinted there by baptism," constantly rubbed them the wrong way. But when Bea's incessant travels began to pay off, they were horrified. On December 2, 1960, John received Geoffrey Fisher, archbishop of Canterbury and leader of the worldwide Anglican Communion. It was the first meeting of a pope and an archbishop of Canterbury since the Reformation. And this was only the beginning. Soon, a veritable torrent of non-Catholic religious leaders began to flow into the Vatican, as John met with Baptists, Presbyterians, Lutherans, Orthodox and Reformed Christians, and, last and most outrageously, Shizuka Matsubara, superior of the Shinto Temple of Kyoto. John loved these comings and goings, not least his meeting with the Shintoists: "The Pope loves to be united with all honest and upright souls, wherever they are, to whatever nation they belong, in a spirit of respect, understanding, and peace." And he loved the "precious robe of bright scarlet" that the Shintoists gave him as their gift.

Like the variety of religious leaders, a wide assortment of heads of state began to make their way to Pope John. Pius had received only ten heads of state in a pontificate that lasted nearly twenty years. John would receive thirty-four such visits in less than five years. With many of these august personages, he found a way of dispensing with protocol and creating a person-to-person encounter. When he received Jacqueline Bouvier Kennedy, wife of the president of the United States, he had been advised to address her as "Mrs. Kennedy" or, if he preferred, as

"Madame" since they would speak French together. But when he saw the beautiful young woman striding toward him, he opened his arms and exclaimed, "Jackie!"

By the end of 1961 it had become clear that John would insist that representatives of the non-Catholic Churches be invited to the council. He saw to it that Roman Catholic observers were allowed for the first time to attend the General Assembly of the World Council of Churches, meeting in New Delhi. John's apostolic constitution convoking what would be known as the Second Vatican Council (or Vatican II) was issued on Christmas Day 1961. It contained a pointed ecumenical (in the Protestant sense) invitation to all Christians; and it stated that the work of the council was to "discern the signs of the times," as Jesus advises in Matthew's Gospel, and to be "at the service of the world"—new vocabulary within the Vatican, however ancient the concepts.

The coming council, especially now that Bea was on board, began to stimulate innovative thinking at an accelerated speed. Such thinking could only have alarmed the slow-paced *intransigenti*—had they been aware of anything outside their Roman cocoon—for they were men used to viewing developments in terms of centuries. No thinking was more innovative or more freshly stated than that of a young Swiss theologian, teaching at Tübingen, Germany, whose name was Hans Küng. His book *The Council and Reunion* (or *The Council, Reform, and Reunion*, as it was published in the United States) became a bestseller in German- and English-speaking countries, as well as in France and the Low Countries, but it had to wait five years—till 1965—for an Italian translation. The Catholic Church was in need of reform, said Küng, but then, in accordance with the Church's own ageless wisdom, *"ecclesia semper reformanda"* (the Church is always in need of reform). If the council carried out its reform properly by admitting that the Protestant reformers had made just demands—for vernacular liturgies, for the centrality of the Bible, for the recognition of the "priesthood of all the faithful," for the extrication of the papacy from politics—if the Church opened a dialogue with other cultures, reformed the Curia, and got rid of inanities like the Index of Forbidden Books, reunion could be achieved. Küng saw Pope John as the man to rouse Christendom from its slumbers, so that, wide awake, it might see as if for the first time the damaging scandal of its divisions, "an immeasurably crippling wound which absolutely must be healed."

Prominent churchmen began to line up behind Küng, men like the widely respected Cardinal Achille Liénart, archbishop of Lille, and the scholarly Cardinal Franz König, archbishop of Vienna, who wrote the introduction to the German edition of Küng's book. Küng's trumpet call would become to a large extent the council's blueprint. John's revolution would not be something he engineered by himself. But his spirit—and key public actions and appointments—were inspiring Catholics and encouraging them to speak and write more freely than they had done in many centuries.

Having extended the hand of fellowship to the modern world, and especially to other Christians, John began to look East—to the supposed monolith of atheistic Communism. Was it possible to create an opening there? This question—or rather, this hope— lay behind John's other end run around the Curia. But John's second initiative, because of the many diplomatic delicacies involved, could not be championed in the bright light of day or spearheaded by a man like Bea. In nothing had Pius XII distinguished himself so in the public mind as in his uncompromising anti-Communism. Voting Communist was still cause for excommunication in Italy. As Ottaviani was fond of boasting, "You can say what you like about the divinity of Christ, but if in the remotest village of Sicily you vote Communist, your excommunication will arrive the next day." Blatant reversal of such an established position would sow confusion among the faithful and hold the Church up to ridicule. In any case, John saw no unalloyed beauty in Communism; he merely wished to act as Christ would to all men, however benighted they might be. *And* he wanted to find a way to spring Catholic bishops out of the Communist world and into the coming council. The council could not be ecumenical without them, but their governments regularly prevented travel to the West. Beyond this consideration, non-Catholic participation in the council would be sorely incomplete without representatives of the Orthodox Churches of Eastern Europe. Could it be possible to negotiate *their* entrance into the council as well?

John began not in the East but in Italy itself. Aldo Moro, leader of the Christian Democrats, was attempting to forge an alliance with the Italian Socialist Party. In the time of Pius XI, it was the Vatican's unbending opposition to such an alliance— between the Socialists, who were thought to be Communists without the name, and the Catholic Popular Party—that had doomed Italy to Fascism. In Italian politics, alliances between parties are an utter necessity in order to achieve parliamentary majorities and stable governments. If the Christian Democrats did not ally themselves with the Socialists, they would have to turn to the Movimento Sociale, who were indeed Fascists without the name. Such a turn of events would have suited not a few Catholic churchmen, especially the ever-outspoken Siri, the right-wingers' candidate for pope in the conclave that elected John. Cardinals like Siri worked hand-in-glove with Confindustria, the association of major industrialists, who had had a long love affair with Fascism. Moro's *apertura a sinistra*, or opening to the left, brought out all the conservatives' guns. He was roundly condemned as a heretic and traitor by most diocesan papers, *Verona Fedele*, the paper of the Verona diocese, going so far as to assert that Moro had already been condemned by God to the fires of hell. In all this hullabaloo, one Catholic paper maintained its silence, as if there were no controversy. This was *L'Osservatore Romano*. Those who kept a finger in the wind detected correctly that there had been a major shift in air current: the silence could mean only one thing—the pope was on Moro's side!

John's next step was to issue an encyclical letter, one of two that he is especially remembered for. The encyclical's title, *Mater et Magistra* (Mother and Teacher), is intended as a description of the Church in its relation not only to Catholics or Christians but to all people. John presents a view of history that has much in common with the work of the silenced French priest-paleontologist Teilhard de Chardin, a vision of humanity coming gradually together from its primitive beginnings—as from "one of those iron-age villages, in which every house was an impenetrable fortress, and people lived among their fortifications," as Roncalli had put it in the Pentecost sermon of 1944— and slowly and haltingly developing a heightened awareness of the necessary interdependence of all human beings. He calls this development of human consciousness, as does Teilhard, "socialization," which put the uncompromising anti-Communists in a rage—it sounded too close to "Socialism." As evidence of this improving evolutionary trajectory, John cites the welfare state, in which a whole society comes to see that the common good demands the creation of extensive social services for the needy that go far beyond the responses possible through individual charity. Socialization, says the encyclical, "is an effect and a cause of the growing intervention of the state even in matters of such intimate concern to the individual as health and education, the choice of career, and the care and rehabilitation of the physically and mentally handicapped."

Siri was livid: here at last was direct contradiction with the august teachings of Pius XII, who had specifically warned against the monstrous Leviathan of state power and "an all-embracing socialization." In the United States, William F. Buckley's conservative *National Review* went so far as to coin the famous reproof *"Mater, sì. Magistra, no!"* It was fine for the Church to be mother, but free-market capitalists knew better than to listen to anything she thought she had to teach them about the organization of society. John, always meditating on history, had taken his title from a phrase in the address of Innocent III to the Fourth Lateran Council in 1215. Innocent was a papal triumphalist if ever there was one, so there was nice irony in John's choice, but it was also true that the Fourth Lateran Council had been the principal reform council of the Middle Ages. Like the Cosmati of the Middle Ages, who made extraordinary new patterns on the floors of the Roman churches by using only chips of colored marble taken from the ruins of antiquity, John's favored style was to reclaim tiny pieces of the past that could be made to serve bold new patterns in the present.

Having sketched out a new papal political philosophy, John turned his attention again to Italy. He wanted bishops, as he put it in his diary, to stop "meddling immoderately in matters that are not their business, and this is why the Pope must admonish them not to take part in any political or controversial arguments, and not to declare for one faction or section rather than another. They are to preach to all alike, and in general terms, justice, love, meekness, gentleness, and the other Gospel virtues"—a program that not a few motor-mouth bishops might still contemplate to their (and our) advantage. John went on: "At all times, and especially at this moment, the Bishop must apply the balm of gentleness to the wounds of mankind. He must beware of making any rash judgment or uttering abusive words about anyone." Quietly, the message went out: the pope wanted a clear disengagement from politics—not by laypeople but by bishops. When he received Amintore Fanfani, Italy's prime minister, on April 11, 1961, it was to celebrate the hundredth anniversary of Italian unification, which he called "a cause of great joy for Italy and for both of us on the two banks of the Tiber," since the river that runs through Rome divides the Vatican from the city center and the government of Italy. He described Church and state as "two organisms that differ in structure, character, level, and aims" and advised that there should be "a certain reserve in the relationship," though it must be based on "courtesy and respect." Here, in the nuanced language of papal diplomacy, was the final end to the hundred-year-old war between Church and state: they were completely distinct but not in conflict. "The Pope in the Vatican is one thing," John would say a year later to Antonio Segni, president of Italy, "the President in the Quirinal [once the home of the pope!] is another." This pope was happy not to be ruler of Italy, nor even to inject himself into partisan political battles. There was nothing left to fight over.

Cardinal Siri was not happy, nor would he relent in his attacks on Moro, whom John came to value more and more. John felt it "very important to insist that all bishops should act in the same way," and Siri would simply not get with the program. In the end, it became necessary to clip Siri's wings—or at least to muffle his cry. The cardinal's most public position was not as archbishop of Genoa but as president of the Conference of Italian Bishops, a Vatican-appointed position from which he was retired. For Siri, John was "the greatest disaster in recent ecclesiastical history"—by which he said he meant the last five hundred years, that is, since the end of the Great Schism and the rise of the Borgia popes. Looking over the same long arc of papal history, the distinguished British historian E. E. Y. Hales comes to a markedly different judgment: John, he writes, "was largely free from the Renaissance habit of using politics to strengthen the papal position in Italy, and from the medieval habit of using politics to build the papal ascendancy over Europe." Years after John's death, Siri too would at last come to a similarly positive judgment.

Having effected a new disengagement between Church and state, John turned to consider his chances with the Soviet Union. In July 1961, he sent a message of approbation to Pax Christi, the international Catholic peace organization, something his predecessor would never have brought himself to do. He spoke of "the worries of fathers and mothers" that their children would be drawn into armed conflict because of the horrible tensions in the world and that these worries "find an echo in our hearts." For his part, John wrote, "we try to be a man of peace in the deepest meaning of the word. And while we suffer from what is happening, we prefer to stress what unites and to walk along the road with anyone as far as possible." This was also meant as a signal to Nikita Khrushchev. One month later, the Berlin Wall went up, physically separating the so-called Free World from the Communist East. It was not an encouraging moment.

In September, nonetheless, John sent off another message, this time to the Conference of Nonaligned Nations, which was meeting in Belgrade, reminding them of their "dreadful responsibility before history, and, more importantly, before God's judgment" to maintain world peace. Little more than a week later, an astonishing interview with Khrushchev appeared in *Pravda* in which the Soviet premier was quoted as uttering the name of a pope. "John XXIII pays tribute to reason" in his desire for peace, claimed Khrushchev. "It is not that we fear God's judgment, which as an atheist I do not believe in, but we welcome the appeal to negotiate no matter where it comes from" The secretary went on to hope that "ardent Catholics like John F. Kennedy, Konrad Adenauer, and others" would "heed the Pope's warning." It was enough to give Catholics like Siri and Buckley a bad case of indigestion. But John was not the naive dreamer they supposed him to be: he wanted a specific result and was not going to let himself be distracted by Communist rhetorical flourishes.

Now John sent his friend and publisher, the priest Giuseppe De Luca, to meet secretly with Palmiro Togliatti, secretary of the Italian Communist Party, in a Rome apartment. De Luca was the perfect choice. Enigmatic, adept at indirection, known as a fast friend of Ottaviani, he would never be suspected of such a mission. Togliatti was about to depart for Moscow, and De Luca asked him to carry a message to Khrushchev that John would welcome closer relations with the Kremlin. If Khrushchev was in agreement, he could signal by sending the pope greetings on the occasion of his eightieth birthday in November. The boldness of the approach is breathtaking. Had even a whisper of this transaction leaked out, it could have ended John's effectiveness within and without his Church. But John felt himself "under obedience" to the Holy Spirit and "had noticed that this disposition, in things great and small, gives me, unworthy as I am, a strength of daring simplicity."

On November 25, 1961, the Soviet ambassador to Italy duly delivered to the papal nuncio for Italy a telegram from the premier, which was in turn delivered to the Vatican secretary of state. John called the innocuous greeting "a sign from Providence" and swiftly telegrammed Khrushchev his reply, sending "to the whole Russian people cordial wishes for the increase and strengthening of universal peace by means of understanding based on human brotherhood" and offering the pope's fervent prayers "to this end." He then sent through the secretary of state a public message to the Vatican bureaucracy, thanking all for their birthday greetings: "The wide-ranging nature of the birthday greetings we have received permits us to embrace, in a single gesture of affection, the beloved children of the Catholic Church and the entire human family." So the pope was no longer father only of Catholics. He embraced everyone, even the unthinkable Communists. As he wrote in his journal, "The whole world is my family."

But despite the Vatican-Kremlin thaw, there were no official relations, and John would need to find an unusual back door if he were ever to pull off the diplomatic coup of getting the Eastern bishops to his council. He summoned Francesco Ladrone, his successor in Istanbul, to Rome for a private discussion, which they had as they strolled through the Vatican gardens away from interested ears. What better back door than Istanbul, which, as John knew only too well, was seldom in the spotlight. When Ladrone returned to his post, he met with Nikita Ryjov, the courteous Soviet ambassador to Turkey, who passed on the pope's request to the Kremlin. Within days, the answer came back: let the pope issue his invitations to the bishops through the mechanisms of Soviet diplomacy and the arrival in Rome of Catholic bishops from the Soviet Union was assured. Ladrone then proceeded in like manner with the ambassadors from the other Soviet bloc countries. With Khrushchev's example before them, all agreed to speed the pope's request to their governments. John was on the point of achieving the impossible.

The next, and surely the most precarious, step was to secure the participation of Orthodox observers from the Soviet bloc. Even the patriarch of Constantinople, who was completely in John's corner, did not feel free to send observers to the council if no one were to come from the Russian Church, since it was by far the largest in all Orthodoxy. If the Russians did not show up, John's hope for a universal representation of all Christians would fail, for the Orthodox would be missing. The pope initiated several top-secret Ladrone-like initiatives, but for the longest time it looked as if there could be no positive response.

Despite the pressures of these delicate global enterprises, John was not neglecting the inner health of the Catholic Church. Much of his doctoring was to individuals. He wrote a chatty letter to Angelo Pedrinelli, once his fellow faculty member at Bergamo, who had been banned from teaching during the anti-Modernist Terror and consigned to parish work. Don Angelo was dying, and John just wanted him to know that at least the pope had never forgotten him. He wrote in similar style to the parishioners of Sotto il Monte; the pope had not forgotten them, either, was sad that he could no longer visit but kept by him photographs of their beautiful hills, which never failed to cheer His Holiness. When he addressed the Lenten preachers about to fan out to the parishes of Rome—and who were known for evoking visions of hellfire in their sermons—he urged them on in this way: "You must remember that you are called to strengthen your brothers" (as Jesus had asked Peter to do), "not to terrorize them."

He was troubled by the fate of priests who had departed the ministry—usually called "ex-priests," though in Catholic theology a priest, whether or not he practices his craft, is a priest forever. He insisted that they not be shunned or judged as traitors, which had been the practice till then, but should rather be treated with "humanity and decency." "No one," he wrote into the decrees of the Roman Synod, "is to be denied the friendship of his fellow priests or consolation in his difficulties or even material help should it be needed." He knew perfectly well that for most "ex-priests" the insurmountable difficulty was celibacy. Nothing, he told the synod, brought him greater pain than "the groans of priestly souls that come to me not just from Rome but from all parts of the world." But he did not feel he had the right to alter this ancient tradition of the Church, nor did he wish to alter a way of life that he believed was part of the Church's authentic heroism. Did he feel a council had the right?

The council was set to open on October 11, 1962. Despite John's urgings, only seven out of the proposed seventy *schemata* were in sufficient readiness for the recalcitrant preparatory commissions to allow them to be sent to the world's bishops for review during the preceding summer. John found the delaying tactics exasperating; and when asked by a visitor "How many people work in the Vatican?" he replied: "About half."

But now the pope became distracted by gnawing discomfort that would not go away. On September 23, after a battery of medical exams, he was given the verdict: like his sisters Ancilla and Maria, he had inoperable stomach cancer and would be dead within a year. He had already confided to Cardinal Suenens during the summer that he knew "what my part in the council will be: it will be suffering"—something the true Christian must always welcome as an unexpected gift because it is his participation in the sufferings of Christ. But the remark also indicates that John had an inkling of what was to come well in advance of the medical verdict. There would be for him but a few months more, and these would be filled with unavoidable pain. Since it was now obvious that the work of the council would require two sessions at the least—it would, as it turned out, require four—and since bishops must govern their dioceses and not be kept forever in Rome, it was evident to John that he could not live to see his council, the great project of his life, to its conclusion.

But this did not ruffle his tranquility, a tranquility building in grace and strength ever since, as a small boy, he had memorized the advice of Saint Bernard of Clairvaux that he found in the study of his parish priest in Sotto il Monte. The life of the world will continue after each of our deaths, and the future is in God's hands, so there is no need to be "curious and anxious about the shape of things to come." "I await the arrival of Sister Death," he wrote in his will, borrowing the language of Saint Francis of Assisi, "and will welcome her simply and joyfully in whatever circumstances it will please the Lord to send her." On the day he heard the news of his impending demise, he descended the many steps into the crypt of Saint Peter's to pray at the tombs of his predecessors and to tell them he would soon be with them.

If John wished to be the world's parent, he saw himself sometimes as father, at other times as mother, often as both. In his September radio address just prior to the opening of the council, he voiced the expectations of a universal parent: "From every people we expect a contribution based on intelligence and experience that will help heal the scars of the two World Wars that have so profoundly changed the face of all our countries." Just as all mothers and fathers hate war, so "the Church, the Mother of all without exception, will once more repeat the proclamation that echoes down the centuries from Bethlehem, *pacem in terris*, peace on earth.'" More and more, as he approached his end, he saw God as mother, relishing especially the calming image in Psalm 131 of the believer as "a child quieted upon its mother's breast." He was abandoning himself, as he put it, *"in Domino, et in sinu Matris Jesu, et matris mei dulcissimae"* (in the Lord and on the breast of the Mother of Jesus and my most sweet mother).

Well, then, he would go on pilgrimage once more—to seek publicly God's blessing on his coming council and privately God's grace on his approaching death. At 6:30 A.M. on October 4, 1962, the feast of Saint Francis, he boarded the presidential train provided for him at the fanciful Vatican station to make the first trip by a pope since 1870. The train bore him north to Assisi, where he reminded his listeners, in the birthplace of *il Poverello*, the Little Poor Man who was patron of Italy, that the Church must become again a "Church of the Poor" and that only when we share with one another "the good and beautiful things that Providence has placed in this world" can there be peace on earth. He had one more stop to make, northeast, almost to the Adriatic, at the village of Loreto south of Ancona where there is a shrine to the Mother of God that he had first visited sixty years before. If the visit to Assisi was for the council, the visit to Loreto, which framed the whole of his adult life, was for him. But even here, he spoke of public things, telling his audience that the Angelus, the noontime prayer commemorating the angel's announcement to Mary that she was to "bear a son" by the Holy Spirit, prompts us to meditate on "the coming together of earth and heaven," which is also the ultimate purpose of the council. The council and his death were becoming intertwined realities, caught up in the great drama of Incarnation and Redemption.

The day was filled with politicians, journalists, and Italians of all kinds, brought out by the fine weather and the unprecedented spectacle of a traveling pope. In small-town Assisi, which was bursting with people, one visitor—who had *not* come to see the pope—found he could not move through the streets, returned to his room at the hostel where he was staying, and ended up reading Matthew's Gospel. The man was Pier Paolo Pasolini, accomplished poet, famous filmmaker, outspoken Communist, flagrant homosexual, anticlerical cynic. This day became the inspiration for his *Il Vangelo secondo Matteo* (The Gospel According to Matthew), Pasolini's most important film and by far the best film ever made about the life of Jesus, full of Pasolini's unconventional genius, especially in the emotion he elicits from the haunting faces of the Calabrian peasants who convincingly dramatize the two-thousand-year-old story. Pasolini would dedicate the work *"alla cara, lieta, familiare memoria di Giovanni XXIII"* (to the dear, merry, familial memory of John XXIII). As an Italian phenomenon, the film stands with Verdi's *Requiem* of 1874, dedicated to the memory of Roncalli's favorite novelist, Manzoni. Both film and musical composition were created by famous secularists, public sinners, supporters of revolution, the virtual embodiments of the cultural and artistic aspirations of their time, inspired to depart from their usual subjects by the unexpected moral force of a believer, a believer who nonetheless shared something of their political radicalism. Both great works, though standing ninety years apart, are keys to understanding Italy, where profound piety can flow like an underground current just below the parched surfaces of worldliness and skepticism.

In the week before the opening of the council, bishops swept into Rome from almost every part of the world. John knew there would be no bishops arriving from China (though he had tried to establish contact with the People's Republic), but he was waiting in hope for the Eastern Europeans. Three days before the council was to begin, Cardinal Wyszynski arrived by train with thirteen Polish bishops in tow, including Karol Wojtyla, the young archbishop of Krakow who would reign as John Paul II. The next day, three Hungarians and two Yugoslavs showed up, and on the eve of the council three came in from Czechoslovakia and one from Lithuania. It was not all the Eastern bishops, some of whom were in prison or under house arrest, but it was a marvelous beginning.

On October 11, John walked up the central aisle of Saint Peter's flanked by two and a half thousand mitred bishops, veiled patriarchs, and hooded abbots, arranged on lofty tiers that ran the length of the aula on both sides of the aisle, all singing *"Veni Creator Spiritus"* (Come, Creator Spirit), praying that the Spirit would descend on their assembly. The basilica had been constructed long before the advent of mass communications and the liturgy was older still, but it was a scene of color and splendor made for photo spreads and television, which signaled to the world that something grand and wonderful had been called into being by the beloved old man. The Mass that followed was in Latin and Greek, the ancient languages of West and East, and soon enough the pope was speaking to the bishops of the world in his resonant, harmonious voice. *"Gaudet Mater Ecclesia,"* he began. "Mother Church rejoices" at this global assembly of her sons, expressing not uniformity but the "reconciled diversity" of true Catholicism. He set aside the neurotic worries of the naysayers, "the prophets of doom." He brushed out of the way like so many cobwebs the conservative demand for condemnations of errors that "often vanish as swiftly as they arise, like mist before the sun." "Today the Spouse of Christ [that is, the Church] prefers to use the medicine of mercy rather than severity. She considers that she meets the needs of the present age by showing the validity of her teaching rather than by condemnations."

He had told them that the council would be a celebration and a series of affirmations, but the content of those affirmations was up to them. It began to dawn on almost everyone, even those whose Latin was rusty, that the pope did not expect them to be rubber stamps but independent bishops in the ancient sense, assembled to address in their communal wisdom the most pressing needs of their Church and their world. Such a mandate was shocking in its novelty, however primeval its forgotten precedents. Hadn't the safe doctrinal haven of papal infallibility done away with the need for bishops to think new thoughts? There rose in the minds of many of these hierarchs the idea that before them waited an unparalleled adventure, not a timeless ritual but a story to be written by *them*. Some were thrilled, some horrified, others vaguely unsettled, many just confused that the measured life of the Church could take such a turn. The next day, as if to confirm the unexpected atmosphere of innovation that had descended on them, there came without warning two representatives so alien and exotic that their like had never before been seen within the walls of the Vatican and had been seldom met with anywhere in the West—official observers from the Russian Orthodox Church. Everyone was surprised; almost no one knew of John's carefully laid strategy, which at the very last moment had succeeded.

That night, fifty thousand people squeezed into Saint Peter's Square, singing and cheering and coaxing the tired old man to appear at his window, which of course he did. "Dear children, dear children, I hear your voices." He pointed out the moon, which hung large overhead and which, he said, was watching them happily. From the moon Earth could be seen as a unity, as the one household it really was. "My voice is an isolated one, but it echoes the voice of the whole world. Here, in effect, the whole world is represented." John had become not only Father of the World but, in his own mind, Ombudsman for Planet Earth. He told them to go home, where they belonged, "and give your children a caress. Tell them it is *la carezza del Papa*" (the caress of the Pope). Many did just that; and to this day in Italy children who received that caress on that night have felt entitled to pass on to their children, and they in turn to theirs, *la carezza di Papa Giovanni*.

The council's first session was a disappointment to anyone looking for an immediate revolution. At the outset, the conservatives were in command: they knew their way around papal

Rome as did few others, they had prepared the *schemata*, they controlled the daily schedule of bishops' speeches in the aula, they had written the procedural rules. The pope continued on his merry way, telling the non-Catholic observers that he "felt comforted by [their] presence" and reassuring them that he didn't "like to claim any special inspiration. I hold to the sound doctrine; everything comes from God." So much for papal infallibility. He told the journalists that they could "bear witness that the Church has nothing to hide." Well, maybe not, but reporters were barred from the debates in the aula and were fobbed off with incomprehensible summaries that took the curial obsession for secrecy to new heights. Flummoxed, most of the journalists departed. John seemed oblivious. Though he did watch the proceedings on closed-circuit television, he stayed out of the aula. Unlike the emperor Constantine at the First Ecumenical Council, he refused to use his presence to influence or stifle debate. The majority of council fathers, unused to such freedom, were not at first sure what they should be doing and were easily led by the Romans.

For most bishops the first session went like a visit to the optometrist: things came gradually into focus. Ottaviani and crew were pressing for a quick council, imagining that the overwhelming majority would see the wisdom of voting yes to all the drafts and then going home, leaving no trace of themselves and allowing the Curia to get back to the business of running the Church. By the time the session ended on December 8, however, the progressives, led by Suenens and Montini, and with some behind-the-scenes backing from John at crucial moments, had gained control. From now on it would be *their* council. No *schema* had been approved; all were sent back for rewriting; and a new organizing committee, the Coordinating Commission, stuffed with a progressive majority, was set up to take control of agenda and procedures and to ensure that work would continue efficiently during the intersession. The next session was set for September 1963, which meant, as John knew, that, short of a miracle, he would not live to see it.

John addressed *his* council for the last time. The first session, he insisted, had not been a failure but "a slow and solemn introduction. . . . Brothers gathered from afar took time to get to know each other; they needed to look each other in the eyes in order to understand each other's heart; they needed time to describe their own experiences, which reflected differences in the apostolate in the most varied situations." It was true; so there was still reason for the optimism that John continued to profess. He told them not to be perturbed that there were disagreements: such clashes were merely a sign of "the holy freedom that the children of God should enjoy in the Church." But all could see sadly that this was not the healthy-looking pope who had addressed them two months earlier.

While the bishops had been deliberating, John had been working on one last project, a final encyclical, his masterpiece. In the course of the first session, the Cuban Missile Crisis had developed and in short order the world stood on the brink of nuclear catastrophe, while Kennedy and Khrushchev took each other's measure. When the crisis was resolved, Khrushchev told Norman Cousins, editor of *Saturday Review,* that "what the Pope has done for peace will go down in history." In the midst of the crisis, John conceived his encyclical.

Through intermediaries, including Cousins, Khrushchev had asked John to make a clear, evenhanded public statement on behalf of continued negotiations between Washington and Moscow. This would give him cover with the military hardliners in the Kremlin who were itching, like their counterparts in

Washington, for a nuclear confrontation. It would be a sign that even so important a figure of the Western world as the pope was for negotiation and against war. John understood what was wanted. "I beg heads of state," he pleaded in his broadcast from the Vatican on October 24, "not to be deaf to the cry of humanity: peace, peace. Let them do all that is in their power to save peace; in this way they will avoid the horrors of a war, the appalling consequences of which no one could predict. Let them continue to negotiate. . . . To promote, encourage, and accept negotiation, always and on every level, is a rule of wisdom that draws down both heavenly and earthly blessings." That should do it: no Kremlin general could believe that a Catholic president was preparing war in the face of such a plea; and John stood patently on neither side of the argument but in the middle. If this was simpleminded thinking, the simplemindedness was on the Soviet side. John's sophistication was in putting together the words that would impress them properly and erase all doubts about the sincerity of his neutrality and therefore of the passionate desire for peace held by many in the West, which Kennedy would have to be mad to ignore.

Two days later, a pope for the first time made page one of *Pravda*, the enormous headline even quoting John's plea to the leaders "not to be deaf to the cry of humanity." By October 28, Khrushchev had blinked first and the crisis was over. He later told Cousins that for days "the Pope's message was the only gleam of hope" coming from the West and, one may infer, the only thing that enabled him to hold the warmongers at bay. In return, John asked for—and got—the release from a Siberian labor camp of Josef Slipyi, Catholic metropolitan of the Ukraine. When Slipyi finally made it into the Vatican, John took him to his private chapel, where they recited together the Magnificat, the pregnant Mary of Nazareth's song in Luke's Gospel in which she rejoices that by the conception of her son God had "pulled the mighty from their thrones and exalted the lowly." Slipyi gave the pope a map marking all the Soviet labor camps—the Gulag—which John kept prayerfully beside him till his death. He was not blind to the sufferings inflicted by tyranny, but he was never satisfied to leave matters at handwringing. He sent off Agostino Casaroli, a *monsignore* working in the Secretariat of State, on a quiet papal probe of Eastern Europe to see "what seeds can be planted here and there" in cracks and crevices that might eventually bring down the walls that imprison human beings. Casaroli would become secretary of state in the next pontificate.

John was to receive two more visitors from the Soviet Union, Khrushchev's daughter, Rada, and her husband, Alexis Adjubei. Ottaviani and Cicognani were unalterably opposed, but John insisted. It was a harmless, albeit touching encounter, for the pope heard Rada Khrushchevska whisper to her husband in Russian to look closely at the pope's hands, which she described as "the beautiful hands of a Russian peasant." She could not know that her host understood her native language, but the pope was deeply moved. Often he had been heard to muse that what he would really like to do was return to the fields with his brothers. The pope then asked Rada to tell him the names of her children, not because he didn't already know them (he did), but "because when a mother speaks the names of her children, something exceptional happens." He then asked her to caress her children for him, especially the one named Ivan (Russian for John). As his gift, John gave her a rosary, saying he knew she wouldn't wish to use it but he wanted her to have it nonetheless "because it reminds me of peace in the home and of my mother who used to say it by the fireside when I was a child." Then he asked the couple to accept his blessing, not the blessing of a pope, which he knew they could not accept, just the blessing of an old man. They left smiling and in tears; and to this day Rada has kept the rosary and calls it "one of my most precious possessions." But the Secretariat of State was unmoved and would publish no word of the encounter. "I deplore and pity those who in these last few days have lent themselves to unspeakable maneuvers," wrote John, but he was growing too weak to counteract such disobedience.

On Maundy Thursday in Holy Week 1963, the encyclical *Pacem in terris* (Peace on Earth) was published. Papal encyclicals are written to the world's Catholic bishops. This one, however, was sent "to all men and women of good will." But this is not its only innovation, for, avoiding the usual papal prose, it is written in a language anyone can understand—in John's own words.

He speaks first of the marvelous order of the universe, given by God but disrupted by sin. Still, it is possible to discern what God had in mind, particularly in the human realm, where good order means principally good relations among human beings. This leads the pope to enumerate a series of human rights: the right to worship freely "in private and in public," the right to take an active part in the political life of one's state, the right of even small and poor nations to self-determination, the rights of minorities and refugees. Evil laws cannot bind citizens to obedience, for "what are kingdoms without justice but great bands of robbers?" These human rights, however, presume a corresponding series of obligations, and the pope enumerates these, from the obligations of larger states toward smaller ones—all states being "by nature equal in dignity"—to the more intimate obligations "to pass on to others the best of [one's] own cultural heritage and to strive eagerly to make [one's] own the spiritual achievements of others. . . . Therefore, venerable brothers and beloved children, human society must primarily be considered a thing of the spirit." The peace of a society must always rest on "the four pillars" of truth, justice, love, and freedom, and these serve as John's "four great themes."

None of the enumerated rights and few of the obligations had ever before been championed by a pope; in truth, most popes from the French Revolution onward had despised such language, even if intellectuals had long ago succeeded in reconciling Catholic theology with the politics of human rights. But John has a "catholic" explanation for making the minority view into the new papal position. He sees his innovations not as novelties but as developments, stemming from a growing worldwide appreciation of the dignity of each human person. It makes sense that the Church should be part of this development in consciousness, since the Church, in its proper role, is guardian of human dignity and must affirm loudly that "by nature, all men are equal in human dignity." John sees everywhere signs of this heightened appreciation of human dignity, but especially in three areas: "a progressive improvement in the economic and social conditions of workers"; "the part women are now playing in political life everywhere" and their "increasing awareness of their natural dignity"; and the demise of imperialism, which "is fast becoming an anachronism." The section on the waning of colonialism also calls resoundingly for "the elimination of every trace of racism" within and between states. The section on women— with its clear admiration and championing of their rights—is unique in the history of papal pronouncements.

The encyclical ends with a beautifully choreographed plea that nuclear weapons be done away with. In the face of such weapons, the old theory of the "just war" is no longer viable, for it is now "meaningless to imagine that war could be a fitting instrument with which to repair the violation of justice. . . . In peace," he concludes, "nothing perishes; in war all is lost." John insisted that *Pacem in terris* be published on Maundy Thursday, because it was the day on which Jesus at the Last Supper had told his disciples, "Love one another," and had prayed to the Father "That all may be one."

Darius Milhaud made a choral symphony of texts from *Pacem in terris*, a transmutation unthinkable for any other encyclical ever written. It was the second time that John had inspired an important work of art. But there would be at least one more. The Italian sculptor Giacomo Manzù—for many the greatest sculptor since Rodin—made several bronze busts of the pope from life. The old priest and the aging radical, both irrepressible raconteurs, had a riotously informal time during the sittings and became fast friends. After John's death, Manzù made the pope's death mask. But his great Johannine masterpiece is surely the awesome *Porta della Morte*, or Door of Death, commissioned by Paul VI for one of the entrances to Saint Peter's, with its monumental bronze panels commemorating John, the council, and martyrdom, and very nearly leading us into another world.

Two days after the publication of *Pacem in terris*, Manzù brought his finished busts for John to inspect. It was their last meeting, and Manzù was shocked to see the change in the face he had endeavored to sculpt: "Most of it had fallen, except the big hooked nose and the immense ears, which were left to ride above all else like alarming sentinels, gaunt towers of a crumbling castle." Sister Death was on her way.

John finds himself attacked as a simpleminded dupe, encouraging Italians to vote for the Communists. He hears of rear-guard tactics from conservatives hoping to "save" the council. The editors of *Time* magazine, who have chosen him as their "Man of the Year," want him in New York for a summit lunch involving Kennedy, Khrushchev, de Gaulle, Adenauer, the Swiss Protestant theologian Karl Barth, and Pablo Picasso. He would love to go, but . . . He is awarded the Balzan Peace Prize (with the concurrence of the four Soviet members of the Balzan Foundation's general council and, therefore, with Khrushchev's approval), and a U.S. Presidential Medal of Freedom is in the works (Kennedy being no less grateful to John than Khrushchev is). He ponders whether there is a way to spring the old cigar-smoking Hungarian royalist Cardinal Mindszenty from the U.S. embassy in Budapest where he took refuge seven years earlier and has been driving diplomats crazy ever since.

But John is finally forced to turn his attention away from the affairs of Italy, the Church, and the world and toward his own pain. By May 23, Ascension Thursday, he rises and dresses for the last time in order to receive his nephew Flavio Roncalli. Once he takes to his bed, he has the task of comforting visitors whose tears stream down uncontrollably on finding him in such a weakened state. Federico Belotti, the lay brother who acts as his night nurse, tells him, when he complains of not being able to say Mass any longer, that "your bed is your altar." He likes that, says "an altar needs a victim" and that he's ready.

But he can't stop the habits of a lifetime, and when Cicognani and Dell'Acqua, an old friend from the Secretariat of State, visit, he sits up in bed and delivers a brief elocution. He used to joke when he first came to the Vatican that, even though he had left Venice, he was still surrounded by Acqua and Canali. But Cardinal Canali, who had introduced him to the world on the evening of his election, is now dead and John is fading fast. "Today more than ever," he tells the two papal diplomats, "certainly more than in previous centuries, we are called to serve mankind and not just Catholics, to defend above all and everywhere the rights of the human person and not just those of the Catholic Church. Today's world, the needs made plain in the last fifty years, and a deeper understanding of doctrine have brought us to a new situation. . . . *It is not that the Gospel has changed: it is that we have begun to understand it better.*" It is a précis of *Pacem in terris*, but it is also a last plea to his middle-of-the-road subordinates that the policies of his pontificate not be reversed.

In his wakeful moments, Capovilla reads to him from the *Imitation of Christ* and from the messages that are pouring in from all over the world, from high and low, from Christians and Jews, from Buddhists and atheists. One writes, "Insofar as an atheist can pray, I'm praying for you"—which brings a smile to the lips of the man in the bed. May 30 is a day of acute abdominal pain, followed by sedatives. The next day, the doctors tell Capovilla that nothing more can be done and that death may be only hours away. Fighting back his tears, Capovilla gives John the news— "doing for you what you did for Monsignor Radini at the end of his life." It was the signal they had agreed upon earlier. Capovilla, overcome, falls to his knees, collapsing into the bedcovers. "Help me to die as a bishop should," whispers John.

The members of the papal household, including the nuns from Bergamo who have served as his housekeepers, the doctors and nurses, Cicognani and Dell'Acqua, are ushered in to witness the pope receive the last rites of his Church. He receives for the last time the bread of the Eucharist, here known as *viaticum*, food for the journey he is about to take. He points to the crucifix opposite his bed and calls it "the secret of my ministry." "It's there so that I can see it in my first waking moment and before going to sleep. . . . Those open arms have been the program of my pontificate: they mean that Christ died for all, for all. No one is excluded from his love, from his forgiveness." He remembers his mentors Rebuzzini, Radini-Tedeschi, Ferrari; he asks forgiveness from anyone he has offended. But he feels "calm and sure that my Lord, in his mercy, will not reject me."

The papal sacristan anoints his body—eyes, ears, nose, mouth, hands, and feet—the Church's last homage to God's living creature, the human body. In his agitation, the sacristan mixes up the order of the anointing, so John helps him get it right. The ritual done, he speaks to each in turn and tells them that he guesses Montini will succeed him. Another round of visits, and then all are gone but Capovilla. "We've worked together and served the Church without stopping to pick up and throw back the stones that have sometimes blocked our path. You've put up with my defects and I with yours. We'll always be friends. . . . I'll protect you from heaven."

More pain, more sedatives. As night falls, John's surviving siblings, Zaverio, Alfredo, Giuseppe, and Assunta, arrive to keep vigil. John drifts in and out of consciousness. Sometimes he thinks he's back in France and speaks French, sometimes he's in Bergamo, then in Sotto il Monte. He murmurs blessings over cities and countries, over communities and individuals alive and long gone, a lengthening litany of remembrance. Sometimes he comes to and greets his family. "I'm still here," he says with a smile.

June 2 is Pentecost, the feast of the Holy Spirit and John's favorite. In the night between June 2 and 3, he wakes at 3:00 A.M. and says with marked emphasis, "Lord, you know that I love you!" These are Peter's words at the close of John's Gospel in answer to the question Jesus puts to him, "Simon Peter, son of Jonah, do you love me?" The gospel scene, set on the shore of the Sea of Galilee, is dreamlike in its unfolding. Jesus, now risen from the dead, asks his question three times. Each time Peter makes the same vehement reply. After each of Peter's replies, Jesus gives him a symbolic mandate: "Feed my lambs"; "Care for my sheep"; "Feed my sheep." Contemporary Scripture scholars theorize that this scene may have been added to the gospel as a coda after the early Christian community that produced it, the

Community of the Beloved Disciple, which had started out as anarchic and freewheeling, finally attached itself to the larger Church of the Apostles. This coda was their admission that they needed more structure and authority if they were to survive in the world. So they accepted a bishop, someone like Peter, to run their community—so long as he was truly pastoral, so long as he saw himself as a provider of nurture and care rather than as a ruler of others.

"Lord, you know that I love you," says John once more—his last distinct words. He drowses off, wakes occasionally, makes the sign of the cross. At 5:00 P.M., an enormous crowd begins to fill Saint Peter's Square. They are coming to an outdoor Mass to pray for the sick pope. Familiar faces—his family, his household, his closest collaborators—surround his bed and listen to the sounds of prayer from the square below. At 7:45, the Mass comes to its ritual conclusion with the chanting of the *"Ite, Missa est,"* which can be translated as "Go, the Mass is ended" or "Go, your mission is completed" or "Go, you are sent forth." It is heard by everyone in the room. The white-shirted figure on the bed gives one last shudder, there is the faint suggestion of a death rattle, the breathing stops.

The men and women gathered around the bed—from farmers to cardinals—begin to sing *"In paradisum"*:

> Into paradise may the angels lead you,
> at your coming may the martyrs take you in
> and bring you to the Holy City, Jerusalem.
> There may angel choirs welcome you,
> and with Lazarus, once poor,
> may you know eternal rest.

PART IV

AFTER JOHN

✚ ✚ ✚

ANGELO GIUSEPPE RONCALLI, late in life Pope John XXIII, saw the life of his Church as a development, rooted in the Gospel, the proclamation of the Good News that Jesus had brought us by his life, death, and resurrection. This idea of development, not original with him, enabled him to view the motley history of the Church, and even of the papacy, with the equanimity that was essential to him and to draw from that history wisdom useful for the present moment. His own life was one of gradual psychological development, an evolution so slow-paced that at times little seemed to be happening. I have called him "Angelo" for most of his life because he is under obedience, seldom free to act independently—though there are spectacular exceptions, such as the effort to save Jews during World War II, that point to an underlying reservoir of spontaneous goodness, ready to spring up and pour forth when tapped. Once he is made patriarch of Venice and awarded adult autonomy, I call him "Roncalli," and here we begin to see what he is capable of. Under his new name, John, he has a final blossoming beyond all expectations; but in retrospect it is a blossoming prepared for throughout his life. This is because of his unique combination of sincerity—he is always, first of all, a priest, who believes he is obliged to live the spirit of the Gospel—and native intelligence, an intelligence that has two aspects: it keeps him ever curious, ever meditating on the deeper truths of history, and it keeps him realistic about people and possibilities. He is never merely cynical: a life of constant prayer and reflection—part of his sincerity—gives him vision and courage that few people are capable of.

The reader may find it remarkable how seldom in the history of the papacy it is necessary to make reference to the Gospel of Jesus. This is because the actions of the majority of popes are more aptly appreciated as the actions of politicians—and we do not need religious inspiration to explain the actions of politicians. As politicians, their actions may be viewed as successful or unsuccessful according to political norms. But once we introduce the Gospel as norm, it must be admitted that most popes have been failures. Perhaps this should not shock us as much as it does. The peoples of the Protestant-influenced societies of northern Europe and North America, where moral rectitude wears a very public face, are always more alarmed by the discovery of character flaws in their official leaders than are the peoples of southern Europe and Latin America, where men of power are never expected to be good. As a Roman chambermaid remarked exquisitely to Hannah Arendt while John XXIII lay dying: "*Signora*, this pope was a real Christian. How is that possible? And how could a real Christian ever get to sit on Saint Peter's Chair? Didn't he first have to be made a bishop, then an archbishop, then a cardinal, before he finally got elected pope? Didn't anyone have any idea who he was?" One could term this comment deeply cynical, impossibly pure, or just realistic.

At any rate, after Gregory the Great in the sixth century—whose masterwork, *Pastoral Care*, was Angelo's principal "how-to" book—there are only a few popes who can be said to have any permanent standing as Christian religious figures—Benedict XIV, Pius VII, Leo XIII, and Benedict XV, all relatively recent, which tends to confirm Roncalli's theory of spiritual development through history, of our gradually coming to "understand [the Gospel] better." Bearing this in mind, we will now glance briefly at the papacy since John to see how close subsequent popes have been able to come to the humane standard set by Papa Roncalli.

Paul VI

As JOHN HAD PREDICTED, he was succeeded by his friend Giovanni Battista Montini, age sixty-five, who took the name Paul to indicate, in a broadly ecumenical gesture, that he saw his mission to be like that of the apostle Paul, who had tried to preach to the whole world, not just to the converted. He made the continuance of John's council, which he could have stopped, his highest priority; and on the council's conclusion in late 1965, he promulgated its decrees and made significant strides in implementing the intentions of the council majority in the life of the Church. In the conclave that elected him, his most notable opponent was the old *intransigente* Siri, but the opposition of his aging faction could not overcome the wishes of the new majority of cardinals appointed by John. When the *intransigenti* began to obstruct the implementation of the council's decrees, Paul was forced to insist on the retirement of all bishops (save himself) at the age of seventy-five and of all curial cardinals at the age of eighty, after which age no cardinal would be allowed to participate in the next conclave. On their way out, Ottaviani and the rest of the Old Guard made their bitterness as public as possible.

The decrees of Vatican II, in which one may everywhere detect the influence of John's "separated brethren," reshaped the Church to such an extent that the English historian Eamon Duffy can call the council "the most revolutionary Christian event since the Reformation." The Church is no longer to be thought of as a hierarchical pyramid but as "the People of God on pilgrimage through time," which means that the Church is capable of making mistakes along the way. Keeping the liturgy and sacraments of the Church in Latin long after the language had become unintelligible to most worshipers is undoubtedly one of those mistakes. (In his introduction to the reformed Sacramentary, Paul even says as much.) Bishops are "colleagues" of the pope, and together they share responsibility for the Church—which is no longer identified as the one and only Church of Christ, thus leaving room for non-Catholic Christians. The Church does not have two sources of revelation, the Bible and the Church's Tradition, long a bone of contention with Protestants; it has the Word of God, which animates the treasures of the Church, both Bible and Tradition. But believers must not concern themselves only with the divine: they have a grave responsibility to work with "all men toward the establishment of a world that is more human." They have a profound obligation, laid on them by Christ, to create unity among all Christians. The Jewish people cannot be held responsible for the execution of Jesus; they are, rather, to be cherished as "the first to hear the Word of God" (according to John's Good Friday liturgy); and anti-Semitism is an abomination. Religious liberty is the right of every human being.

This last, though exceedingly simple, is the most revolutionary of the council's changes. It sweeps away for all time the older notion that "error has no rights" and that, therefore, the Church (or the state) has the right to impose belief. The council's Decree on Religious Liberty was largely the work of the American Jesuit John Courtney Murray. Like the Frenchmen de Lubac, Chenu, and Congar, the Swiss-German Küng, and the German Karl Rahner, Murray had worked under a cloud of suspicion and silencings during the pontificate of Pius XII; but now all these men received their validation: they became the intellectual fathers of Vatican II. With Murray should be listed a little-known Polish archbishop, Karol Wojtyla of Krakow, who would become John Paul II. Wojtyla, in fact, disapproved of the open disagreements among bishops at the council, which scandalized him, but he saw the Decree on Religious Liberty as a weapon that could be used against the Communist regime under which he grudgingly lived. He brought the Eastern bishops to support the decree, which helped, with North American, French, Dutch, and German votes, to enable it to achieve a conciliar majority against the solid bloc of Spanish, Portuguese, and Latin Americans (and not a few Italians) who couldn't—at the time—begin to imagine their societies adopting such a program.

The son of a leftist, Paul came from a familial tradition of political and intellectual engagement. He had a deep attachment to the idea of Christian reunion, as well as a lifetime of friendships with non-Catholic Christians. As pope, he met several times with the ecumenical patriarch Athenagoras—one of the most open-minded and greathearted figures in the history of Orthodoxy—and together they expunged the mutual excommunications that their predecessors had hurled at one another a thousand years before. To Michael Ramsey, archbishop of Canterbury, Paul gave his own episcopal ring as a gift and spoke freshly of the Anglican and Catholic Churches as "sister Churches." His 1967 encyclical, *Populorum progressio* (The Progress of Peoples), building on Leo's *Rerum novarum* and John's *Mater et Magistra*, remains to this day the most radical social encyclical ever written, condemning the gap in prosperity between rich and poor nations, insisting that God made the abundance of this earth for everyone without distinction, and declaring that "the new name for peace is development" and that no one should expect there can be peace without a just sharing of the world's resources. All this was written with an economy of expression seldom matched in the history of papal documents, for Paul exhibited a clean and pointed literary style, whether he was writing in Latin, Italian, or French, the language in which he memorably addressed the United Nations in New York. He was the first pope to travel beyond Italy since the eighteenth century, making a dozen or so trips to such places as Israel, India, the United States, Portugal, Turkey, Colombia, Switzerland, Uganda, the Pacific islands, Australia, and the Philippines, where a madman, dressed as a priest, attempted to knife him.

Despite these many positive initiatives, however, there was a side to Paul more in league with Pius XII, whom he had served for many years, than with John XXIII. Like Pius, he could not let go of the image of the pope as unique and lonely spokesman for God, uttering inspired oracles to a disbelieving world. He suppressed a movement by the council fathers to declare John XXIII a saint by acclamation, because he feared it would compromise papal authority (even though, as he knew, papal "canonization" of saints is a relatively recent phenomenon). Under conservative pressure, he had a "prefatory note" appended to the council's Dogmatic Constitution on the Church, in which he claimed that nothing in the constitution in any way diminished the supreme authority of the pope, very nearly negating the doctrine of episcopal "collegiality" contained in the body of the document. When he set up the continuing body mandated by the council—the periodic World Synod of Bishops—he made sure to give it only "consultative" status and, therefore, no real power. (Similarly toothless status would be accorded the parish councils of laypeople set up "in the spirit of the council" to advise pastors.) He pulled two issues out from under the council's consideration, clerical celibacy and birth control, reserving both to himself. He must have felt that the council was in danger of making the "wrong" decision about these matters—something that would never have occurred to John, with his trust in the Holy Spirit. Unsurprisingly, Paul ended up affirming lifelong celibacy for priests and the ban on artificial birth control for married couples—this last despite the fact that the commission that he himself appointed to advise him on birth control (a topic that he admitted caused him "embarrassment") voted overwhelmingly to allow contraceptives. Once again, Karol Wojtyla makes an appearance, posing as the sexual expert Paul knew himself not to be and convincing the wavering pope that the commission is in error and that "the constant Tradition of the Church" can permit no change in doctrine.

The encyclical in which Paul reaffirmed the ban on contraception, *Humanae vitae* (Of Human Life) appeared in 1968, little more than a year after *Populorum progressio,* canceling out much of the positive impact that the earlier encyclical would otherwise have made and provoking such a storm of protest that Paul resolved never to write another encyclical. In the Western world, and particularly in Germany, Holland, and the United States, the protests were fierce and unyielding. We know from sociological surveys that, where contraceptives are available, sexually active Catholics make use of them just as often as their non-Catholic counterparts. (This was not the case before the release of *Humanae vitae,* so we may deduce that the papal ban has had something of the same effect that Prohibition once had on American drinking habits.) But the encyclical seems also to have precipitated the departure of many who found they could no longer in good conscience remain Catholic and some diminution in financial support among those, especially in the United States, who continue to attend Catholic services. Laypeople, permitted no voice, may be voting in significant numbers either with their feet or with their wallets.

Paul became less and less effectual as he lost confidence in his own insight and judgment. In the last year of his life—he lived to 1978, dying of a heart attack, a weary old man just weeks short of his eighty-first birthday—he had to preside at the memorial service in Saint John Lateran for his friend Aldo Moro, the leader of the Christian Democrats and a former prime minister of Italy, who was kidnapped and executed for complicity in "the crimes of the capitalist state" by the Red Brigades, an underground movement of Marxist-Leninist terrorists. Paul had tried to free Moro prior to his execution: he wrote to the Red Brigades, proposed a large ransom, and offered himself in exchange, but could not bring himself to do the one thing that might have saved Moro—public papal intervention with the State of Italy in favor of the exchange of prisoners that the Red Brigades were demanding. That, he feared, would go against all the principles of "disengagement" so carefully set in place by his recent predecessors and faithfully promoted by him through his entire life. He could not now intervene in a "foreign state." The Moro family, believing that neither Church nor state had done enough to save their husband and father, refused to attend the Lateran service.

Paul was often called "Hamlet" because of his bouts of indecision. It was said that his favorite word was *but*. Now, at his life's end, many Italians, with whom he had never been especially popular, wondered if a life had been lost by his hesitation. Though he had spent his early priesthood as a chaplain to students, the new crop of young people was beyond his comprehension, not just the wild-eyed Red Brigades, but the radical Catholic students who now populated the waves of protest demonstrations and the angry young priests and nuns who were leaving their posts in droves. Coupled with his hesitations, the spirit of the time—individualistic, centrifugal, sometimes hysterical—robbed him of effectiveness long before his death.

John Paul II

THE MAN ELECTED to succeed Paul VI was Albino Luciani, patriarch of Venice, who lasted only a month. He was genial but unprepossessing, the cardinals seeming to have decided they needed a pope who looked less austere and worried than Paul. Known as "the smiling pope," Luciani made history by being the first pope to take a double name, John Paul I, and to refuse coronation. His smile apparently hid tensions and pains that he kept to himself. Early on the morning of September 28, 1978, he was found dead in his bed by his inquisitive housekeeper, Sister Vincenza, who had earlier left the usual cup of coffee at his door but opened the door and invaded his bedroom sometime later on discovering that the coffee remained at the door, cold and untasted. The Vatican could not admit that a woman was the first to see the dead pope in his pajamas (what might people think was going on in the Vatican?), so they put out the story that he had been found by his (male) secretary. This story quickly unraveled and led to baseless media speculation that the pope had been poisoned. He had died of a heart attack, while reading in bed.

The cardinals gathered once more. They already knew the field of *papabili*, since they had looked them all over but a month earlier, and they soon found they had run out of possible Italians. The aging and all too willing Siri was of course pressed into service by the remaining conservatives but he had no chance; and the cardinals, in any case, could not risk a third papal heart attack in three months. This time they were looking for vigor, something their ranks did not possess in superfluity. An alliance of German-speaking and Latin American cardinals, led by Franz König of Austria and Aloisio Lorscheider of Brazil, settled on the man who would become history's first Slavic pope, the cardinal archbishop of Krakow, Karol Wojtyla, still in his fifties, a handsome, athletic philosophy professor with a graceful, confident manner. They thought him a political pragmatist, able to get along with Communists (in contrast to unbending *ancien régime* types like Mindszenty) and a theological progressive—his interventions at the council had left this impression—but they would learn in time that they had badly misjudged their man. Wojtyla took the name John Paul II, out of "reverence, love, and devotion to John Paul and also to Paul VI, who has been my inspiration, my strength." Ominously absent from this encomium was the name of John XXIII.

What the electors could not know about Wojtyla was that he had grown up in a most peculiar household, his mother dead by the time he was eight, his only sibling, an elder brother he admired, succumbing to scarlet fever when Wojtyla was twelve. The family was a solitary one with few relatives and friends; and now the boy was left only with his father, a taciturn military man, who kept his son to a rigidly structured schedule that permitted but three pleasures: study (especially of German, in which the boy soon became fluent), soccer, and prayer. The prayer was omnipresent: friends of Lolek (his nickname in childhood) remember discovering father and son on their knees in the middle of the day; and summer vacations tended to be extended pilgrimages to Marian shrines. In 1941, when Lolek was twenty, his father died, after which the young man was often found in his bedroom, prostrate in prayer, his arms stretched out on the floor in the form of a cross. As one wanders through Wojtyla's early history, it seems almost the opposite of Roncalli's. They had Tridentine Catholicism in common, of course, but Roncalli's is of the gentle, affectionate, merry kind, dependent on God's grace, whereas Wojtyla's seems morose, even morbid, with little place for laughter or enjoyment, dependent on the training of the human will to create a hero who always does what is most difficult.

A personality forged like this in a culture of scarcity and coming to manhood in the brutal circumstances of wartime Poland is bound to have, if he survives, more than the normal allocation of steel in him. A self-denying athlete is unlikely to value a shuffling and voluble gourmand. It is even understandable why a man like Wojtyla might resent the playfulness of a man like Roncalli and the evident ease with which he enjoyed others and was content to let them be themselves—to the point of allowing bishops to disagree hotly and publicly. It would also be understandable—though far from certain—that this Pole of Poles may have resented John's friendly *Ostpolitik* as unworthy of the blood and misery of so many Polish Catholics. At any rate, Wojtyla emerged into adulthood as a kind of superman: skier, mountain climber, oarsman, gifted actor in his spare time, double-shift factory worker during the war, secret seminarian under Nazi rule, run over by a German truck and left for dead, offering his life as a Christ-like victim, rising to new life as a priest, doctor of philosophy, and bishop, always noticed by others for his amazing single-mindedness and indomitable will, always in complete control of himself and whatever environment he found himself in.

As pope, John Paul II never doubted that he was God's choice, Poland's reward for its faithfulness through so many oppressions—colonialism, Nazism, Communism—and a rebuke to the degenerate West. With unwavering courage he used the papal throne as an invulnerable position from which to pull on the sleeve of the Polish Communist state and unravel the whole fabric as if it were so much knitted wool till, in the end, the Warsaw Pact and even the Soviet Union lay in shreds. Historians may long debate how large was John Paul's role in the fall of

Communism, but there can be no doubt that his election was the catalyst that encouraged the rise of Solidarity and that his un-flinching presence—by radio, film, television, and fax—helped fuel every step of the subsequent destabilization and collapse. At the Yalta Conference, Stalin had derided the idea of taking the pope's opinion into account, asking, "How many divisions has the pope?" Now a pope had answered Stalin's question.

After John Paul was shot down at point-blank range in Saint Peter's Square on May 13, 1981, he saw his survival as God's doing, May 13 being the feast of Our Lady of Fátima, named af-ter an apparition of Mary that occurred at Fátima, Portugal, on that date in 1917. The apparition spoke to three shepherd chil-dren, entrusting to them a "terrible secret" that they could reveal only to the pope. The secret has recently been publicized by the Vatican: a vision, confided to Pius XII by the only surviving shepherd, subsequently a cloistered nun, of a "bishop in white" under a cross and surrounded by martyrs. The bishop falls down "as if dead." In John Paul's mind, the martyrs are the Christians of Eastern Europe persecuted by the Communists and the white-clad bishop is their champion, the Slavic pope, who, like them, is unjustly marked out for death but saved by Jesus's mother. Well, maybe; but the very things that impress some about this sort of "prophecy" give others the creeps. It is all of a piece with the pope's idiosyncratic Polish Catholicism, which he seemed at times to mean to impose on the whole world, or rather on the whole Catholic world.

This pope, despite the fact that he was by far the most traveled pope in history, all but stopped trying to speak to the whole world. His ecumenical gestures were few, and the ones he made—almost all toward Orthodoxy—have had little effect. Toward Protestants, he was generally cold and unbending; and his Grand Inquisitor, Cardinal Joseph Ratzinger—the Roman Inquisition having been renamed first the Holy Office, now the Congregation for the Doctrine of the Faith (CDF)—instructed Catholics that they may not properly speak of Protestant communities which lack bishops in apostolic succession as "Churches," nor may the Roman Catholic Church be called "a sister Church" of any other Church, since she is always the Mother. This, of course, condemns the innovative and fraternal usage of Paul VI, as well as the whole ecumenical project of Pope John and Cardinal Bea. It is impossible to imagine John Paul II bestowing his episcopal ring on an archbishop of Canterbury (as Paul VI did) or his precious breviary—a lifelong priestly possession—on an Anglican priest (as John XXIII once did). Such actions imply recognition of legitimacy. Rather, under John Paul, Ratzinger was allowed to reaffirm Leo XIII's judgment on the illegitimacy of Anglican orders in nearly infallible terms. Ratzinger also issued a warning to those involved in interfaith dialogue that they are not to take dialogue as an invitation to compromise, for it must ever be borne in mind that non-Christian religions are so "gravely deficient" that Christians have nothing to learn from them—which, of course, vitiates the whole point of dialogue. We have come full circle and are back in the pontificate of Pius XII.

Likewise reminiscent of the waning years of Pius XII is the leeway John Paul gave Ratzinger to impose sanctions on theologians who have anything new to say. Several of the key theologians of Vatican II have been hounded by the CDF. Küng, in particular, who is almost John Paul's *Doppelgänger*—handsome, athletic, certain he is right—has been deprived of his license to teach as a Catholic theologian. Latin American espousers of Liberation Theology, a mixture of Christianity and Marxism, have especially suffered from papal displeasure. A new loyalty oath, reminiscent of the anti-Modernist oath of Pius X, has been imposed on bishops, seminary professors, and new priests; a *mandatum* (or obligation) to teach only what the Holy See teaches has been readied for imposition on all theology faculties of Catholic universities. This doctrinal policing, which occupied much of the energy of John Paul's pontificate, has lessened papal influence on non-Catholic Christians. Whereas the pontificate of John XXIII gave us a pope who more and more spoke not only for the world's two billion Christians—a third of the planet—but for humane aspirations everywhere, this pope in his contentiousness found it harder and harder to convince anyone that he speaks even for the world's Catholics. It may be that the pope can be Universal Father only if he stops trying to be Universal Policeman.

In nothing did his policing effort fail so spectacularly as in his preoccupation with sexual issues. In 1960, soon after his days as a philosophy professor, then bishop Wojtyla published a book about sex, *Love and Responsibility,* that was something of a *succès de scandale* in its time, not only because a bishop was writing about sex but because the book contained accurate information about female orgasm and how it may be achieved, a subject not then widely understood in *any* Polish circles. It is tempting to speculate how Wojtyla might have come by this information in the doubly repressive atmosphere of Catholic-Communist Poland. He certainly had nothing more than book knowledge of his subject, which I conjecture was achieved by reading the work of an early-twentieth-century European sexologist such as Van de Velde, whose books were widely available. Whatever he read, it was not reading approved by his Church. As far as it goes, *Love and Responsibility* represents progress over anything else then on offer: it advocates "the equality of man and woman in marriage" and urges that the man has a responsibility to satisfy the woman. Its author, however, was also certain that the interposition of any means of "artificial" birth control would represent a flight from responsibility by the partners in the sexual act.

In *Love and Responsibility,* one can see all Wojtyla's contradictory impulses. He was no puritan; he was, if anything, too romantic and idealizing of sexual love—and far too attached to notions of sexual "complementarity," which floated him far from the real world of male-female partnerships. He was utterly fearless and sublimely sure of his own self-control—how else could he have waded through whatever banned sex manuals he studied? But he lived in a world of his own ratiocination, doubly removed from everyday realities by his celibacy and his penchant for philosophy. He believed with the Platonists that he could reach the truth by thinking about it—and once he reached it, he would instruct lesser mortals. Wojtyla felt himself to be gifted with infallibility long before he became pope.

It was this habit of certitude that made the man so impossible, for in nothing was he more certain than in the realms where his experience was least: sex and women. If thinking about something can bring you to the truth, thinking about something you know nothing about is sure to bring you to the truth even faster and more certainly. John Paul was certain that the Church could never change its mind on such subjects as premarital sex, birth control, divorce, homosexuality, married priests, and women priests. He was so certain of this that he would not promote anyone who disagreed with him on any of these subjects—which, after more than two and a half decades of his papal reign, has given us a worldwide Catholic episcopate with an unusually high number of duplicitous sycophants and intellectual incompetents. Who else would sign on to such a list of certitudes?

John Paul ignored the ancient litmus test of "reception," the idea that a doctrine must be actively accepted by the whole Church if it is to be considered valid and that a bishop must be similarly accepted by his people if he is to be considered validly appointed. The fact that several of his teachings were not "received" by believers hardly encouraged John Paul to alter course; and he forced reactionary new bishops on dioceses in Holland, Switzerland, Germany, and Austria in the teeth of general opposition. (The Austrian appointment—to the see of Vienna—turned out to be a notorious pedophile and had to be removed.) But all Catholic bishops, whether appointed by John Paul or not, have suffered a demotion in importance. Once again, as in the papacy of Pius XII, they have been there simply to carry out papal policy. The World Synod of Bishops, which was already degraded in importance when Paul VI made it merely "consultative," became a rubber stamp assembly worthy of the most repressive Communist regime, with the pope prominent and taking notes at all sessions and the topics approved in advance. All such assemblies and public meetings tended to be orchestrated down to the smallest detail to exclude even a whisper of spontaneity, let alone an original thought. No wonder John Paul was reduced to speechless fury when Sister Theresa Kane, an American nun, managed to insert a plea for women's ordination into one of these carefully controlled gatherings.

John Paul promulgated the reform of the Code of Canon Law initiated by John XXIII, as well as a Catechism of the Catholic Church to replace, at long last, the Catechism of the Council of Trent. The new Catechism is a lucid document, marred in its English translation by offensive servings of sexism—the result of execrable linguistic advice Ratzinger took from his right-wing American pals. John Paul was vigorous in promoting new lay movements in the Church, but these run the gamut from the secretive and unwholesome Opus Dei, hatched in Franco's Spain, to the open and unconstricted Community of Sant'Egidio, inspired by the Gospel to befriend the poor. John

Paul's social teaching did not advance beyond that of John XXIII and Paul VI, but it was not a retrenchment, either, except in the brusque exclusion of the liberation theologians. But John Paul's forceful and sometimes eloquent teaching—in favor of the redistribution of wealth and the protection of migrants and minorities, against the death penalty and armed conflicts of all kinds—has been overshadowed, at least in the world media, by his championing of the rights of human zygotes, embryos, and fetuses. In nothing did John Paul distinguish himself so gracefully as in his loving regard for the Jewish people, though even in this effort there are a couple of strange and needless blots on the record.

In 2000, he beatified John XXIII, which means that John may now be officially invoked in Catholic prayer as an intercessor with God; it is the last step before sainthood (or "canonization"), which raises the individual so honored as a public model of heroic sanctity. It was the least John Paul could do, since the whole Catholic world long ago declared John a saint. The shock was that John Paul, at the same time, beatified Pio Nono, a man whose beatification no one wanted, except perhaps a few ancient representatives of the deposed Italian nobility and the proprietors of Il Papa-Re, a Trastevere pizzeria named for Pio Nono, the last "pope-king" of Italy. Virtually all other Italians, however, would tend to applaud the Romans of Pio's day who attempted to throw his corpse into the Tiber. The carefully maintained fiction about a pope's actions is that, even when he is at his most willful, he is said to be acting "on behalf of the Church." There is no way this second beatification was "on behalf of the Church," since no one wanted it but the pope and no one will ever invoke the intercession of Pio Nono. But John Paul was sending his usual message: he would bless the humility and humanity of individuals only if he could at the same time exalt the intransigence and triumphalism of the official Church. John Paul had to defend the historic purity of the papacy because he was a committed institutionalist, who never admitted that the institution had ever done anything wrong. When he apologized for the burning of Jan Hus and the condemnation of Galileo, he blamed these catastrophes not on a duplicitous Church (in Hus's case) or an ignorant papacy (in Galileo's case) but on "some Christians," "some theologians." The Church is spotless, the papacy all-knowing. There were, nevertheless, limits even to John Paul's canonizations: he did not canonize Pius XII. A man of John Paul's extraordinary courage and inner strength could hardly admire a man of Pius's weakness.

John Paul beatified and canonized far more souls than any other pope, a record of more than one per week. Unfortunately, the vast majority have been priests and male religious, not a few of them Polish, few of them laypeople, save for the occasional martyred catechist. With all his might, this pope has been engaged in reclericalizing the Church that John XXIII had opened to all. Whereas popes like Pio Nono were locked in a fortress of their own devising, this one seemed trapped in an earlier time and place—Poland in the first half of the twentieth century, virtually no one's cultural ideal—as if he were petrified in amber. His lasting legacy to his Church may prove to be the alienation and unease that so many Catholics now harbor toward Catholicism, a sensation of no longer feeling at home.

John Paul II died on April 2, 2005, a month short of his eighty-fifth birthday and after more than twenty-six and a half years on the papal throne. He succeeded in displacing Leo XIII, who (at twenty-five and a half years) had previously held the title of second-longest-lived pope. (No one has yet managed to exceed Pio Nono's thirty-one years.) The cardinals in conclave, virtually all of them appointees of John Paul II, made the unsurprising choice of Joseph Ratzinger to succeed John Paul. Ratzinger, who has taken the name Benedict XVI, has performed rather as his electors expected him to and as his previous performance as John Paul's Grand Inquisitor would lead us to expect. He has forcefully restated his opposition to the ecumenical courtesy of calling non-Catholic Christian communities "churches." His language toward non-Christian religions (Judaism excepted) can be patronizingly superior. In a gratuitously spectacular insult to Islam, he has bumbled into territory that John Paul was smart enough to avoid. In his bearing, however, Benedict is kindly, often seeming to have the distracted air of a retired professor. Now past eighty, he was elected to stay the course that John Paul set and not upset the cardinals by introducing anything novel or unexpected. He is likely to play according to plan.

EPILOGUE

What Next?

TO ANYONE who studies the origins of the papacy it soon becomes evident that it is a Christian invention that evolved under the pressure of historical events. The belief that the papacy was somehow "given" by Christ cannot stand up to scrutiny. But, then, the role of the bishop (on which the papacy is ultimately based, since the pope is nothing other than "bishop of Rome") is also a Christian invention. In the gospels, Jesus uses the word *Church* (*ekklesia*) only twice, both times in the same section of Matthew (chapters 16 and 18, flanking the account of the Transfiguration), which leads most Scripture scholars to the sensible conclusion that Jesus may never have uttered the word and that these passages represent a retrojection by the primitive Church— what it was imagined Jesus would have said about "Church" had the notion ever occurred to him.

In the first passage, Jesus says he will "build [his] Church" on the Rock, that is, on Peter. The gospels present Peter as lovable but wishy-washy, hardly a "Rock"—Jesus's affectionate, semi-ironic nickname for him. Peter's literary function in the gospel stories is as representative believer, someone who means well, who gets crucial things wrong, and whose courage often fails him. If Jesus did indeed mean to build his Church on Peter, the obvious sense of the passage is that he will build his Church— that is, the new Assembly of God's People, the new (or reformed) Israel—on ordinary, fallible human beings. It is a long way from this scene to the erection of Saint Peter's Basilica with the words of this passage incised in enormous gold letters, over-whelming the visitor with his own littleness. Here the words blast like trumpets and roll like thunder: "Thou art Peter . . ."

But if in fact bishops are a Christian invention, developed by the primitive Church because of its need for unity in the face of bizarre heresies like Gnosticism, may it not also be legitimate for the Church to invent other forms of organization? What, in the end, is the norm for legitimate change and development in the Church? The answer of John Paul II would have been "the *magisterium*," but the *magisterium* is nothing more than the teaching authority of the Church, embodied especially (John Paul would no doubt have said) in the pope and the other bishops. If, how-ever, the Church in its earliest forms lacked bishops, what was then the norm for development? It can only have been the Gospel, the Law of Love explained and exampled in the stories that became the New Testament, and as interpreted by the whole Church—that is, by the community of faithful believers—for Christ gave the power to "bind" and "loose" not only to Peter (Matthew 16:19) but to the Church as a whole (Matthew 18:18). In the final analysis, it is the Church that must decide what the Church is or should be. Bishops, including the pope, can act validly only as the representatives of their people. Such a view cannot be labeled theological innovation: it was put forward by William of Occam in the fourteenth century and was the com-mon view of ancient Christians, propounded even by so head-strong a bishop as Cyprian of Carthage, who in the third century vowed "to do nothing on my own private opinion without [the] advice [of the clergy] and the consent of the people."

The Church is always in need of reformation because it is al-ways in danger of becoming a mere self-protecting institution like all other institutions. When this happens, it follows not the Law of Love but the Law of Institutions, by which it tends to do the opposite of what it professes to do. Just as banks can make people poor, hospitals make them sick, and schools make them ignorant, Churches can make them evil—and the history of the papacy is embarrassingly full of examples. More often, however, the papacy has simply taken on the coloration of its time and place: congregational and democratic, oligarchic and imperial, monarchic and absolutist. The hope of John XXIII was to return the Church to Pentecost, to a time when the Spirit of God flowed freely through the congregation, inspiring *all:*

> *I shall pour out my Spirit on all humanity.*
> *Your sons and daughters shall prophesy,*
> *your young people shall see visions,*
> *your old people dream dreams.*
> *Even on the slaves, men and women,*
> *shall I pour out my Spirit,*

proclaimed Peter in his Pentecost sermon (Acts 2:17–18), quoting the prophecy of the Hebrew prophet Joel.

A thoughtful Jesuit predicted to me recently that it would take the Church two hundred years to recover from John Paul II's pontificate. But this assessment, though it surely speaks of immense dissatisfaction in the ranks of the Church's frontline troops, may be needlessly pessimistic. The ancient Church was the world's first true democracy, and it can be so again—not a democracy of campaigns and runoffs, of parties and platforms, but a democracy of the Spirit, in which every human being, male and female, young and old, rich and poor, is accorded the "equal human dignity" of which John wrote so movingly. Only as the ombudsman for such a universal assembly—which has at least the potential to include the whole world—could the pope begin to fill the role discovered for him neither by theology nor by history but by the express yearning of the world's peoples during the pontificate of John XXIII: Father of the World.

According to Loris Capovilla, John's whole life is summed up in the saying of Jesus "Happy the merciful for they shall be given mercy" (Matthew 5:7). This, coupled with John's abandonment to Providence—his willingness to let go in God, to let God be God, to be "carried by the Lord" and thus bring him to others—is the large and open spirit to which the Church is always invited to return. Whether it wells up in the next conclave or in the prayer of the next pope or in the refusal of Christians to be excluded from the full life of their Church (perhaps a refusal to accept bishops they have had no hand in electing), it surely breathes just beneath the surface of the present.

After the visitor to Saint Peter's Basilica has stared for a time at the great gold letters pronouncing Peter's primacy, he can lower his gaze to the splendid window of stained glass, designed by Bernini to light up the sanctuary. The window depicts the dove of Pentecost, the ardent Spirit of God, entering his temple. Below the dove, statues of amazed saints and martyrs surround the papal altar, their draperies lifted and swirling majestically in the wind of the Spirit. Even the four great pillars of the *baldacchino*, the canopy suspended over the altar, are in motion, each swiveling in ecstasy on its axis. All this is part of Bernini's plan, a portrayal in tableau of the effect of the Spirit on the Church. As at Pentecost in Jerusalem two thousand years ago, as at the council convoked by John more than forty years ago, the Spirit will descend again, the foundations will tremble and the statues come to life.

NOTES AND SOURCES

THIS BOOK is a biographical essay and not in any sense a definitive biography, which remains to be written when all the extant documents of Roncalli's life are made available. I have based my essay on currently available sources, all of which are incomplete. My purpose is to give an interpretation of my subject that sets him in his time and in the history of papal Catholicism, so that his uniqueness may show itself and his relevance to our time become vivid. The history of Christianity is so long and full of incident that it may yield at times diverse and even opposed interpretations, any one of which may appear valid, depending on how one marshals the materials. My interpretations of papal history will please neither anti-Catholic bigots nor ultra-Catholic crusaders. I have tried to steer a middle course between the two extremes; but since the papacy serves only as frame to my central narrative, it is necessarily sketched in broad strokes and lacks the refinement of detail that would be essential if my chief subject were papal (or theological) history.

Three books were exceedingly useful in constructing my brief tour of papal history before and after John: Thomas Bokenkotter, *A Concise History of the Catholic Church* (New York, 1990); Eamon Duffy, *Saints and Sinners: A History of the Popes* (New Haven, Conn., and London, 1997); and Richard P. McBrien, *Lives of the Popes* (San Francisco, 1997). If Bokenkotter and Duffy occasionally find more reason to praise a papal action than I do, McBrien seems a tad more dismissive. For the life of Paul VI, I consulted Peter Hebblethwaite's admirable *Paul VI* (New York and London, 1993). For my sketch of

John Paul II's early life I am especially indebted to research Marco Politi amassed for *His Holiness* (New York, 1996), the book on John Paul II that he wrote with Carl Bernstein.

Indispensable to my portrait of my main subject was Peter Hebblethwaite's *Pope John XXIII* (Garden City, N.Y., 1985), which remains the single richest source of general information. Needless to say, John's own *Journal of a Soul* (London and New York, 1965), the selection from his lifelong diaries edited by Loris Capovilla, was essential reading, as were additional selections, remembrances, etc., published by Monsignor Capovilla at various times over the last four decades. Of these one volume, *L'Ite Missa Est di Papa Giovanni* (Padova, 1983), partly concerning the last hours of Pope John, was especially valuable. I have felt free to emend the available English translations of both Italian and Latin texts and occasionally to translate from scratch. I have also relied on personal recollections Monsignor Capovilla imparted to me during a series of interviews at Ca'Maitino in Sotto il Monte, as well as on oral recollections from a number of other witnesses to Roncalli's life, some of whom would prefer not to be identified. Pope John's instructions to Agostino Casaroli for his mission to Eastern Europe were conveyed to me by their recipient, afterward Cardinal Casaroli, in November 1992 during an interview in the apartment of the secretary of state in the papal palace. A study of Roncalli during the Istanbul years—Alberto Melloni, *Fra Istanbul, Atene e la Guerra: La missione di A. G. Roncalli* (Genova, 1992)—contains information far beyond my needs but is a model first step toward the creation of a definitive biography.

A papal document is usually referred to by its first Latin words, which serve as a kind of title. Where possible, I have given an English translation of such titles in parentheses immediately after their first occurrence in Latin. Occasionally, however, the first Latin words do not constitute a translatable phrase, on account of Latin's reliance on declension rather than word order. In such cases, I have had to forgo translation.

An orthographical puzzle I encountered was the capitalization of the word *church*. At the outset, I intended to capitalize the word only when it referred to the universal Church or, at least, to a substantial part of it (say, the Eastern Church). But this proved an impossible distinction to maintain, so in the end I capitalized the word wherever it occurred, except when it referred to a building rather than a congregation. If this leaves the impression that the Church is whole and complete wherever it manifests itself, my usage would certainly please Yves Congar, the principal theologian of Vatican II, and, *uti mihi videtur*, Pope John himself.

ACKNOWLEDGMENTS

AT THE HEAD of my list is Archbishop Loris Francesco Capovilla, whose precise and poignant remembrances (and corrections of the stories of others) have been for me pearls of great price. Nor can I overpraise the gracious help given me by Marco Roncalli, great-grandnephew of a great pope. I am much indebted to my research assistant, Paul Lipkowitz, and to all those who read the first draft of the manuscript—my wife, Susan Cahill, John E. Becker, Thomas Bokenkotter, Paul Dinter, Mario Marazziti, Marco Politi, Richard Somerset-Ward, Nan A. Talese, David S. Toolan, and Robert J. White—as well as to Nancy Allen, Andrea Ginsky, and Diane Marcus for last-minute fact checking. Each reader was able to correct many errors that would otherwise have gone unchecked, but needless to say only I am responsible for whatever errors and imperfections remain.